D0554183

Financial
and
Economic
Journalism

Analysis, Interpretation, and Reporting

Financial and Economic Journalism

Analysis, Interpretation, and Reporting

DONALD KIRSCH

New York • New York University Press • 1978

/ 0 3/ 2 0

Grateful acknowledgement is made to the following for permission to reprint excerpts from their published material:

To the WALL STREET JOURNAL for permission to reprint 19 articles appearing in issues dated July 29, 1977 and August 1, 2, 3, and 4, 1977. Reprinted by permission of the WALL STREET JOURNAL, © Dow Jones & Company, Inc., 1977, All Rights Reserved.

To the NEW YORK TIMES for permission to use three articles from issues dated July 30, 1977 and August 1977, © 1977 by The New York Times Company. Reprinted by permission.

To the JOURNAL OF COMMERCE for permission to reprint an article appearing in that publication.

To THE NEW YORK SOCIETY OF SECURITY ANALYSTS for permission to use material appearing in the appendix.

To THE NATIONAL BUREAU OF ECONOMIC RESEARCH for permission to use an excerpt from MEASURING BUSINESS CYCLES by Arthur F. Burns and Wesley C. Mitchell, published in 1946 by that organization.

To THE FINANCIAL ANALYSTS FEDERATION for permission to reprint the list of their member societies in the appendix.

To the AMERICAN STOCK EXCHANGE for permission to include a page from their pamphlet on requirements for original listing applications.

To the SECURITIES AND EXCHANGE COMMISSION for their assistance regarding the material appearing in the appendix, which is all in the public domain.

Library of Congress Cataloging in Publication Data

Kirsch, Donald, 1931-
   Financial and economic journalism.

   Bibliography: p.
   Includes index.
   1. Journalism, Commercial. I. Title.
PN4784.C7K57   070.4'49'33   78-55415

ISBN 0-8147-4569-5
Project Editor: Nat LaMar

Manufactured in the United States of America

For Dorothy,
a "blue chip" in anyone's book.

Preface

The Hasids have an interesting custom. When a boy reaches the age of three he is given a party by his religious teacher, and all of the youngster's male friends are invited. The child is seated on a pillow, a black skull cap on his head, a prayer shawl draping his tiny shoulders; strands of hair on either side of his head are cut, shaped, and curled.

And then his rabbi holds before the boy a parchment scroll with the Hebrew alphabet on it. The teacher smears honey over the first letter, has the boy lick it off and then verbally repeat each letter of the alphabet.

At the last letter, the rabbi smears honey once again, and the three-year-old licks the parchment clean. This ceremony introduces the boy to learning, and the concept that study is sweet and always rewarding.

I wish I could smear honey on the front and back of this book, for the subject is indeed sweet to me. But it is also complex, at times dry, surrounded by an undeserved mystique—and always rewarding. I hope you find it so.

I have spent much of my life in communications and finance, working on a daily basis with financial journalists and research analysts. I respect them both more than I can describe. I consider a financial journalist to be among the elite of a profession which I honor above all; and in the world of Wall Street and finance, I find the stimulating mind of the financial analyst the mirror image of the financial journalist.

The two, strangely, frequently consider themselves adversaries. The financial journalist looks at the analyst with skepticism, often accusing him or her of obtaining and using inside information from corporations for the gain of one's clients, and therefore, one's own advancement. The analyst, in turn, often wonders why a newsman reports a story months after the information has been floating freely around Wall Street, or why, in the reporting of a story, observations and conclusions of great importance are excluded.

Financial reporters and financial analysts are natural allies. Each profession demands men and women of great intellectual capacity, analytical ability, insight, diplomacy, reportorial, editorial, and interpretive skills—all built on a foundation of healthy skepticism. In good financial journalists and analysts, skepticism is congenital; the rest must be learned.

Some things which have to be learned have nothing to do with skill. In teaching a course in financial journalism at the New York University Graduate School of Arts and Sciences, I try to impress upon my students the need for empathy, not sympathy, for their news sources: the company treasurers, presidents, association executives, and economists whose careers and family lives can immediately be reshaped by the reporter's tapping fingers. This is a heavy responsibility. After all, the bad businessman—the liar, the cheat, the fraud, the impostor—often sounds, looks, and behaves outwardly the same as the businessman who has made an honest business error. How to tell the two apart is an interesting problem.

The outstanding financial reporter is a financial detective. He reads financial statements as expertly as a financial analyst does, and searches for discrepancies between an executive's spoken comments and his company's financial figures. In discrepancy, there is always a story.

There are enormous time pressures on the working journalist. Most often he or she does not have the time to analyze a financial statement while meeting a deadline. But when this is possible, the journalist's weaponry should include an ability to read financial statements.

Those who come to financial journalism bring with them trained reportorial minds. Although financial statements are complex, they are not difficult. No great mathematical skills are required, only the ability to understand *concepts* and to work with the ordinary computational skills developed in grade school.

This book has been written as a text for graduate journalism students interested in financial reporting. It has also been written as a handbook for those assigned to business pages who would like an introduction or refresher course in the elements of financial and economic newswriting.

The Foreword to this book presents an overview of business since the founding of the nation. It gives some perspective to our national psyche and our inherent commitment to a business society.

Chapter 1 traces the parallel growth of business and business journalism. Business cannot grow without information, and the business journalist has played an important role in the economic growth of this country.

Chapter 2 sets the stage for the core of the book. It deals with a mythical company, founded by two young journalists who have moved into the field of magazine publishing. It traces the development of the corporation, the problems it has in financing its expansion, and its ultimate decision to become a "publicly owned" company—one with numerous investors supplying capital for its expansion. In doing so, the two founders are faced with basic analytical and philosophical decisions, ranging from how much of their company they're willing to give up for what amount of capital; how to project the pace of their own growth; and the sudden impact on their own estates of the valuation others are willing to give to the property they are building. We see in this chapter the new demands made upon the two journalists as to reports they must make to their shareholders and to the general public; the types of news stories they must release, and with which the journalist must deal. We also see them interfacing with the professionals who surround, guide, beat upon, and massage the executives who run corporations—the accountants, the lawyers, the Wall Street community, the public relations men, and the governmental authorities such as the Securities and Exchange Commission.

Since the journalist must also deal with all of these profes-

sionals, he or she must know who they are, how they work, *what
they expect of a financial journalist,* and how the journalist is
perceived by other professionals.

Chapter 3 deals with the ten basic stories which recur most
often, and with which the financial or economic reporter must
deal routinely.

Chapter 4: Our mythical company is impacted not only by
events in the industries it serves, but by the overall economic
climate of the nation. Economic news has in recent years become
a front-page story. (Has anything in recent years gained as much
front-page attention as oil?)

This chapter is devoted to an explanation of the economic
statistics released from Washington, and to the headline stories
which are created by these reports. It covers the workings of the
Federal Reserve Board and the banking system, and defines each
of the signals, commonly called "indicators," which can foretell
whether or not the economy is moving into a decline or is
expanding.

Chapter 5 goes beyond the ten top stories which routinely cross
the newsman's desk. By studying each line of the balance sheet,
each line of the profit and loss statement, the notes to the balance
sheet and accountant's statement, we come to an understanding of
how these financial documents can reveal *new,* more subtle, and,
often, more important stories than those which the companies
themselves reveal in their news releases. There are stories to be
found in every line of the profit and loss statement and the
balance sheet. Moreover, financial statements are comparative
and the financial journalist must learn to go back over several
years looking for *changes*—adjustments, restatements. There is
always a story behind a change or discrepancy between currently
reported figures and previously reported figures. This section tells
how to find them and what they mean.

As I said earlier, financial statements are *complex,* but not
mysterious. This section will take some reviewing, and close
attention. But don't be put off by it. Although I am not an
accountant, I am a reasonably good analyst of financial statements. Yet, after a quarter century of work in this field, I still find
it necessary to review and think about new accounting regulations.

You may have to return to this section a number of times, but ultimately it will provide you with a foundation for deep insight into financial and economic news.

Chapter 6 is a collection of comments by leading financial analysts who present their insights in specialized industry analysis. It is well to remember that in addition to understanding financial statements, the reporter assigned to a specific industry must learn the financial ratios which have particular meaning in that specialized business. Ratios which seem to be excellent in a technology business might be awful when applied to a retail business. Working financial analysts break the corporate universe into some 40 industrial spheres, each with its own set of applicable ratios for analytical purposes. Although all 40 industries are not covered in this text—that would transform our book into a primer for financial analysts rather than for journalists—enough groups are covered so that the working journalist or student journalist can easily recognize how specialized ratios are useful in covering these varied industries.

Chapter 7 deals with the Securities and Exchange Commission and is related to Appendix A which appears in the Supplement, and which includes the SEC acts of 1933, 1934, and 1940. These are valuable to have on hand since many prominent news stories revolve around violations of SEC regulations.

Chapter 8, the Glossary, contains the financial and business terms most commonly used in financial and economic news stories. The journalist should consider the Glossary a tool to be continually expanded. As he shifts from industry to industry, he should add the special language of the business he is now covering.

Chapter 9 is devoted to research materials and reference sources. All publicly owned corporations—this includes some 15,000 actively traded companies, and many thousands of others—must file reports on a quarterly or annual basis with the Securities and Exchange Commission. This public information, available from the SEC, is valuable to the financial journalist. A review of this chapter will give the financial journalist a full understanding of what public information is available. The extent and variety is astonishing.

I have brought to this book my personal dedication to two professions, journalism and financial analysis. Over these past 25 years, I have been privileged to work alongside some of the finest talents in these two crafts, and I owe thanks to so many teachers that a recitation of their names would fill a book alone. However, I owe special debt to Professor John Tebbel, a great scholar, teacher, and journalist, formerly Chairman of the New York University Department of Journalism; to Robert E. Bedingfield, recently retired from the *New York Times* as Assistant to the Financial Editor; and to Sidney R. Winters, Senior Vice President of Lehman Brothers, and Past President of the New York Society of Security Analysts.

I must also thank those special friends who were so diligent in critiquing my manuscript, offering incisive comments and many suggestions for its improvement. From the working press: Harold Gold, Editor of *The Journal of Commerce;* William Giles, Editor, *The Detroit News,* and until January 1977, Director of Management Programs of Dow Jones & Company. From the academic community: Dr. David Rubin, Chairman of the Journalism Department, New York University; Dr. Robert Kavesh, Chairman, Department of Economics, New York University Graduate School of Business Administration; Richard Elfenbein, Professor of Business Communications, Rutgers University and Fairleigh Dickinson University. From the financial community: Sidney R. Winters, Senior Vice President, Lehman Brothers, and Past President of the New York Society of Security Analysts; George Weiss, former Chairman, and Director Emeritus, Bache Halsey Stuart Shields Inc.; Raphael Yavneh, President of Forbes Investors Advisory Institute Inc., member of the board of directors of Forbes Inc., and Doctor of Law with a special knowledge of Securities and Exchange regulations. From the legal community: Robert Haines, partner, Zimet, Haines, Moss & Goodkind. From the accounting community: Paul Neuwirth, partner, Alexander Grant & Co.

And finally, my thanks to Malcolm Johnson, Director, New York University Press; to Nat LaMar, who edited this volume; to Florence L. Ocker, my assistant, who labored over this manuscript; to Mary Bleakney, who typed it; to Herbert L. Lanzet,

Charles F.X. McCarthy and Thomas L. Wilkerson of the Wall Street Group, Inc. for their invaluable advice; to William and Eva Kirsch and Edward and Sylvia Tejw, for so many things; to Mark Adam, Karen Rebecca and Jonathan Bradford, my children, who would be unhappy if they did not see their names in print; and to my wife Dorothy Ann Kirsch, who made the task easier by her encouragement.

Donald Kirsch
New York, NY

Contents

Introduction:
An Overview of United States
Business History

The discovery of America transformed the world from a barter economy to a cash economy. It also laid the groundwork for individual liberty and for the eventual focus on human rights—but these only as an afterthought.

Originally, the discovery of America simply presented Spain with a marvelous business opportunity. It was perceived in exactly that manner by Spain's political and economic rivals, Portugal, France, England, and the Netherlands.

Queen Isabella was no fool. Although Adam Smith had not yet written *The Wealth of Nations* (1776), and the Scots had not yet introduced the concept of chartered accounting (1850), Isabella intuitively understood what every contemporary corporate raider and conglomerate manager knows: a new acquisition means a new stream of profits from a diversified source. She quickly sent the "Gold Dust Twins," Cortez and Pizarro, to audit the new enterprise, and to begin upstreaming dividends (as we term it today) from the new subsidiary to Spain, the parent holding company. Cortez quickly siphoned off the Aztec gold in Mexico, and Pizarro pulled all the silver out of the Inca vaults in Peru.

The success of this endeavor can be easily measured: in 1492 there was only $200,000,000 of gold and silver in *world* circulation (about $2 for each person then living). By 1600 this had increased eightfold to approximately $1.6 billion ($3.20 per person), and by 1700 it had risen to some $4 billion ($4.00 per person), an increase of 20 times.

EUROPEANS EYE THE MARKET

No wonder the competing European monarchs looked at America with the same sense of adventure and excitement that Tom Watson had when he recognized the potential of computers to transform IBM from a staid maker of timeclocks (believe it or not, only *30* years ago) into a monolith of innovation. The European scramble for this new business opportunity began in earnest, in the same way that hundreds of large and small companies jumped into the computer business to challenge IBM. As happens in a new industry, some of the newcomers were big names, while some were small crapshooters taking a chance in the big time, hoping by ingenuity, daring, and skill to knock off the leader. Within a few years, Portugal, England, France, Holland, Sweden, Denmark, Prussia, and even Scotland had formed their own versions of the East India Companies. (Remember, Columbus was seeking India!) Each wanted as large a piece of the new market as he could take and hold—not unlike a modern business enterprise.

And what a prize they were after! Sixteen million square miles of property with virtually no population, compared to 3,750,000 square miles in all of Europe, with 100,000,000 residents.

Preferring temperate climates, Spain moved to colonize the western and southeastern areas of America. The Dutch and the British moved towards the big money prize—the Atlantic Seaboard—almost simultaneously.

DUTCH FORM STOCK EXCHANGE

The Flemish traders and merchants appreciated the symbiotic nature of national and private interests. Understanding the need to pool capital for investment purposes, the Dutch in 1531 established the world's first stock exchange in Antwerp. The flourishing Antwerp exchange and the active trade in the shares of the early joint-stock companies provided the Dutch with a workable machinery for raising capital, and laid the groundwork for the funding of the Dutch West India Company and the founding of New Amsterdam.

Through pooled capital, the Dutch hired English explorer Henry Hudson to investigate America for them, and to find a shorter route to the Pacific. Hudson found no Northwest Passage, but did issue a favorable business report on the prospects for fur trading. As a result, a group of Dutch merchants set up trading posts in the New World in 1614, and in 1624 the then three-year-old Dutch West India Company brought a group of colonists to the territory at the mouth of the Hudson River and named the site New Amsterdam. Two years later, in 1626, the director-general of the Dutch West India Company, Peter Minuit, bought Manhattan from the Indians for 60 guilders—the equivalent of $24. (Had the $24 been invested at prevailing bank interest rates, it would be worth more than $20 trillion, enough to buy Manhattan back—or the world. The current tax assessment for Manhattan is approximately $18.3 billion, and the wealth of the world is estimated only at $5 trillion.)

BRITISH ESTABLISH JOINT-STOCK COMPANIES

To sponsor their interests in the new territories, the British copied the joint-stock company technique of the Dutch, granting two such charters in 1606. The crown granted to a group of 715 investors led by Sir Walter Raleigh the right to develop 1,800,000 square miles of property—what now constitutes 18 states and parts of 14 more—which Raleigh named Virginia, in honor of the virgin Queen Elizabeth.

The 715 investors paid £50,000 sterling for their stock, equivalent to $218,000 in United States currency when dollars were issued for the first time late in the 1700s. Known simply as "the Virginia Company of London," the full and proper title was "the Treasurer and Company of Adventurers and Planters of the City of London for the First Colony in Virginia." The London group founded Jamestown.

The second charter was granted to a less wealthy group from the Plymouth area who petitioned for the same privileges of overseas investment as granted the London group. The Plymouth group soon founded Plymouth, Massachusetts.

Though both investments seemed promising, neither proved to be so. Each company went through many reorganizations, with investors putting in good money after bad.

FORTUNES IN LAND

Although Sir Walter Raleigh's land scheme failed, the earliest American fortunes were indeed made in land, with the first arrivals acquiring the choicest parcels, generally along rivers and the seashore. The economic base of early America was, for some 200 years, land-oriented and mostly agricultural, with some 95 percent of the New World population working as farmers in the 1600s and 90 percent in the 1700s.

Although land was plentiful, labor was at a premium. Farmers and merchants were eager for workers, and the monarchy obliged by emptying the English prisons of its thieves, debtors, vagabonds, and paupers, and shipping them to America as indentured servants in bondage for from seven to ten years. It is estimated that half of the white migrants to America arrived as indentured servants and that, by 1776, three-quarters of the populations of Pennsylvania, Maryland, and Virginia had come to the colonies in this way.

THE ECONOMICS OF SLAVERY

In 1619, a Dutch privateer arrived at Jamestown carrying a cargo of black slaves from Guinea. The commander offered the slaves for sale at $80 to $150 a head. For many hard-pressed farmers the economics were compelling enough to overcome morality. An investment of less than $150 provided a lifetime employee plus clear title to his children at no additional cost. Compared with $10-to-$20 annual overhead required to provide for an indentured servant who gained his freedom just when he was becoming most productive, the investment made sense.

The Dutch did not exploit this business opportunity as vigorously as they had other aspects of trade, and half a century after the first slave cargo was sold in Jamestown, less than 2000 slaves were to be found in the colonies. At this point American traders broke the Dutch monopoly, and slavery grew rapidly. By 1790, the time of the first census, there were some 700,000 slaves in the United States, accounting for some 20% of the country's total population, and about 40% of the population of the South.

As the colonies became productive, surpluses were generated, enough to begin an international trade. The southern colonies were producing—along with rice and indigo—tobacco, which became the most profitable product in the New World. The northern colonies were principally producing forest and seafood products; and the middle colonies began exporting agricultural items.

While fortunes were being made rapidly in trade, wealth was quickly transferred into land. The colonies lacked a system of coinage, and although the New England colonies experimented with paper money secured by real estate, most trade was conducted with Austrian thalers supplied by the British government and with Spanish and French coins received in trade. This reflected the British attitude that the colonies existed to serve the commercial interests of the Empire. Colonial manufacturing was forbidden, and trading was restricted to territories within the British Empire. The British wanted the colonies to have as primitive a monetary system as possible.

NO CURRENCY

As a result, the burgeoning trade of America was conducted by barter and by Letters of Credit, a system of banking conceived in thirteenth-century Italy whereby credit was exchanged and interest charged without currency changing hands. This was quite a hindrance to the spirited colonialists, and it was just one of the many burrs pricking them as the concept of economic liberty evolved.

As the innovative Americans expanded their agricultural base and began to diversify into manufacturing, they began to produce more than was needed for their own use and more than the Empire wished to buy. They turned to other foreign buyers, and American exports began to compete with goods manufactured in England. British merchants and manufacturers were furious at the competition, and demanded legislation from the Crown that would protect the home industries. The stage was being set for independence.

The 37 colonial newspapers operating before the Revolution were filled with news of the latest economic outrage pressed upon an agrarian society anxious to sell its surplus farm and forest products on international markets, and audacious enough to want to upgrade raw materials into finished goods and compete overseas with manufacturers in the Mother Country. The various English mercantile guilds, which agitated for Parliamentary regulations to halt exportation of finished goods from the colonies, brought the two nations increasingly into conflict, until finally the only resolution was total independence, with America free to produce and compete internationally without restriction.

ECONOMIC INEQUITIES

An illustration of the economic inequities which proved to be the bellows for the Revolutionary flame can best be seen by the British treatment of colonial tobacco growers. John Rolfe (who married Pocahontas) developed a better method of curing the tobacco leaf in 1612, and so great an international demand developed for this product that it quickly became the mainstay of the American agricultural industry. Economic cooperation was developing between the colonies, and New England seamen were sailing their small boats into the narrow inland waterways of the tobacco-growing colonies, picking up their cargo and transporting it to overseas markets.

British merchants were enraged at the competition from American ships, and fostered legislation known as the Navigation Acts, the first of which was introduced in 1651. It forbade the importation into England, Ireland, and the colonies of any products not carried in English bottoms and manned primarily by English seamen. This economic noose was further tightened ten years later when, in 1661, the newest Navigation Act restricted the American export of tobacco, sugar, wool, and indigo to any destination but England.

By limiting the market for tobacco, the British also limited the source of credit to the plantation owner. He had to borrow in England. By 1700 many of the planters were heavily in debt to their overseas creditors. One angry planter commented that planters themselves had become property as business debts passed from father to son. The planter who made the remark was Thomas Jefferson, and his irritation was later to be stated in more direct style.

That the new lands in America were something to be exploited for the benefit of the Mother Country was graphically demonstrated by the Navigation Acts. But the exploitation of colonial lands was not a new phenomenon. *Exploitation* was the purpose of *exploration.*

The economic bondage to which Jefferson referred was felt increasingly by all Americans in commerce, and this included a significant part of the population of this new commercial nation. This country was conceived not only "in liberty" but in debt.

There is no need to recount here the political and military acts leading to independence. The bedrock of our discontent was economic.

AFTER THE REVOLUTION

In 1776, the vise was broken. A unique, independent nation had been formed, created by an aristocracy committed to class mobility, backed by a people infused with a Calvinistic appreciation of the rewards of hard work.

No single institution benefited more from independence than

the Manufacturing Societies, established to provide a framework for the financing of new ventures. In 1790 Alexander Hamilton issued his important *Report on Manufactures* in which he stated "a hope that the obstacles to the growth of industry are less formidable than they were apprehended to be." Hamilton himself helped organize the Society of Establishing Useful Manufactures, a colonial conglomerate whose aim was to manufacture cotton, linen goods, paper, run printing shops, and engage in various other public works. Stockholders invested $250,000 to fund the Society.

A financial and industrial society soon burst forth from the Revolutionary chrysalis, flexible enough to adapt to the permutations required in a new civilization in which each generation expected to advance its standard of living from the preceding— and in which each generation desired its progeny to have more material possessions, and a supposedly easier life.

Corporations similar to the Dutch joint-stock companies of the mercantile era, but more adaptable to the needs of an industrial manufacturing society, were chartered to enable investors to pool capital. By 1800 more than 300 corporations were chartered. (Today there are more than 1,750,000 in the United States, with 75,000 being added annually and some 60,000 dying each year.) The great majority of the new corporations were chartered for purposes which today might classify them as public utilities, such as roads, bridges, canals, and watersystems. But a growing number were established to produce products which filled a market need and made a profit.

Private wealth was put at risk in the hope of making a profit. Men of wealth also speculated in scrip, buying what might prove to be worthless I.O.U.s from farmers and veterans hard-hit by the Revolutionary War. The trading center for scrip focused on Manhattan, in what eventually became the New York Stock Exchange. Colonialists were used to trading in scrip and commodities. Since Parliament had forbidden issuance of bills of credit as legal tender in New England in 1764 in an effort to keep the new territories dependent upon Mother England, the American tradesmen had developed unusual skills in evaluating risks and property, and in negotiation.

HAMILTON'S FORESIGHT

Alexander Hamilton assumed the role of Secretary of the Treasury in September, 1789, and immediately began to work on a comprehensive program to spur industry, create a monetary system for the new nation, and lay the foundation for the economic growth of the United States. Hamilton was one of the few men of his time to grasp the nuances of the Industrial Revolution, and his vision of America as an industrial giant was a bold and visionary one.

In his *First Report on the Public Credit,* Hamilton proposed that the new government accept the obligation for all foreign debts and monies owed to veterans and merchants. Some $77 million was involved, and there was much opposition to Hamilton's proposals. A tradition had already evolved of nonpayment of taxes, and those opposed to Hamilton wanted to abrogate such debts. Additionally, some opponents were against rewarding speculators who had been buying scrip for as little as 12¢ on the dollar.

Also, most of the state debts were Northern, and the Southerners objected to the Federal Government assuming these obligations because it would penalize those with little or no debt. Hamilton bargained with Jefferson for the two Southern votes he needed in Congress to approve the assumption of debt: States which had paid their debts would receive a subsidy, and the new national capital would be on the banks of the Potomac.

As a result of the compromise, a national debt was created. Congress authorized the issuance of $80,000,000 in government bonds to fund the new debt, and trading began in these securities as the financial needs of the investors changed.

OUR FIRST STOCK EXCHANGE

Brokers, or "stockjobbers" as they were then called, traded these securities, as well as scrip and certificates in some of the newly formed corporations. They conducted their business on street corners in lower Manhattan, continuing indoors at nearby coffee houses when the weather was poor.

The trading of securities was at best haphazardous, and based more on intuition than on sure knowledge regarding the underlying value of the securities. As a result, some issues did not trade at all. Marketability was poor, and liquidity of investment erratic.

This began to change when, on May 17, 1792, a group of 24 stockjobbers and merchants met under a buttonwood tree at what is now 69 Wall Street in Manhattan (marked by a plaque in the curbstone) and signed the following agreement:

> We, the Subscribers, Brokers for the Purchase and Sale of Public Stocks, do hereby solemnly promise and pledge ourselves to each other that we will not buy or sell, from this day, for any person whatsoever, any kind of Public Stock at a less rate than one-quarter per cent Commission on the Special value, and that we will give preference to each other in our negotiations.

In 1793, the signers of the Buttonwood Agreement moved their business indoors to the newly built Tontine Coffee House, and in 1817 formalized their association with a constitution and the name "New York Stock & Exchange Board." The initiation fee (for a "seat") was $25. In 1929, a seat on the Exchange sold for an all-time high of $625,000, and a contemporary low of $14,000 was reached in 1942. More recently, a contemporary high of $515,000 was paid for a seat in 1968; by 1977 the value of a seat had declined to $35,000, 30% less than the cost of a medallion license to own a New York City taxicab.

THE CAPITAL-RAISING MECHANISM: BANKS, INSURANCE COMPANIES, AND PRIVATE INVESTORS

At last, the latticework was in place for the stitching together of the unique capital-raising mechanism which has enabled the United States to finance its industrial growth through banking, insurance companies, and the public stock market. The life blood of industry is capital. Without money and credit our industrial society would come to a halt. Alexander Hamilton clearly understood this, and under his ministrations our nation evolved its extraordinary system of capitalism—a unique blend of venture funding from large numbers of individual investors and combined financing from banks and insurance companies. The colonial feeling of isolation and spirit of independence; the anger and humiliation at the economic injustices perpetuated by England; the appreciation of the Calvinistic doctrine of God's approval of hard work and its earthly rewards; and the evaluating and negotiating skills required in building a barter economy—all contributed to the entrepreneurial character of the emerging nation. Together, the innovative financial machinery and the special temperament of the people produced a new society, *a business civilization.*

BANKS

For more than a century before the Revolution, colonialists had been talking of the need for banking. The lack of currency had been a great hindrance to the expansion of the colonies. The success of the Revolution permitted the establishment of local banks, and groups of merchants and others quickly moved to fill this need. The Bank of North America in Philadelphia was founded in 1781; the Bank of New York and the Massachusetts Bank in 1784. These early banks were conservative and inspired trust—the true basis on which the banking business runs.

Almost all of American industry and commerce is financed by credit, a term derived from the Latin *credo,* "I believe." Those who extend credit believe they will be repaid. The merchant who accepts a promissory note from a buyer believes he will be paid at the time stipulated in the note. If the merchant needs financing to purchase additional goods, he can sell the note to a bank, which also expresses its faith that the signer of the note will meet his obligation at the proper date. The paper currency the bank gives the merchant in exchange for the note is simply a substitute for a silver or gold coin. In this fashion, money and credit are created.

Moneylending is an ancient profession. Its earliest limitation was that the moneylender could lend out only what he possessed in valuable metal. When he had loaned it all out, he could do no more until some of the debt was repaid. The advent of banks changed that. By substituting paper money for metal, credit is created, and the prudent extension of credit by banks has enabled many now important industries to grow from embryos.

Banks in America are deposit and credit agencies, however, not investors. And when they loan money, even to major industries, they want it back in a relatively short time—generally five years or less. The earliest American banks worked on an even shorter cycle (at times only 90 days) and in some cases made loans only with the unanimous consent of all directors. At the Massachusetts Bank, as an example, the directors voted on all loans by dropping white or black balls into a box. If one black ball appeared, the loan application was denied. (This bank also charged depositors a fee for keeping their money.)

The First Bank of the United States was chartered for 20 years in 1791 at the strong urging of Hamilton, who recognized the importance of a national bank to control the overall supply of money and to act as an intermediary between public and private financial interests. The Bank was quite successful, although Jefferson and the Republicans were much against it, feeling that it provided the industrialists of the Northeast with an opportunity to transfer even more of the nation's capital to their provinces.

As the West grew, regional pressures caused difficulties for the national bank. The needs of farmers proved to be different from those of the industrial East. New lands being put to crop would not pay off for several years, and the thirty-day notes used by Northern and Southern merchants were of little assistance: The farmers needed longer term mortgages. Frontier banks who met the needs of the local communities found themselves in a delicate position: When loan payments were not met because of crop failure or sharp price fluctuations in the commodities markets, they could not easily foreclose for fear of causing panic or earning the hostility of the community. Yet if they did not foreclose, they faced the possibility of financial difficulty themselves.

As a result of the problems caused by the frontier banks, the Republicans fought the renewal of the bank charter for the First Bank of the United States, and it expired in 1811. Only five years later, a new national bank was chartered. This was the Second Bank of the United States, chartered also for 20 years, and its stern behavior during a period of inflation, unstable currencies, land speculation, and a financial panic in 1819 caused many smaller banks and overextended merchants to go out of business. The feeling grew that banks did not serve the interests of the common man, but instead were dedicated to the interests of the manufacturers and larger merchants.

INSURANCE COMPANIES

As manufacturing enterprises grew, a second source of funding became available—insurance companies. Insurance companies today have more than $434 billion in assets, and have industrial loans of some $108 billion outstanding. Whereas banks seek loans of less than five years and do not take stock as a part of their compensation, insurance companies make loans for as long as 20 years and frequently seek stock positions in the businesses to which they are lending.

Insurance is one of the world's oldest businesses. The ancient Chinese, Normans, and Romans commingled assets as protection against loss by fire or drought. In 1218, an English guild offered to help any of its members with financial aid if they lost property through fire or robbery. And in 1769, sea captains, ship owners, and merchants who met daily in Edward Lloyd's coffee house in London drew up policies evidencing participation in newly formed syndicates which shared both the profits and losses of trading voyages.

Insurance companies specialize in five categories: life, fire, casualty, marine, and surety. The first insurance company in America was founded in 1735 at Charleston, South Carolina, to specialize in fire protection and claims. Benjamin Franklin established a marine company in Philadelphia, in 1752. Life insurance was not introduced until 1759.

SECURITIES

The third spoke on the wheel of finance was the public market, and the New York Stock & Exchange Board was to become an increasing force in this area. Although trading before 1830 was slight, it did offer a marketplace for companies wishing to sell securities. The 1830s witnessed the introduction of steam railroads in the United States, and railroad and canal issues soon became the most active stocks on the exchange. They also helped to attract foreign investors, who had felt comfortable investing in America ever since Hamilton had won his battle in 1790 to have the Federal government assume certain colonial debts.

TREMENDOUS INDUSTRIAL EXPANSION

The opening of the Western territories, the unleashing of manufacturing to produce for domestic and export markets, and the creation of a three-pronged financing apparatus spurred the development of basic industries and encouraged inventors to seek new approaches to solving industrial problems. The Patent Office recorded an average of 77 new patents per year between 1790 and 1811. From 1820 to 1830 this number jumped to 535 a year, against only 145 for Great Britain, at that time the world's most industrialized nation. By the 1850s the number of new patents granted each year in the United States averaged 2525.

The diversity of inventions was staggering. James Watt's improvements in 1769 on Thomas Newcomen's steam engine were the basis for Robert Fulton's successful steamboat in 1806. The growing opportunities in steam engine transportation moved a young Staten Island ferryboat operator, Cornelius Van Derbilt (later spelled "Vanderbilt"), to build his own steamboats, becoming one of the largest steamboat builders in the nation before moving on to railroads. In 1830 Peter Cooper, a New York merchant who later founded Cooper Union College, built a steam engine named "Tom Thumb" from scrap iron, and in a 13-mile race against a horse, convinced the management of the Baltimore & Ohio Railroad to switch from horse-drawn trains to steam. By 1835 the Eastwick & Harrison Company of Philadelphia had developed coal-burning engines, opening an international market for American railroad equipment.

The sale of government lands in the West sucked population

from the East, causing some labor problems in the East, but also opening the market for vast amounts of agricultural products. In the 1840s John Deere, a blacksmith, improved upon the cast-iron plow; and Cyrus McCormick perfected a reaping machine in 1834, offering it to farmers with payment on an instalment basis, sharply improving the agricultural productivity. In 1842 Joseph Dart invented a granary which kept grain insulated from heat and moisture and which could be filled directly from a docked ship. Moses Brown, businessman and founder of Brown University, had established the great New England textile industry in 1789 with the introduction of equipment developed by Samuel Slater, an English spinning mechanic; and by the mid-1800s the New England mills had moved to steam power and had increased spindle speed to 11,000 rpm through the use of John Thorpe's "ring spinner," compared with 50 rpm earlier in the century. Iron factories switched to coal from wood as the forests in the East thinned out, bringing about strong growth in an unrelated industry, cooking stoves.

And, so it continued. Edison, Marconi, Ford, the Wright Brothers—from pony express to Western Union telegraph to giant computers; from steamboats to railroads to jet aircraft.

BUSINESS NEWS COVERAGE

With all this activity came an expansion in business news coverage. Investors and businessmen alike required as full disclosure as possible, and as rapidly as possible. From the earliest days of the colonies, economic news had been treated as the most vital kind of information. With financial and industrial expansion, there was a need for specialization in this type of news and for concentration of news space devoted to this aspect of America. Newspapers began to allocate separate sections for the reportage of financial and economic news.

As our $1.8-trillion-dollar economy moves onward, the need for even more comprehensive financial and economic coverage grows. The major front-page stories—OPEC, welfare, medical costs—are economics-oriented. If one digs deeply enough, virtually any financial or economic news story can be turned into a human-interest feature or a story of local implication. And conversely, by thinking through noneconomic stories to see if they have local impact, or if they affect a company with public stockholders, many interesting and important business stories can be found.

Calvin Coolidge said it best. "The business of America is business."

Financial and Economic Journalism

Analysis, Interpretation, and Reporting

CHAPTER ONE

Business And Business Journalism: Parallel Tracks

Since the Renaissance, business and business journalism, in their most primitive forms, have moved on parallel tracks. The need to know is inherent in the making of business decisions; information is the lifeline of the businessman.

Today's daily pages in local newspapers, with their multiple columns listing stock transactions on the New York, American, and regional stock exchanges, have antecedents in publications first issued almost 400 years ago. The Dutch, flourishing in the world of art, were at the same time the most aggressive of Renaissance businessmen, pushing their trading fleets to the limits of the then-known world, and hiring adventuresome sea captains to explore as yet unknown territories.

With their expansion of trade came a requirement for information about commodity prices, the goods they were selling and shipping, buying, and exchanging. Merchants and brokers in Amsterdam, founders in 1531 of the world's first stock and produce exchange, made the first move toward resolving the problem of price information by introducing a "price-current" publication, *The Rate of Commodities Valid in Amsterdam (Cours van der comenschappen soo die hier in Amsterdam geldende sijn),* in 1585. The commodities were printed in type, but the prices were handwritten.

Within a quarter of a century these price-current publications formalized into a journalistic art, with both prices and commodities being set in type, providing uniform information to a broader public. The oldest existing such publication is dated November 23, 1609, carrying information on more than 200 commodities as traded by members of the Amsterdam Produce Market.

The English introduced their own price-current publications some 75 years later, the earliest known one being published about 1667. By 1681, the English price currents had begun to make their first transformation, expanding to include stock prices of the earliest publicly owned companies (then known as "joint-stock" companies). The addition of the trading prices of shares of the East India, Africa, and Hudson's Bay companies triggered the evolution of price-current publications to broader, financially oriented papers.

Price-current journalism received its biggest thrust from the growth of the American colonies. As business began to expand along the eastern coast of America, price currents followed. The first to be published in the New World was introduced in 1752 in Halifax, Nova Scotia, printed on behalf of the merchant firm of Nathans and Hart by Joseph Bushell, a Philadelphia printer who had recently moved to the area. A second publication was not introduced for 22 years, until the advent of the Carolina *Price-Current* in Charles-Town, in 1774.

Suddenly, price currents began flourishing throughout the colonies. With important business centers sprouting in Boston, New York, Philadelphia, Baltimore, and Charleston, the need for news of commodity prices was great. These publications, however, did not depend upon advertising or subscriptions for support. Rather, they were subsidized by the merchants who considered them an integral business tool.

With eight price currents being published in Philadelphia in the late 1700s, that city became the center of business publishing in the colonies. The Revolutionary War and the British Blockade sharply impacted American business and reduced the number of price-current publications, but with the end of hostilities American shipping interests expanded to the major ports of the world. As a result, price currents responded with still another innovation, the introduction of shipping news. Especially important to readers was the notice of mailbag pickup and delivery by the sailing ships.

On July 11, 1791, Vincent Pelosi of Philadelphia founded *Pelosi's Marine List and Price Current,* and for the first time charged subscribers for a U. S. business publication—$4.67 for 52 weekly issues. He quickly learned what all publishers know—that publishing is a precarious business. The publication lasted only 42 issues. (Few of the Colonial price currents lasted as long as five years.)

By the early 1800s, price-current publishers were looking to advertisers to help support their publications. Thomas Hope, a former grocer, changed the name of his publication to *Hope's Philadelphia Price-Current and Commercial Record,* and in 1811 opened the pages to lottery advertising. At that time, lotteries were an important method by which capital was raised for expanding businesses and public works. From 1811 through 1830 many colleges were financed almost entirely by lotteries.

On September 1, 1827 the *Journal of Commerce* made its appearance. Despite its name, it was a general daily with only a modest business news section. The founders selected the name, however, to appeal to the merchants whose advertising was required to keep the paper afloat. A century and a half later, the *Journal of Commerce* is one of the leading all-business dailies in the world.

The first daily paper devoted entirely to business appeared in New York on November 1, 1815. *Daily Items for Merchants* lasted for only a year, and was not followed by another daily until 1869, when William Dodsworth founded the *Daily Bulletin,* as a spin-off of the successful weekly *Commercial and Financial Chronicle.*

SHIPPING LISTS

Commodity-price information shaped the character of the earliest business publications. By the 1800s, the importance of shipping information had supplanted commodity news as the greatest need of the greatest number of business people. Price currents, as we have seen, gradually expanded to include shipping news, but by 1810 the requirement for shipping information was so great that maritime news began to dominate these publications.

As is so often the case, business-paper publishers and newsmen are themselves excellent businessmen, with sufficient insight to spot new opportunities. The founders of the *General Shipping* and Commercial List, New York printers Mahlon Day and Charles Turner, foresaw a strong increase in shipping as a result of the Treaty of Peace, signed in December, 1814, and founded their newspaper in 1815 to offer "a faithful record of all the floating commerce of the world."

The paper prospered as shipping boomed following the War of 1812, and for more than 100 years *General Shipping* reported the growth of New York shipping. During that span the paper expanded to include coverage of business and commerce, and in 1927 merged into the *Journal of Commerce*.

By the mid-1820s, *General Shipping* had introduced a series of departments offering specialized information to a variety of industries: marine lists, commodity prices, stocks, auction sales, and a new innovation—a bank-note table which reported on the rate at which notes could be exchanged for cash. As always, business news mirrors current political and social activities: State banks were proliferating as a result of decisions made some 20 years earlier by Alexander Hamilton, who recognized the need for an independent system of currency and banking for farmers and merchants.

Other shipping papers emulated *General Shipping* but none were as extensive in news coverage. Still, they offered local businessmen the information they needed on arrivals and departures of vessels in local ports, and the all-important information about pickup and delivery of mailbags to and from overseas ports.

AUCTION REPORTS

One of the earliest journalists to recognize a gold mine in shipping news was Peter Pane Francis DeGrand of Boston, who started a weekly in 1819 to report on merchandise being offered for auction in public sale. In the early 1800s auction sales were an important method of wholesaling products to merchants or merchandise brokers, and DeGrand knew that prices of past sales and notices of future offerings would be of interest to merchants. DeGrand informed his readers that his publication would not only advise them of forthcoming sales, but that by comparing previous sales they could determine seasonal fluctuations in certain products, and even determine how to price their existing inventory during uncertain economic times. DeGrand's *Boston Weekly Report* did well, and was the precurser for imitators.

GENERAL BUSINESS PUBLICATIONS

By 1865, the business press was maturing in America. Specialized publications followed the growth of individual industries—mining, railroading, shipping—and price-current publications had expanded to cover a variety of business news. *Hunt's Merchants' Magazine,* a monthly founded in 1837 by Freeman Hunt, an experienced Boston journalist who yearned to have his own publication, became the first nationally distributed business journal in America, and introduced a strong editorial posture. Hunt chastised political leaders for actions which he considered detrimental to business interests, and the paper quickly developed a strong support in the commercial world.

Hunt had a wide personal horizon. As the nation expanded, his magazine covered the emerging industries, with experts in many fields writing on their specialized areas. The monthly developed an international reputation and readership, and became an influential shaper of thought. Hunt died in 1858 at age 54, and the publication was taken over three years later by William B. Dana, a lawyer from Utica, New York. In 1865 Dana founded a weekly business paper, the *Commercial and Financial Chronicle,* which became enormously popular, and in 1870 he merged *Hunt's* into it, ending a publication whose founder was one of the giants of business journalism in America.

FINANCIAL JOURNALS

With the growth in importance of banking and capital, a new group of publications arrived in response to a new economic need—information about banking, stocks and bonds, and money conditions. Bankers became editors and started successful publications, the first being the *Bankers' Weekly Circular and Statistical Record* in 1845 (still published in Boston as the *Banking Law Journal*). Founders Isaac Smith Homans and Edwin Williams acted as responsible overseers of the public interest, among other things calling to task those bankers who fought against the introduction of a national currency. Homans, in particular, took positions which were unfriendly to his banking audience, editorializing that bankers were making personal profit on their own bank notes, and demanding that the government issue a standard bank note. In 1863, the government responded to his fifteen year campaign by adopting his proposals, passing a bill establishing the National Banking System. Following the *Banking Law Journal* numerous excellent bank publications were founded throughout the states, with their editors and reporters making important contributions to the development of a sound banking system in the United States.

The diversity of financial publications was great in the mid-1800s. For instance, the first paper to defend stockholders was published in 1862, two months after Lincoln issued his Preliminary Emancipation Proclamation. F. D. Longchamp introduced *The Stockholder: Monitor of Finance and Industry* in New York City as a weekly, and immediately attacked entrenched managements for their disinterest in their shareholders. Longchamp printed much information about stocks and bonds, and wrote editorials about the national debt of the United States and commentary on how political leaders affect corporations and their shareholders. He particularly took out after railroad managers, commenting in one editorial that "railroad managers have been accustomed ... to consider the roads they manage as their own property. Salaries and other expenses swollen to exaggeration are the consequence, and stockholders have been often deprived, as a matter of course, of income of their property." This, at a time when railroad barons tolerated criticism from no one.

Following in Longchamp's editorial footsteps, stockholder-oriented newspapers were formed in New York (the *American Circular,* and the *Banker and Broker)* and in San Francisco (*Weekly Stock Circular).* Each operated successfully, and helped create a body of readers for newer and even broader business newspapers which contained news of finance and other matters of economic interest.

Until the founding of the *Commercial and Financial Chronicle* in 1865, and the *Wall Street Journal* in 1889 there were no newspapers devoted entirely to finance—although the earliest papers, the price currents, set the stage for specialized commercial publications.

The first major financial newspaper, the *Commercial and Financial Chronicle,* was founded as a weekly in 1865 by lawyer William B. Dana, who five years later merged the prestigious business monthly, *Hunt's,* into it. In his first issue he stated "No comprehensive paper devoted wholly to the great mercantile and commercial interest has yet appeared.... It is to fill this place in the ranks of the public press, and supply this want, that the *Commercial and Financial Chronicle* aspires." The *Chronicle* continues today as a weekly statistical paper.

What was to prove to be the most important event in financial journalism was the founding in 1882 of Dow Jones & Company, organized by two New England reporters, Charles H. Dow and Edward H. Jones, to collect information of importance to brokerage houses. The first Dow Jones publication, a one-page newsletter, proved of immediate and immense value to banks, brokerage houses, and businessmen. In 1889 the partners expanded into newspaper publishing with the *Wall Street Journal.*

Actually, there had been two previous newspapers entitled the *Wall Street Journal,* neither of which was related to the Dow Jones national financial daily. A *Wall Street Journal and Real Estate Gazette,* founded in 1852, was devoted to finance, real estate, and mining. A second *Wall Street Journal,* whose earliest available issues date from 1867 (but include a comment that publication began in 1852) may have been a descendant of the earlier publication. The *Wall Street Journal and Real Estate Gazette* (1852), was published by Robinson and Company, and edited by Frederick D. Robinson. The 1867 paper, published by

John Hillyer, was frequently referred to as "Hillyer's *Wall Street Journal.*" Throughout the 1860s and much of the 1870s it was important for its coverage of finance and those newer industries into which capital was rushing. Hillyer's was published until at least 1879, three years before the founding of Dow Jones & Company and ten years before the start in 1889 of the contemporary *Wall Street Journal.*

The *Wall Street Journal* was sold in 1902 to another legendary financial journalist, Clarence W. Barron, an imposing-looking gentleman, weighing 300 pounds and wearing a full beard. Barron, founder of *Barron's Magazine,* had started a service similar to Dow Jones in Boston and had also served as the *Journal's* Boston stringer. Under Barron's leadership, the *Wall Street Journal* extended its coverage to the entire country. In 1929, a year after Barron's death, the *Journal* started a regional edition in San Francisco, and today has others in Chicago, Dallas and an Asian edition in Hong Kong.

The *Journal* best exemplifies the consistent growth in business and financial news. At the beginning of World War II, the *Journal's* circulation was around 30,000. Today it is better than 1,500,000.

Dow Jones's influence is felt everywhere. In addition to the *Wall Street Journal,* stockbrokers and businessmen subscribe to the famous *Dow Jones Newswire,* which five days a week sends forth a continuous stream of current news from 8 A.M. to 6 P.M. (or later, as required). *Barron's,* its weekly magazine of finance, is among the best-read financial periodicals in the country. And the Dow Jones Averages are the indices most popularly followed as an indication of stock market behavior.

Financial and economic news today has come of age. With the Arab oil boycott, commodity prices and their effect upon consumers' lives have become front-page news; unemployment, inflation, the decline of the New York Stock Exchange, and women's rights all tie into the changing environment of business. Business reporters who cover the financial and economic news have their fingers on the pulse of the public. They feel the immediate reaction to political, environmental, and societal news, and at the same time find that their assignments frequently alert them to non-business stories which end up on page one.

Major newswires—the *Associated Press Business Wire,* the *United Press International Business Wire, Reuters, Dow Jones Newswire*—rush the business news to readers. Daily newspapers are beginning to devote more pages to the subject, and the specialized papers—the *Wall Street Journal,* the *Journal of Commerce,* the *Market Chronicle*—are expanding their coverage, while business magazines such as *Forbes, Fortune,* and *Business Week* intensify their own efforts to present the reader with an accurate understanding of what is happening to his most sensitive indicator, his pocketbook.

In the decades ahead, financial and economic journalism may well be the most exciting place to be.

CHAPTER TWO

The Creation and Growth of a Corporation

The race for riches in the New World was fueled by capital. As we have seen, the Dutch were the first to realize that pooling capital was essential to create the sizable funds needed to build settlements.

The mechanism they choose—the joint-stock company—permitted individuals to purchase shares in a single venture, or in an ongoing enterprise. These joint-stock companies issued shares to the investors, and these shares rose in value or fell as the fortunes of the venture improved or declined. If the investment was in a share of a new sailing ship, and the ship was much overdue in reaching its destination, those who were fainthearted might try to unload their shares at reduced prices; news—or even rumors—of a ship returning with a rich cargo might cause speculators to offer a shareowner a nice profit before his ship came in.

To facilitate the exchange and trading of shares, the Dutch merchants formed a stock and produce exchange in Antwerp in 1531.

Some 75 years later, the English monarchy, hard pressed for cash, recognized the joint-stock technique as a valuable method to permit more rapid exploitation of the New World. As a result, investors were permitted to pool their capital, receive shares in exchange for their pounds, and risk their personal fortunes in the hope of significant gains. Jamestown, Virginia and Plymouth, Massachusetts were, in effect, company towns founded by real estate developers who were managing the funds of a group of investors in what we would today consider "publicly owned" companies. In fact, had those companies been formed today, the Securities and Exchange Commission would probably have sued Sir Walter Raleigh and other members of management for abuse of privilege. In each case, investors lost all their money.

The concept of pooling capital to form a company of investors was readily accepted and sponsored in America by that most innovative of Revolutionary patriots, Alexander Hamilton. His 1790 *Report of Manufacturers* urged the joint-stock technique— ultimately called a "corporation"—on the American public. He helped organize what today is termed a "conglomerate," a company with eclectic interests and holdings in many different trades and industries.

Shares in these American-style joint-stock companies were subject to the same types of pressures as those of the Dutch and English varieties. They rose or fell in price on rumor, speculation and news. News was vital to the investors.

In 1792, traders in these American variety shares formed a stock exchange for the orderly trading in these securities. By doing so, they provided a three-part service: a method of buying and selling shares of existing corporations; a method by which an inventor or founder of a new company could raise capital by selling shares to the investors who were customers of the traders; and an opportunity for monied speculators to cheaply buy into a new enterprise at groundfloor prices, with attendant risks inherent in all new ventures.

It has not changed much in almost 200 years. Life has become more complex, sophisticated and analytical; so has investing.

The fewer than 300 corporations existing in the United States in 1792 have grown to 1,750,000 today, with an estimated 15,000 of these having sufficient shareholders to qualify as "publicly owned" rather than "family-owned" companies, with active, daily trading in their securities. An estimated 35,000 more qualify as "publicly owned" corporations, but their shares trade less actively.

This universe of 15,000 actively traded publicly owned corporations is a prism through which our society can be observed and studied. There is no industry—no matter how shrouded with military secrecy—in which some management has not sought investor funding to sponsor growth. Many have "gone public," and succeeded, based only on an idea—and many, of course, have failed.

As expendable income has grown in our nation, some of it has entered the speculative arena as investments in new companies ("new issues," if newly public, or "venture capital" if the companies are privately owned), or in already "public" companies where the trading market has already been established. And an important specialty has evolved within the spectrum of business journalism to cover this significant portion of corporate America— financial journalism, which is the reportage of all material news which affects publicly owned corporations and their 25,000,000 owners, the stockholders of America. *Everything* is of importance to the financial journalist, for *everything* impacts on the public company, from the doings of unrelated private companies to national economics, politics, and even fads.

As is true in all specialties, a private lexicon has developed in financial journalism, no more difficult than in any other profession. And an allied profession, financial analysis, has evolved with different objectives: the evaluation of these "public" companies, measured by many different yardsticks, to determine their safety as investments, or their potential as speculations.

These yardsticks are also useful to the financial journalist. They help him expand his weaponry and sharpen his investigative skills. With financial analysis, the basic grouping of ten stories which recur routinely can be broadened to hundreds.

To explore the psyche of the men who run public companies, and the structure of such organizations, a fictional corporation has been created—a magazine company run by two young journalists. (Is there a journalist anywhere who doesn't dream of owning his own publication?) But it could be a manufacturer of anything— frisbees or "whatchamacallits." Put yourself in their shoes; give the company *your* name; and see what happens.

YOURNAME PUBLISHING
585 Madison Avenue, New York, NY, 10017

January 11

Mr. Robert Cass
Cass, Josephs, Cook
1104 Park Avenue
New York, New York 10017

Dear Bob:

I too enjoyed our chance meeting last
Saturday at Ted and Mary's party. Your remarks
about financing were of particular interest and,
in repeating them to my partner, Ed Frank, we
both concluded that we ought to pursue this
subject with you. Could we get together?

Before we do, let me give you some further
information about our company, Yourname Publishing
Company, Inc. Our company is now seven years old
and was founded by the two of us to publish trade
magazines aimed at narrow industries which need
specialized information on a consistent basis.

Ed and I have news backgrounds but, in the
past seven years, we have had to learn a great
deal about management — everything from
negotiating printing and delivery contracts to
Subchapter S corporations. It has been quite
an educational process and I sometimes think
we have only begun.

We now publish three magazines, each of
them a result of our own work background. Ed was
a reporter, then an editor, at Electronics News,
a Fairchild newspaper; and, as I mentioned to you,
I worked for one of McGraw-Hill's technology
magazines before moving over to The Wall Street
Journal as a reporter.

Ed and I spotted the growth in microcircuitry and started a monthly newsletter to cover this field, operating it from our homes while continuing our regular jobs. As the newsletter took hold we saw the need for a quarterly journal devoted to management, and this became our second property. Microcircuitry News, our newsletter, has since become a controlled free monthly magazine (circulation 11,000) and our journal, Microcircuitry Management, is now a bimonthly with a 24,500 paid circulation. We expect next year to increase MM's frequency to a monthly.

With the introduction of the Management quarterly Ed and I, of course, had to leave our jobs. We must have been out of our minds: We had $6,500 between us — and 3 children and $2\frac{1}{2}$ wives (Ed was in the midst of divorce but already engaged! I guess if we had more cautious temperaments, we would never have attempted to go into this business.)

No need to explain how difficult it was to raise money. Banks won't accept $2\frac{1}{2}$ wives as collateral and, as to family financing, $2\frac{1}{2}$ wives simply meant that we had 3 sets of in-laws who thought we were crazy. Why don't business histories tell you how really difficult it is to come up with bucks to back the immodest ambitions of two modest, but ambitious, embryo publishers. How did Xerox make it? Or, better yet, Luce?

Chemical Bank, thank God, loaned us $10,000 against various types of personal collateral, along with a stern explanation that banks only make secured loans and, on a short-term basis, three to five years. (We were fortunate in our astute choice of a lending officer — the first desk we were ushered to — a young, assistant vice-president with personal authority to lend up to $20,000 without going to committee. Since he only loaned us ten, I guess he was only half-sure of us!)

And two of the three sets of in-laws made reluctant investments (guess which one didn't), adding another $5,000 to the $5,000 Ed and I were putting in. We talked a printer into two months' credit (the typesetter wanted to be paid immediately) and we were in business.

I'm attaching our latest financials (unaudited). Although we have had a nice growth we have always been tight for cash, reinvesting our profits as much as possible, and therefore we have never spent the additional dollars necessary to have our statements "certified." But they will hold up. Our banker scrutinizes them and our accountant — though not a "Big 8" firm — is a partner in a major regional practice with some important local publicly-owned companies as clients.

The reasons for our immediate interest in financing are twofold. First, we have always been undercapitalized, and more so now that we have started a third publication, MiniComputerworld, a monthly newsmagazine aimed at an exciting growth market. It already has a good advertising base and we are attempting to convert our 9,000 controlled free circulation to a paid basis. Second, we have spotted an emerging technology market for which there is no publication, and we would like to be first in. (We certainly are not timid! Do you think we are stretching ourselves thin?)

We also repackage our best articles and publish them as yearbooks. They do well and additional money would be welcome in this operation. But enough! We could spill our plans over your desk every minute of the day for the next year and we wouldn't come to the end of it.

Review our financials and then let's have a meeting and tell us if you are the lawyer/ financier/advisor/messiah we have been looking for. The door is open and the glass of wine awaits you.

Sincerely,

Bill

William Bart

CASS, JOSEPHS, COOK
1104 Park Avenue. New York, N.Y. 10017

January 20

Mr. William Bart, Pres.
Yourname Publishing Co., Inc.
585 Madison Avenue
New York, N.Y. 10017

Dear Bill:

Frankly, I'm overwhelmed.

My partners and I have never seen such a torrent
of ideas. Our legal practice is more directed towards
manufacturing companies, and the smaller ones nurture
one new engineering idea at a time — occasionally
several, but never the profusion of new business
activity that you and Ed danced before us. No wonder
you are so impatient! I would be too if I had as
many prospects to explore.

The growth of Yourname Publishing, your protests
to the contrary, has been excellent. If anything,
you may be growing too rapidly. (To answer your
question, I do think you are stretching yourselves
too thin. Not a criticism, mind you, just a yellow
blinker at an intersection.)

I'm not sure you need financing. Your own cash
flow seems to be good, your return on invested capital
would make Luce blush (are you planning to buy Time-
Life?), your profit margin is much better than the
industry average. Why don't you and Ed double your
salaries, pay a good dividend to your in-laws, hire
some additional editorial talent and take Fridays
off to play golf. I'll be happy to sponsor the two
of you at my club.

Cordially,

Bob

Robert Cass

CASH FLOW. Net profit after taxes, plus the replacement cost of machinery and
other equipment that wears out.
RETURN ON INVESTED CAPITAL. How much was earned on the capital the
company had available.
PROFIT MARGIN. Percentage of profit made on sales.

P.S. If you're foolish enough to want additional
investors, our firm represents a venture capital
group which would be interested. And, yes, we would
be happy to be lawyer/advisor. As to financier, our
firm subscribes to the Code of Ethics of the accounting
profession which forbids an auditor to have an
investment in a client company, for obvious reasons;
even though we are attorneys, not accountants, and
the Bar Association permits counsellors to invest in
clients, we are against it. As to being a messiah,
Quien Sabe?

DIVIDEND. A portion of net income after taxes given as profit to the shareholders.

VENTURE CAPITAL. Money put up at risk, generally in a new venture.

AUDITOR. An accountant who comes in periodically to review and certify the company's financial statements.

YOURNAME PUBLISHING

585 Madison Avenue, New York, NY, 10017

January 24

Mr. Robert Cass
Cass, Josephs, Cook
1104 Park Avenue
New York, New York 10017

Dear Bob:

Let's do it!

Ed and I want to run a larger company, not play handicap golf. Our mothers didn't send us to college so that we could spend our lives getting tan. They wanted us indoors, sallow and prosperous. So let's be getting on with it.

Cash flow and return on invested capital? What in the world is that? All we know is that we still haven't gotten back the $5,000 we invested in the company seven years ago, our in-laws haven't been repaid their money, we now have five kids and 22 employees, all of whom think we exist to make their lives better and each of whom would bet their bottom dollar we couldn't live without them.

I <u>hate</u> business! But I <u>love</u> business! Boy, would I love to tackle Time-Life.

Bring on the investors, Bob.

Sincerely,

Bill

William Bart

CASS, JOSEPHS, COOK
1104 Park Avenue, New York, N.Y. 10017

January 27

Mr. William Bart, Pres.
Yourname Publishing Co., Inc.
585 Madison Avenue
New York, N.Y. 10017

Dear Bill:

    I have arranged a meeting with two principals
of Federal Investment Company, a venture capital
client of this office, and would appreciate it if
you, Ed and your accountant could attend, February 3
at 3 P.M. We will be discussing a private placement
of up to $1,000,000. Although we are permitted to
represent both parties, we hesitate to do so and
request that you bring along another counsel to
handle your interests in this matter — but don't
hire him permanently, for goodness sakes. I want
the job!

                Cordially,

                Bob

                Robert Cass

PRIVATE PLACEMENT. Sale of new shares in a company to a single buyer or
a small group.

memo YOURNAME PUBLISHING CO., INC
585 Madison Ave., New York, NY
212 254 3110

from William Bart   date: **February 1**

to: Robert Cass

What's private placement?

Bill

MEMO Cass, Josephs, Cook, 1104 Park Avenue, New York, NY 10017

to:

When you started the company and sold stock to
your in-laws you had a "private placement," although
for very little money. Simply, it's selling a large
block of stock in a company to a small number of
investors, either individuals or institutions, as
opposed to having a Wall Street house sell shares
in your company to hundreds or thousands of
individuals.

Advantages are that you don't have to apply to
the Securities and Exchange Commission and go
through the legal and accounting headaches involved
with a public offering of stock. Negatives are that
you end up with a very large partner. It's like
mating a canary to a lion. Don't know what you get,
but when it chirps you listen!

B.s

Robert Cass

YOURNAME PUBLISHING
585 Madison Avenue, New York, NY, 10017

February 6

Mr. Robert Cass
Cass, Josephs, Cook
1104 Park Avenue
New York, New York 10017

Dear Bob:

I'm perturbed and don't know what to do about it. The meeting went poorly and you didn't help any.

I understand that you are not yet our counsel, and that in this transaction you had to stand behind your client. And I recognize, too, that Ed and I are not financially sophisticated. But your friends from Federal tried to rip us off! What is this business about "investing only at book value"? Do you realize that if they invested "only at book value" Federal could buy 100% of our company for the liquidation value of the business — and pay us off after taking control by using our own cash, and getting a bank loan against our receivables and inventories?

Federal must think we're fools. If they wanted to <u>loan us</u> $1,000,000 for expansion, on a <u>very</u> long-term basis (say 20 years) at <u>very</u> low interest rates (say 5%), they might ask for an option on a <u>small</u> percentage of the common stock of the company (say 10—15%) at book value.

I'm surprised you would introduce us to such rapacious people.

Are we ignorant? Naive? Or what?

Sincerely,

Bill

William Bart

BOOK VALUE. The true value of a company after all debts are paid. (The amount the company could be sold for if the desks, chairs, and other assets brought the value they are carried for on the balance sheet.)

LIQUIDATION. Termination of an operating business, and sale of its assets.

OPTION. The right to acquire property at a future date for today's price.

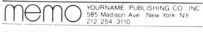

memo   YOURNAME PUBLISHING CO. INC
585 Madison Ave. New York, NY
212 254 3110

from William Bart

to: Ed Frank & Files   date: February 7

SUBJECT: Financing

        Cass called today upset at the tone of my
letter of Feb. 6. Implied we were indeed ignorant
and naive. Said it was "too harsh a deal" but that
we "had to understand it was an opening negotiation."
And that he "had to protect the interest of his
client, Federal, just as he will protect Yourname
Publishing" in the future. Said that's why he
advised us to have independent legal counsel and our
accountant present. Suggested we have a second
meeting.

Bill

YOURNAME PUBLISHING
585 Madison Avenue, New York, NY, 10017

February 16

Mr. Robert Cass
Cass, Josephs, Cook
1104 Park Avenue
New York, New York 10017

Dear Bob:

I'm glad we had the second meeting. The new proposal is very much better, but we still find it hard to give up so much for so little.

Federal's offer of a $500,000 20-year loan at 7% bears thought, although the interest rate still seems high. I know that it's less than we would pay for money on a <u>short-term</u> basis at the bank (and we certainly couldn't get that amount), but it's more than Federal could get if it left the money in the bank. Since they are also suggesting investing an additional $500,000, they should be interested in making their profit on the <u>investment</u> half rather than on their loan half. As to the investment half, Ed and I are still having trouble accommodating ourselves to their formula: $500,000 for 50% of the company's common stock.

This, Bob, places a value of $1 million on our entire corporation. We're not financial analysts, but it doesn't take much research to dig up information on publishing companies which have raised their capital through brokerage houses in public issue. On a <u>comparative</u> basis, the offer seems very low.

Perhaps it's our news background which has made us so probing, so unwilling to accept the seemingly conventional without investigation. But it's really more than that. Ed and I have put our lives into this business and we think it's <u>worth</u> more. Beyond that, we don't want an equal partner in anything. We want absolute control of our own company. We want to write our product, edit our product, and decide for ourselves whether to reinvest our profits in new publications or pay the monies out as dividends.

So where does that leave us? Looking for another partner, I suppose.

But before we follow this route, let me make a few points and see whether or not Federal will reconsider:

(1) We earned $135,000 after taxes last year. Federal is offering to pay us the equivalent of 8x earnings. Dun & Bradstreet has just purchased Technical Publishing Company — much larger than we are, granted — for about 20x earnings.

(2) The average price/earnings ratio for publicly-owned publishing companies is 15x. And for companies growing, as we are, better than 15% annually (what Wall Street, we're told, calls a "growth company") the price/earnings multiplier is more like 17x.

(3) Our balance sheet is pretty liquid — enough so that we could pay all our current liabilities out of cash and receivables alone, not having to sell our inventories **for** anything but full retail price. I'm told by our accountant that this is the "acid test," and we pass it. In the late 1960s there was a slogan, "Go public or go bankrupt," and many companies went public for this reason. We're pretty

GROWTH COMPANY. A "public" company whose sales and earnings are growing at a compounded annual rate of 15% or more.

PRICE/EARNINGS MULTIPLIER. The numbers of years of earnings you are willing to pay for a company, broken down in its simplest form to a single share in the company.

solid — though small. We simply want money so that
we can grow more rapidly. We would even agree not
to raise our salaries or declare dividends until our
earnings doubled — or tripled, if necessary.

So here's our counterproposal. Value the
company at 30% less than the average growth company
in the publishing field. We realize we're not public
and will take a discount for it (although when I
review the volatility of stock prices, and
price/earnings ratios over the past 15 years I think
we deserve a premium for staying privately owned).
At 12x earnings our company would have a total value
of approximately $1.6 million.

We would be willing to sell 31% of the company
to Federal for $500,000 plus the 20-year use of
their additional $500,000 at 6% annually.

This, Bob, is really a good deal for Federal
and a fair one for us. Ed and I have plans, as you
know, for a new publication and we are convinced it
will do as well as our other three. It will take
us two years to put the new $1,000,000 to work but
we believe we can earn the same return on this
capital — 17% — that we now do on our surplus.

If we are correct, and we continue to grow at
15% annually as we have in each of our past seven
years (sometimes double that), next year's after-tax
earnings should be about $155,000 and in two years
our base from existing properties only should rise
to almost $180,000 after taxes. But that's the year
we believe the $1,000,000 will begin to earn profits
for us as several new properties come on stream.
If we are right, and we earn 17% on this capital,

BALANCE SHEET. A financial picture of the company at a particular date.

INVENTORIES. The amount of product the company has on hand, not yet
   shipped to customers.

ACID TEST. Refers to whether a company can pay all current debts out of
   available cash, salable securities, and immediately liquidatable receivables.

we'll add another $170,000 after taxes to our income — doubling our earnings to about $350,000.

If we chose to "go public" at that time, and got 12x earnings, our company would be valued at $4.2 million, of which Federal would own 31% worth (about $1,700,000) — a more than tripling of their investment in two full years.

Why not think about it and let us know?

Sincerely,

Bill

William Bart

CASS, JOSEPHS, COOK
1104 Park Avenue. New York, NY. 10017

February 20

Mr. William Bart, Pres.
Yourname Publishing Co., Inc.
585 Madison Avenue
New York, New York 10017

Dear Bill:

The counterproposal you made was a good one,
but not consistent with the investment philosophy
of Federal. They will be returning your financials
to you shortly, along with your cash-flow
projections and a letter of regret.

Federal is truly a "venture" firm. It seeks
out opportunities for "big hits" — the one-in-
twenty opportunity which will bring them at least
a return of eight to ten times their investment —
which makes up for their many losses. As they see
it—they would be tying up $1,000,000, not just
$500,000, for a very long time. And having $1,700,000
on paper after two years is not as great as it seems.

The stock market analysis you did, though
superficial, made several important points. But
I suspect there are some things you overlooked or
haven't been exposed to as yet. Most good
underwriting houses (they are the ones who market
your new issue of stock by putting together a
syndicate of brokerage houses who have full-time
salesmen) will not allow insiders to sell stock on
the first offer. In Wall Street's parlance this
would be a "bail out," and they prefer management
to demonstrate its faith in the company by holding
onto its stock a while longer. If the company does
well, and the market holds up, management can consider
a "secondary" offering. (Primary is for the corporate

account; <u>secondary</u> is for insiders, and a <u>combination</u> offering is a little of each). Management, therefore, shares the risk of the marketplace with the new public shareholders. I know this is not <u>always</u> the case, and that sometimes even good underwriters allow insiders to turn the first issue into a "combination," but this is not the best underwriting market, and Federal isn't willing to gamble on what the market might be like in two or three years.

If they can't sell any part of their interest in the public offering — and they certainly won't be able to sell <u>all</u> $1,700,000 worth (if your valuation turns out to be correct) — they will be subject to the vagaries of the market. You described these well when you questioned whether or not Yourname deserved a premium for staying private, since the price/earnings multipliers most often reflect investment <u>sentiment</u> rather than a perception of true value. If stock market <u>sentiment</u> is negative, your price/earnings multiplier could be 4x when Federal wanted to sell, even if your earnings had tripled. I know of many companies whose earnings have risen dramatically through natural growth and the prudent use of monies raised from the public, while their stock has declined to a level where the entire company had a market value of much less than the proprieters could have received by selling out when they were private — and smaller.

Federal doesn't want to take this risk. They don't want to put up $1,000,000 for a basically illiquid minority position which will yield them, if all goes <u>superbly</u> well, a 70% "paper" gain which they can't take. They feel they need more leverage than that.

        At any rate, we tried. Should you wish, I'll
    explore other avenues for you — on a "finder's fee"
    basis (which would entitle us to 5% of the first
    million raised on your behalf. The standard formula
    calls for 4% of the second million, 3% of the third,
    2% of the fourth, and 1% ad infinitum) or on a time
    basis, if you still intend to become a client of
    this office. Are we to go ahead in our relationship?
    Or has the Federal experience soured this possibility?

                        Cordially,

                        Bob

                        Robert Cass

FINDER'S FEE. Paid to an individual who arranges a financing, a merger, or an
    acquisition for a company in need of one.

YOURNAME PUBLISHING
585 Madison Avenue, New York, NY, 10017

February 27

Mr. Robert Cass
Cass, Josephs, Cook
1104 Park Avenue
New York, New York 10017

Dear Bob:

No, the Federal experience hasn't soured us. But it has caused some strain.

Ed and I agree that you put your cards on the table. You did ask us to get other representation, and you didn't make it easier on us because we were prospective clients. You represented Federal in the strongest fashion possible and, I guess, that's what Yourname needs as well.

So. We'd like you to become our counsel. But we would like the relationship to direct itself toward <u>legal</u> guidance and the <u>mechanics</u> of the law (drafting documents, etc.) and <u>away from business</u> guidance and negotiation. Although we value your insights, we prefer to come to our nonlegal judgments ourselves and, as to negotiations, we feel comfortable coming to those backed by our accountants. No offense.

When would you like to start?

Sincerely,

Bill

William Bart

from William Bart   date: May 11

to: Ed Frank

SUBJECT: Financing

    As you requested, I have undertaken and spent
the better part of the last two months reviewing
various approaches to financing the expansion of
this company. This memo will recite them.

    But, even before that, perhaps we ought to
address ourselves to a corporate philosophy. I
find it impossible, Ed, to come to a conclusion
as to the course to follow because I'm now less
sure of the risks I'm willing to take for the
sake of size. Perhaps I've come to enjoy the
security of our stable little business. Or maybe
I've settled into a premature middle age. (Are
publishers like ballplayers? Do they fade early?
Is there some life-chart equivalent of a periodic
table which can measure the half-life creative
potency and energy of a publisher?)

    As Bob Cass pointed out many months ago we
can have an easy life should we choose it! By
doing nothing. By letting nature take its course.
We're in a good field. Electronics, microcircuitry,
and mini-computers are growing rapidly, and we
have the number one books in each area. So here
are our alternatives:

(1) We stay privately owned and if we continue to
grow at 15% annually (we have actually grown an
average of 30% in each of our seven years) we'll
double our profits in just under five years, and
continue to double every five years or less
thereafter. Of course, if we continue to grow at
30% per year we'll double our profits every 2½
years, but that's being too optimistic. It's
harder to double off a growing base. I discovered,
in my Wall Street research, that this is one
reason great growth companies don't always continue
to be great growth companies. As they take more
of their market, and reach higher volume bases, it
becomes more difficult to continue growing at 15%
or more per year.

At any rate, if our three books continue to dominate
their markets until we're ready to retire — and
I'm assurming we'll both want to work at least
another 25 years — and our profits grow 15% per
year, we'll end up earning $4.4 million per year in
25 years. Doesn't seem possible does it? I wouldn't
bet on it, but don't numbers like that make you
happy? Makes daydreaming seem worthwhile. I've
checked out the trade associations and they tell me
they see this type of growth for the industry for
at least ten years but they won't forecast beyond
that. If all this came about we could have an
estate problem that could probably be resolved by
selling out to a major public company — a la the
Technical Publishing merger into Dun & Bradstreet —
for cash or stock of — get this — $40 to $80
million (using today's yardsticks which might not
hold true). What a parlay on a $5,000 investment!

PRIVATELY OWNED. Means that the company's shares are owned by an
individual or a small group, and are not traded openly in a barter market.

(2) Why consider any alternatives? Because, as we both know, a million things can happen. The market might not grow this rapidly. We might slow down. Competition might come in. And we may make some poor management decisions. And the underlying curse? We both are enjoying building so much, and there are so many new publications to start, that it would be a crime to stop here — to say we have reached our personal zeniths at this early age, and that we will simply conserve rather than build from now on.

We can therefore fund more rapid growth (and take more risks) in the following ways:

(1) Bank financing: Although the banks won't loan on earning power alone (they want assets either from the corporation, or by having the two of us personally guarantee the company notes as collateral), they look to earnings for repayment. And earnings we seem to have. They'll loan us 80% of our net worth, since we have no other debt, and will continue to expand it each year by adding 80% of the increase in net worth. (If we earn $150,000 after taxes next year they'll loan us an additional $120,000.)

But we'll have to set up a repayment program so that we are clean every three or four years. This can be arranged by borrowing, as well, from a second bank and having them come into the full loan those times we must be out of the lead bank.

(2) Private placement: We went through that routine with Federal. If we wish, however, we can solicit friends or have an investment banking firm put a small group together. An investment banker, I've learned, is not the same as an underwriter or brokerage house, although he can have departments which offer all three services, and many more.

NET WORTH. The assets of a corporation minus its liabilities.
LEAD BANK. Among a syndicate of banks, the bank which extends the largest part of the loan or credit to the borrowing company.

The investment banker, Ed, is the other side of
the coin from the commercial banker, such as
Chase or Citibank. The investment banker analyzes
the company, draws up a memorandum for investors,
brings us to and negotiates for us with such diverse
potential investors as wealthy individuals, venture
capital groups, insurance companies or an underwriting
firm to take us public (or he might do it through
his own underwriting department).

(3) Insurance companies: You wouldn't believe how
rich they are. I never stopped to think about what
they do with the money we pay in premiums. After
all, on a regular life insurance policy they have
to return some balance with interest to you at the
end of the insurance period. So they can't <u>spend</u>
the money. They <u>invest</u> it. Insurance companies,
Ed, may be the biggest investors in America. I
spoke to one about lending us some money, and they
said we had all the ingredients they like in a
long-term loan — good growth; dominant position
in a marketplace; young management; good balance
sheet, excellent return on invested capital. But
they said we're too small for them to invest in —
come back when we're double this size. And they
feel we need more management; a couple of more
executives who are just like us. (Can you clone,
Ed?)

(4) The public market: After all is said and done,
Ed, this is the best way if we are seeking additional
capital. Granted the market is a crazy barometer
of <u>confidence</u> rather than a real reflection of
corporate earning power. But I've reviewed price/
earnings multipliers over a 60-year period (I've
been living at the economics room of the 42nd St.
library), and in every decade there are half a
dozen opportunities to sell shares at good prices.
I've evolved a simple financing philosophy if we

go public: negotiate the highest price/earnings
multiple for our initial sale since we will never
again have the opportunity to set the price of
our stock. The free-market mechanism takes over
after that. And, every time our stock enjoys a
very high multiplier, sell more shares for the
company and put the money in the bank. That way
we won't be begging for expansion funds when the
stock market is ridiculously low.

If we can find an underwriter of good
reputation, who will give us the sort of deal we
wanted from Federal, we would have many partners,
none of whom would own enough stock individually
to create a problem. We could have an open avenue
for further financing, a market for small pieces of
our own ownership so that we could create some
liquidity in our own estates, a stock with which
we could acquire other publishing companies, and
and opportunity to share our growth with partners
in the most meaningful way — our partners will be
able to sell at any time they wish and hopefully
make a big profit.

What do you think?

Bill

memo YOURNAME PUBLISHING CO., INC.
585 Madison Ave., New York, NY
212-254-3110

from Edward Frank   date: May 11

to: Bill Bart

SUBJECT: Financing

I choose "4".

memo   YOURNAME PUBLISHING CO., INC
585 Madison Ave., New York, NY
212-254-3110

from William Bart   date: June 27

to: Ed Frank

SUBJECT: Financing

Here's what's happening.

I checked Standard & Poors industry survey for the
publishing group and got a list of all public companies.
(S&P is one of the largest reporting services devoted
to public corporations, and also runs a stock market
forecast business.)   I took the list of the public
publishing companies to the Manhattan office of the SEC
and photostated all their original registration statements,
all of which I have studied in detail.   Some, surprisingly,
went public with no properties — just ideas.   There's
an S2 form for "development" companies; since we're not
a "start-up" we would file an S1.   An S1 or an S2 can be
used to raise as much money as the underwriter wishes
to try for.   But there's a short form — called a Reg A
(Regulation A filing) — for companies that want to
raise less than $500,000 (maximum Reg A used to be
$300,000 and may soon be raised to $1,000,000).

I have spoken to each of the underwriters who were
involved in the financings of the already-public
publishers, as well as a half a dozen more who have been
recommended to us.   Would you believe that of the
approximately 4,500 brokerage houses in the U.S., only
some 600 are underwriters? — although any that want to
do an underwriting can, if they adhere to rather strict
regulations of the SEC and the National Association of

Security Dealers.

The securities industry, by the way, is quite large — some 1,575 stocks listed on the New York Stock Exchange, about 1,140 on the American Stock Exchange, approximately 3,700 on so-called regional exchanges, Boston, Cincinnati, Philadelphia — Baltimore, Chicago, Spokane, Salt Lake City (mostly mining), Pacific Stock Exchange (floors in San Francisco and Los Angeles), and Honolulu. When companies first go public their shares are traded "over-the-counter" and many major companies — some large banks and insurance companies among others — choose to remain there because it is a real barter market with traders at different over-the-counter specialist houses "making markets" in the stock. For those who wish to move up to an exchange, and meet the more stringent requirements regarding number of shareholders and shares outstanding and earning power, the barter market is exchanged for an auction market — one specialist on the floor of the exchange making a market in the stock, and buyers and sellers bidding, just as at an auction.

I've just about selected an underwriter for us, subject to your review and agreement. It's Samuels, Higgonson & Allen, a member firm (New York Stock Exchange), with a good syndicate department and its own retail power — their brokerage department employs some 1,700 brokers in 80 offices throughout the country.

They're willing to do a deal at 12x earnings, but would like us to put a dividend on the stock to help them sell the deal. They say investors are once again interested in yields. They have suggested that we recapitalize the firm in the following way: authorize 1,000,000 common shares, but issue only 322,000, holding

SYNDICATE. A group of several underwriting houses, each of which attempts to sell shares in the company to its own customers.

YIELD. The shareholder's dividends expressed as a percentage either of the current price of the stock or the price paid for the stock.

the balance in the treasury of the company for
registration and sale at a later date, hopefully at
higher prices, or for issuance in case we want to
acquire another publisher. Of the 322,000 shares
outstanding 100,000 would be sold to the public for
$5 per share, representing 31% of the company. Our
in-laws would each exchange their current 10% interest
in the company for 22,000 shares each of stock, worth
$110,000 at issuance to each of them, an increase of
more than 44x on their original investment of $2,500
some seven years ago. And you and I would exchange
our 80% interest in the private company for 177,600
shares — or 88,800 shares each — worth $444,000 to
each of us at market, and representing a 55% share
in the public company.

The dividend suggested is 2.5¢ per quarter, or
10¢ annually, which would yield each shareholder a
2% return on his investment. Doesn't seem much to
me, but the investment banker said it would show our
intent to share with the stockholders. That, however,
would cost us about $32,000 after taxes each year,
or almost 25% of what we are now earning. It seems
to me that someone who wouldn't buy the stock of a
company growing at our rate wouldn't buy it to get a
2% return.

It occurs to me that the insiders could waive
their dividends, and therefore the payout could be
reduced to only $10,000 per year. I'd like to have
the additional $22,000 to reinvest in the company,
but two things bother me in such an action: It's
not fair to our in-laws, and I'm concerned about the
precedent set by such a decision.

I've interviewed executives of several companies
that went public recently to get their views on the
process, and their suggestions. They all note that
our stock becomes our corporate currency, and that

we will have to make an effort to communicate with
our shareholders so that they don't become exasperated
and dump the stock, depressing the price for a long
period to come. They also suggest that we demand of
the underwriter that in so small an issue he not sell
more than a couple of hundred shares to any one
stockholder — and that the potential stockholders
be selected from as broad a geographic area as possible.
We need a certain level of activity in the stock to
be listed in the daily price quotations in the <u>Wall
Street Journal</u>, and other newspaper lists, and <u>this</u>
is more likely to happen if we have a greater number
of stockholders. Also, brokers don't like to recommend
new stockholders to an issue in which the "float" is
small — "float" being a term every one mentioned.
In our case, the entire 100,000 shares will likely be
float. I can't imagine any of our friends saying they
will never sell. But most brokerage houses, and
especially funds, consider a float "light" if it's
less than a million shares. (What are we getting
into?)

The reason that stress is made on a broad
geographic dispersion of the stock is that it makes
it harder to pick up easily should an unwanted suitor
come knocking on the door. Can you imagine Time, Inc.
getting so excited about us that they would go scurrying
around the country to buy up our stock against our
wishes? (Why have I got this thing about Time and
Luce?)

Lastly, the company executives I've talked to
keep mentioning "aftermarket support." They say there
is no such thing and term it "underwriters' bullshit."
Seems all underwriters promise to buy stock on the
open market after the company is public, and have
their over-the-counter department make a good trading
market in the stock, buying it for inventory if large
blocks appear which can drive down the price of the

FLOAT. The actual number of shares available for purchase and sale at the
current price level.

stock. It rarely happens. If the underwriters kept
their promise to all the companies they underwrote,
they wouldn't have enough money to commit to future
underwritings. It would all be tied up in inventory
of old underwritings (I checked out, by the way, the
capital structure of the various underwriting houses
in the annual Finance Magazine directory and ours
ranks within the top ten).

Two more things: the cost and the procedure if
we go ahead. We will have to absorb our legal and
accounting costs. We will need three years of audited
financial statements for the SEC filing, and that will
be expensive. We also must pick up the cost of
printing the registration forms filed with the SEC
and ultimately the red herring and the approved
prospectus, which must be sent to prospective shareholders
before they buy the stock. Bob Cass has warned me that
the prospectus is an insurance policy — it lists every
negative the attorneys and underwriters can think of
— so that a shareholder does not come back and sue
for fraud. Bob says not to get upset when we read
the document — also that we must keep a list of
anyone to whom we send the red herring (a preliminary
prospectus which has red printing on the left side
to warn everyone that this is not a final document).
Everyone who receives one must then get an approved
prospectus. Better to turn all such names over to
the underwriter.

The underwriter will charge us 8% (I've seen some
as high as 12%) from which he pays the salesmen and
makes his profit. It means we'll net only $460,000
from which we have to pay printing, legal, and accounting
charges, perhaps another $40,000. Oh, well.

The procedure: Should we both agree to the deal,
the underwriter will prepare a "letter of intent"
which outlines the terms. It means nothing, really,
and I don't know why such a big deal is made of it.
It has no teeth: After we've laid out funds for
printing, legals and auditing, the underwriter can
walk away for many different reasons, including a
down stock market — even after giving us a "firm
letter of commitment." (Some deals aren't "firm,"
but ours will be.) If the underwriter feels conditions
have changed and he can't do the deal we have no
recourse, and can't get our costs back.

At any rate, once we have this "firm commitment,"
the underwriter puts together his "selling group" of
brokerage houses which will join him in retailing the
stock. Since ours is such a small issue, and our
investment banker is also our underwriter, he could
do it alone — and perhaps will.

Once the issue is sold, and the syndicate
"released," the underwriter will give us our check.
Then, I'm told, our real headaches begin — reporting
to stockholders, the SEC and living in a fishbowl.
We can't run any personal expenses through the
business — not even little ones, such as personal
lunches — and we have to bear in mind an SEC doctrine
called "full disclosure." That means that we must
report promptly any action or activity that could have
a material effect upon the price of our stock, or on
how the company is evaluated or perceived. I can't
imagine that either of us will have any difficulty
with that — our news sense ought to tell us what's
"material" and subject to "full disclosure."

The immediate goal is to get a go-ahead from
us so that the underwriter can begin doing his "due
diligence," an investigation that goes beyond a

SYNDICATE "RELEASED." The five-day period, after new shares are sold in an underwriting, during which salesmen are not permitted to accept sell orders on the shares from the new purchasers.

reading of our various documents. He'll probably
check us out at the banks, in the publishing business,
review our ABC records and so forth. He also will
turn one of his securities analysts loose on doing
a comparative review of our company to justify the
12x price/earnings ratio he's putting on the stock —
even though we have already had an informal "pricing
meeting." At the same time Bob Cass will begin
working on the S1 form to be filed with the SEC so
that the red herring can be out as quickly as possible.
The SEC will make comments on the registration, to
which Bob will respond with changes, and ultimately
we will have an approved document with which the
underwriter can sell our shares.

This whole process can take 60 to 90 days after
Bob and our accountants prepare the S1. In the
1960s, the SEC was so clogged with filings that it
sometimes took four to five months to get a comment
back. Ours should go much faster.

I feel rather badly that I haven't been able to
help you these past few months with the management
and editorial chores that seem to be piling up.
I'll be free as soon as this project is done.

What do you say?

ABC. Audit Bureau of Circulation, which testifies as to the accurate circulation
of each publication which is a member of the organization.

SECURITIES ANALYST. A person employed by a brokerage house to
evaluate financial statements and determine which companies are more likely
to grow rapidly.

from Edward Frank   date: June 27 P.M.

to: **Bill Bart**

SUBJECT: Financing

Let's go ahead.

Why are your memos getting longer while mine are getting shorter? I'm inquiring only because I'm embarrassed at sending you another one-liner.

YOURNAME PUBLISHING CO., INC.
585 Madison Ave., New York, NY
212-254-3110

To The Files   date: October 9

SUBJECT: Financing

We did it!

We went public today. The underwriter tells us we will have about 700 shareholders in 42 states, from New York to Alaska. We collect the money on October 16. Let's hope we look back on this as a milestone.

Bill

FOR THE FILES

From the Financial Observer (August 19)

YOURNAME PUBLISHING ISSUE

New York, N.Y.—Yourname Publishing Co., Inc. yesterday completed a successful primary offering of 100,000 shares of common stock at $5 through a syndicate led by Samuels, Higginson & Allen. The magazine publishing company will use the proceeds for the development of new publishing properties and for additional working capital.

memo   YOURNAME PUBLISHING CO., INC.
585 Madison Ave., New York, NY
212-254-3110

from Edward Frank   date: October 26

to: Bill Bart

Since you are the resident expert on publicly-owned companies, don't you think you ought to prepare: (1) a press release on third-quarter earnings; (2) a shareholders report covering the third quarter and nine months; and (3) begin planning the Annual Report to Shareholders. After all the current year _does_ end December 31.

---

memo YOURNAME PUBLISHING CO., INC
585 Madison Ave., New York, NY
212 254 3110

from William Bart   date: October 26, P.M.

to: Ed Frank

Me? Why me?

Bill

---

memo YOURNAME PUBLISHING CO., INC
585 Madison Ave., New York, NY
212 254 3110

from Edward Frank   date: October 27

to: Bill Bart

Because, Blue Eyes, I don't know enough about those things and you, after all, worked at the _Journal_. Financial reporters know about such things.

memo   YOURNAME PUBLISHING CO., INC.
585 Madison Ave., New York, NY
212-254-3110

from William Bart   date: February 17

to: Ed Frank

Don't know how to phrase this delicately —
but, old friend, I'm beginning to feel abused. Not
by you, but by my new role. Mind you, I'm delighted
we're public. But look at my work schedule:

I have six separate appointments this week with
people from the financial community — two stockbrokers
and four securities analysts, who say they are doing
reviews of the publishing industry, one of them
focusing on us as a "hot" new company.

I am deeply involved in the production and
writing of our annual report. (What happened to
my involvement in magazines?)

I now have the assignment of working with Bob
Cass on the agenda for the annual meeting. Why don't
you become president and let me be chairman so I can
get back to <u>work</u>?

Or better yet, Why don't we hire: (a) a
treasurer who can <u>really</u> handle this himself (our
treasurer doesn't know anything about a public company,
and the forms he has to file are driving him crazy);
(b) and/or a financial public relations agency.

Bill

memo YOURNAME PUBLISHING CO., INC
585 Madison Ave., New York, NY
212-254-3110

from Edward Frank   date: **February 17 P.M.**

to: **Bill Bart**

     Because **a** treasurer with public-company experience will increase our costs for this function by about $20,000 per year above what we are currently paying. And, because <u>also</u>, a financial public relations firm will cost us another $20,000 or more. This combination is equivalent to 7¢ per share, after taxes, or more than a point at our current p/e ratio (we're above 15x, if you haven't noticed). In total market value you're talking about $320,000 just for this. (Don't I learn <u>fast</u>!) If we were selling out, this little extravagance would cost our stockholders $320,000 — and 55% of our stockholders is us.

memo YOURNAME PUBLISHING CO., INC
585 Madison Ave., New York, NY
212-254-3110

from William Bart   date: February 18

to: **Ed Frank**

SUBJECT: **Financing**

     Well, half of the 55% of our stockholders just voted to hire a Treasurer!

Bill

FOR THE FILES

From the Financial Observer (April 10)

ROBERT PINTER NAMED
TREASURER OF
YOURNAME PUBLISHING

New York, New York—Robert Pinter
has been named Treasurer and Chief
Financial Officer of Yourname Publishing Co., magazine publishers. He was
previously Comptroller of Valley Magazines.

FOR THE FILES

From the Financial Observer (May 21)

YOURNAME FORECASTS RECORD
EARNINGS AT ANNUAL MEETING

New York—Yourname Publishing
Co., Inc., magazine publishers, expects
record profits and revenues in the current year, William Bart, president, informed stockholders at the company's
first annual meeting. Although he did
not give projections, he termed the
anticipated gains "significant."

Reasons for the gains include the
"successful introduction of Electronics
Age, the company's newest publication,
whose paid circulation should shortly
cross the 30,000 level at $10.00 per year
per subscription." He said the company's three other magazines are
"growing rapidly, and are on target to
meet our internal budgets."

He stressed the "excellent balance
sheet, capable of supporting strong internal growth for the company."

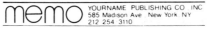

memo YOURNAME PUBLISHING CO. INC
585 Madison Ave. New York. NY
212 254 3110

from William Bart   date: August 11

to: Ed Frank

SUBJECT: Financing

As a result of the sharply increased trading
in our stock we have received an inquiry from the
SEC asking if we know the reasons or the source
of buying. I told them that nothing unusual had
happened, that earnings were up by about 30%, and
that I had spoken to a group of financial analysts
and brokers last week at the Stockbrokers Club.
I pointed out that I had not made any projections
at that meeting, and suggested they get in touch
with Bob Cass. Bob later told me the protocol was
for him to get in touch with the Commission, and
he's doing so.

Reuters Financial, reflecting this activity,
has called for an interview. I think we should
both be present. Here's a suggested outline:

(1) Yourname Publishing is having another record
year. For the eighth consecutive year sales and
earnings will be up sharply — sales by some 40%,
earnings by 30%.

(2) The Board of Directors, as a result, at its
next meeting will consider a modest increase of
dividend.

(3) The sales and earnings increases reflect the
successful introduction of our newest monthly
magazine, Electronics Age, which already has a
paid circulation of 31,000 at $10 per year, plus

the publication of two new books on electronics
management by our newly expanded book division.
Our three existing magazines have each grown by
more than 30% in revenues this year, and we
expect this to continue for the next half-year
at least.

(4)   We are in the process of joint-venturing a
seminar on minicomputers with a seminar company,
but are not projecting any of these earnings in
our full-year estimates.

(5)   We have no specific acquisitions in mind,
but we are beginning to look for publications
to buy if they have good managements willing to
stay on.

(6)   Our balance sheet is in the best shape ever —
good enough to support a modest acquisition program
even if we use cash. Our current ratio is now
better than three-to-one; our quick ratio alone
is better than two-to-one. Our receivables are
running 32 days; we have completely repaid our
bank loans, and have a line of credit with Chemical
for more than $500,000.

Bill

CURRENT RATIO. The number of times the current liabilities (due to be paid
   within 12 months) are covered by the current assets (cash, securities,
   inventories, and the like).
QUICK RATIO. Another definition of the "acid test."
LINE OF CREDIT. The amount of money a bank is willing to extend as credit.

memo YOURNAME PUBLISHING CO., INC.
585 Madison Ave., New York, NY
212-254-3110

from Edward Frank   date: August 11

to: Bill Bart

Several things.

First: OK on the Reuters interview. I'll
join you, but let's bring along our new Treasurer —
or will three-on-one seem too formidable. It always
bothered me when I was interviewing — seemed more
like a rally. Perhaps only the President and the
Treasurer should sit for the interview. You tell
me.

Second: I agree that we ought to raise the
dividend at the next Board meeting by about 20% to
3¢ quarterly from 2½. Granted it's not much of a
yield for investors, but it represents a payout of
about 23% by us and I think that's a fair distribution
of the profits. I'd like to also suggest a stock
dividend. We have to increase the float — and
perhaps the stockholders will sell the stock dividend
and create more float. How about a 10% dividend?
What do you think?

Third: Friend of mine mentioned a privately-
owned publishing company, growing nicely, that he
thinks would be available for purchase. Old
management but young editorial staff. Four books,
all in engineering, profitable. Should we look?

STOCK DIVIDEND. Given as a substitute for, or in addition to, a cash
dividend, and truly meaningless except for a psychological effect on shareholders and, at times, on the market.

memo   YOURNAME PUBLISHING CO., INC.
        585 Madison Ave., New York, NY
        212-254-3110

from William Bart   date: August 12

to: Ed Frank

"Yes," to all three.

Bob Cass says that we must have a press release ready to issue to the Dow Jones Newswire and Reuters immediately after the dividend action. We also have to have a company contact, an officer, to whom Dow Jones and Reuters can speak for verification.

Bob also reminds me that there must be a gap of ten days between the declaration of the dividend by our Board of Directors and the date at which new shareholders can buy the stock and get the dividend (the "record" date). We made a mistake last time, and it was embarrassing, as you recall. We had to telephone a correction.

The newspapers will carry the record date, as well as the payable date (the date we stick the dividend check into the mail), and even the "ex-dividend" date (four days before the "record" date, so prospective buyers of the stock know that after four days before the "record" date, they can't get the dividend. It goes to the former owner of the stock.)

Here's a version of the release:

New York, N.Y., August 19 ... The Board of Directors of Yourname Publishing Company, Inc.

(over-the-counter) today increased the regular
quarterly dividend by 20% to 3¢ per common share
from the 2.5¢ paid previously. The dividend is
payable September 13, 1977 to shareholders of
record at the close of business on September 3, 1977.

The Directors also declared a 10% stock dividend,
payable September 15, 1977, to shareholders of
record at the close of business September 5, 1977.
The increased cash dividend will be paid on the
expanded number of shares. There are currently
320,000 common shares outstanding.

William Bart, president, said that "the
increased cash dividend reflects management's desire
that shareholders participate in the prosperity of
the company. It is our hope that the stock dividend
will help broaden the ownership of the company."

FOR THE FILES

From the Financial Observer (August 20)

New York, N. Y.—Yourname Publishing increased the regular quarterly dividend by 20% to 3¢ per common share from the 2.5¢ paid previously, and also declared a 10% stock dividend. The cash dividend is payable September 13, 1978 to shareholders of record at the close of business on September 3, 1978.

The stock dividend is payable September 15, 1978 to shareholders of record at the close of business on September 5, 1978. William Bart, president, said management hoped "the stock dividend will help broaden the ownership of the company."

YOURNAME PUBLISHING
585 Madison Avenue, New York, NY, 10017

November 12

Mr. Robert Cass
Cass, Josephs, Cook
1104 Park Avenue
New York, New York 10017

Dear Bob:

Sometime ago a friend of Ed's brought to us a most interesting acquisition possibility. The original asking price was so far out of line that a second meeting wasn't warranted. Talks have now, however, been revived, and on a much more realistic basis.

We thus have a problem. Should this come about it will certainly be "material." As I understand it, we should at some point issue a release and make our shareholders — and potential shareholders — aware of the negotiations.

But what if they fall through? Don't the shareholders get hurt? And what about those who purchased the stock on the announcement in anticipation of the acquisition going through? Can't they sue us?

And, lastly, the prospective seller is disturbed. He doesn't want anyone to know he is considering selling unless the deal is firm. What do we do?

Sincerely,

Bill

William Bart

"MATERIAL." Information required by the Securities and Exchange Commission to be released about any change in a company which might affect an investor's decision to buy, hold, or sell securities.

CASS, JOSEPHS, COOK
1104 Park Avenue, New York, N.Y. 10017

November 14

Mr. William Bart, Pres.
Yourname Publishing Co., Inc.
585 Madison Avenue
New York, New York 10017

Dear Bill:

Not to chastise you, but you should have
informed us of these informal talks at the very
beginning. I understand your desire to do your
own negotiating. But in disclosure matters you
need guidance.

The intent of the disclosure regulations is
clear: to permit current and prospective
shareholders to have full access to information
which might affect their investment decision.
That does not mean you have to issue a press
release every time you think about an acquisition,
or a financing, or a hike in dividend. But it
does mean you have to make an announcement when
you have reached the point where it really seems
the acquisition might take place — even if the
final terms haven't been arrived at.

As to law suits from stockholders who bought
in anticipation of a deal that never materialized,
you have no real liability. As long as the prospective
acquisition was announced in good faith you have no
problems.

And, as to your new partner, he must understand
the different types of obligations which a public
company must meet.

Let's get together immediately and see if we
are at the stage where we must draft documents.

Cordially,

Bob

Robert Cass

memo   YOURNAME PUBLISHING CO. INC.
585 Madison Ave. New York, NY
212 254 3110

from William Bart   date: November 19

to:

Cass says we have to get a press release out
although we haven't even arrived at conclusive
terms. It seems clear, though, that we are going
to have a deal — whether stock or cash depends
upon our banks or insurance companies. Bob says
if we are going to make the rounds of money sources
we certainly have to inform the public that a deal
is in the making, because it will surely leak out
anyway.

Here's a proposed release:

New York, N. Y., November 20, 1977 . . .
Yourname Publishing Company, Inc., (over-the-
counter), has entered into a preliminary agreement
to acquire Acme Publishing Company for an undisclosed
price, William Bart, Yourname president, announced
today. The 37-year-old Acme publishes four
engineering magazines.

Yourname publishes magazines for the
microcircuitry, minicomputer, and computer fields.

Bill

FOR THE FILES

From the Financial Observer (November 23)

YOURNAME TO ACQUIRE ACME

New York—Yourname Publishing has signed a preliminary agreement to acquire Acme Publishing Co. for an undisclosed price. Yourname publishes three technical magazines, and Acme four engineering magazines.

memo   YOURNAME PUBLISHING CO., INC
585 Madison Ave., New York, NY
212·254·3110

from William Bart   date: November 23

to: Ed Frank

      Here's what is available to us in terms of financing for the Acme acquisition:

(1) The bank: says it will loan us $500,000, against the combined receivables of Yourname-Acme, at 1.5% above prime for five years.

(2) Insurance company: more interested now that we are larger. Will loan us $1,500,000 for 20 years, constant interest rate of 8.5%, but wants "kicker" (added incentive) of an option to purchase 25,000 shares for ten years at today's price — $9. If we do an all cash acquisition of Acme, the 25,000 shares will represent dilution (a reduction of our ownership percentage) of some 7.3% — but our earnings will more than double even after taking into account the $131,250 in annual interest (deductible from our pre-tax profits).

(3) Underwriting: Our underwriter is willing to sell another issue for us — this time a "combination." To raise the $1,500,000 for the Acme acquisition, plus the 8% underwriting commission, plus the fee to audit us and Acme, plus printing and legals, we need more than $1,800,000, which requires the sale of about 200,000 shares — not counting any shares you and I and our in-laws might want to sell. The dilution, which comes only from issuing <u>new</u> shares

PRIME. The lowest rate a bank will charge its best customers who want to borrow new funds.

CONSTANT INTEREST RATE. Applies to the funds borrowed by a company from a bank at a given interest rate which will not change for a given period of time, dependent upon the negotiations.

"KICKER." Refers to additional things one must give a lender, above the interest rate.

from treasury, would be substantial: 200,000
new shares added to our current 354,200 would
reduce our ownership to about 34% and our in-laws'
to about 8.5%.

We'd be out of control for the first time,
not that I'm worried about being taken over, but
it does present something to think about. Cass
assures me — and I think he's right — that one
does not need absolute control; that public
companies are sometimes controlled with as little
as 10% ownership. The broad distribution we have
in the stock, and the fact that so many of our
holders are in 100-500 share lots, would make it
costly and difficult for someone to pick up. Also,
we've done a pretty good job, and our shareholders
might just be loyal enough to vote against a raider.
But I wouldn't bet on it; not if someone offers a
good premium over the current price.

Here's a more graphic illustration of the
possibilities, and what they mean to us personally
and the stockholders proportionately:

Yourname is running ahead 30% in profits this
year, and based on ad contracts in hand and our
known expenses for next year should gain another
30%. That means after-tax earnings at Yourname
of about $175,000 this year, or 50¢ per common
share (divide $175,000 into our currently
outstanding 354,200 shares, which includes our 10%
stock dividend of August). Acme, on its volume of
$3,500,000, is only earning $200,000 after taxes/
We can't expect to close the deal before January 1,
so we have to look to its effect on next year's
earnings. Let's be conservative and assume it has
no growth in its first year under our management

(although there's some fat we can cut). This
would give us combined income of $375,000 after
taxes, and, if the Yourname group grows 30% we
have to add another $52,000 of profits, for a
total of $427,500.

If we take the insurance deal, we have to
subtract one-half the interest charges (Uncle Sam
picks up the other half since interest is a
deduction from pre-tax income). One-half of
$131,250 is $65,625, leaving us with after-tax
income of $361,875, or $1.02 per share (income
divided by shares outstanding). Our current
price/earnings multiplier is 18, ridiculously high
in the light of current stock market conditions.
But, if it holds, our stock price sometime next
year should reflect the $1.02 of projected per
share earnings and sell at around 18½, double
the current market price. With the 10% stock
dividend, you and I each own 97,686 shares. Our
market positions would be worth about $1,800,000 to
each of us, and our in-laws would have a market
position of about $440,000 each, and our original
public shareholders who contributed paid-in capital
of $500,000 would have shares worth about $2,000,000
— in less than two years. Not bad!

This, of course, presumes the borrowing of the
$1,500,000 from the insurance company and, therefore,
no immediate dilution except for the 25,000-share
option to the insurance group. Prudence would
require that we set up a sinking fund (an escrow
account used to retire debt on a programmed basis)
and put aside one-twentieth of our debt each year —
about $75,000. This is a good deal for us and the
stockholders, Ed. By using someone else's money,
we buy a company that throws off enough profit each

PAID-IN CAPITAL. The amount of money investors originally paid to get the
company started.

year to amortize the debt at the rate of $75,000
each year, pay the $131,250 of yearly interest,
which costs us half — after taxes (and the
interest payments sink each year as we reduce the
amount owed), leaving us with a profit each year
of $59,375 after all costs. The deal costs us
nothing.

If we go the public route the impact is this:
Another issuance of 200,000 new shares would bring
our outstanding to 552,220 shares. We would have
no interest payments to an insurance company, so
the entire combined earning power of $375,000
would be ours. Add to this the anticipated 30%
growth at Yourname, and none at Acme, and we come
up with an additional $52,500 for a total of
$427,500 after taxes. On 552,220 common shares
outstanding this works out to a per share figure of
77¢ and, at 18x earnings, our stock would be selling
at 13 7/8 — bringing our personal market worth to
$1,367,520 each, our in-laws about $339,000 each,
and the original public shareholders to a little
more than $1,500,000.

Going public gives us more equity and, if things
get bad, we have no one we have to repay. Borrowing
from the insurance company gives us an annual debt
and, if things go bad, we're in trouble. Our balance
sheet will be highly leveraged (large debt-to-equity
ratio). Conservative financial people tell me a
well-managed company should have total pre-tax
income seven times its fixed charges. With pre-tax
income estimated at about $800,000 next year, and
interest charges of $131,625, we just about do it.

But I'm torn.

Bill

LEVERAGED. Refers to a company's debt compared to the amount of equity
invested in that company.
DEBT-TO-EQUITY RATIO. A ratio used to determine the leverage involved in
a corporate balance sheet.

memo   YOURNAME PUBLISHING CO., INC.
585 Madison Ave., New York, NY
212-254-3110

from Edward Frank   date: November 24

to: Bill Bart

I've spent the morning analyzing your memo of
yesterday, and that worries me more than the
decision we must make. We're both spending too
damn much time with our calculators and not enough
with our typewriters. If this keeps up we won't
have a company to worry about.

No carping, mind you. You're doing a
fantastic job in the public arena. I wouldn't
want it — and couldn't handle it. But we started
out as newsmen, not as stock promoters. I, too,
love being a paper millionaire (Mister, could this
public company of ours advance me $1,000 in cash?
My kid needs some orthodontia work.) but why must
everything focus on this?

Here's what I think. Let's do both and then
return to running magazines.

Let's borrow the insurance money and, if the
stock does indeed ultimately reflect our new
earning power, let's sell enough to completely
repay the insurance loan (make sure we have
prepayment privileges). If your analysis is correct,
and we have an $18 stock after the acquisition, we
could sell only 100,000 shares to repay the

insurance company — instead of the 200,000 shares we would have to sell now. And we could even sell a little bit for us, so I wouldn't have to beg $1,000 for my kid's teeth.

What do you say?

PREPAYMENT PRIVILEGES. The right to prepay a debt to an insurance company or institution before the due date of the payment.

memo   YOURNAME PUBLISHING CO., INC.
585 Madison Ave., New York, NY
212 254 3110

from William Bart   date: November 25

to: Ed Frank

Makes sense to me. I simply hadn't thought
of doing both. I'm notifying Bob Cass, and I've
put in a call to the insurance company. I'll also
notify the accountants and our bankers.

Sorry, though, about the thousand bucks. You
know we can't hit the corporate treasury for
personal items — can I loan you some? Or, if
you wish, you can sell a little bit of stock
without registering it, under SEC Rule 144, which
says an insider can sell from his personal holdings
in a six-month period stock equal to the lesser of
1% of the total number of outstanding shares but
not more than the average week's trading in the
stock during the four weeks previous to the sale.
Translated, that means you personally can sell
3,520 shares every six months, although the "four-
week" trading formula reduces this to 700 shares at
the moment — enough to raise $6,300.

I'm told, by the way, that once we make the
acquisition it's likely the Federal Reserve Board
will include Yourname stock on its approved list
for margin. Means that under present margin
requirements you can borrow up to 50% against it
at the bank and new buyers can purchase the stock
by only putting up 50% and borrowing the rest from
their brokers.

YOURNAME PUBLISHING
585 Madison Avenue, New York, NY, 10017

Summary: Yourname Publishing (OTC) acquires Acme Publishing for $1,500,000; company forecasts record year.

Contact: William Bart
President
(212) 344-9131

FOR IMMEDIATE RELEASE:

NEW YORK, N. Y., January 5 — The acquisition of Acme Publishing Company, Inc. by Yourname Publishing Company, Inc., for $1.5 million cash was announced today by William Bart, Yourname president. Said Mr. Bart: "The addition of the prestigious engineering magazines published by Acme to the high technology periodicals of Yourname makes us an increasingly important factor in the trade magazine market. The addition of the Acme editorial management further strengthens our organization."

Mr. Bart forecast "new records this year in revenues and profits." He said his projection is based upon "an increase of some 30% in the profits of Yourname magazines plus a contribution from Acme equal to its last year's earnings."

Acme last year earned $200,000 after taxes on $3.5 million in revenues. Although it will be some weeks before Yourname's audited year-end figures are available, sales revenues rose to approximately $3.7 million and earnings to the vicinity of $175,000, or 50¢ per share, against $135,000, or 38¢ per share, earned the year before.

Mr. Bart noted that the $1,500,000 purchase price would be paid for from the proceeds of an insurance company loan, the terms of which are now being concluded.

# # #

CASS, JOSEPHS. COOK
1104 Park Avenue. New York, NY, 10017

January 6

Mr. William Bart, Pres.
Yourname Publishing Co., Inc.
585 Madison Avenue
New York, New York 10017

Dear Bill:

Congratulations on the successful completion
of the Acme acquisition. I'm pleased we were able
to be helpful.

In looking through the press release which
came in this morning's mail I noticed you expanded
on the version which our office had approved. By
adding a forecast you, in effect, "preconditioned"
the market for another stock issue. This means
you're out of the box for several months.

This might prove to be academic. Your interest
in a public issue might diminish, or the stock
might remain in the current $9 range. But we'll
talk further as the year progresses. In the future,
please issue no releases without our review — and,
for heavens sakes, don't make any editorial changes
without telling us. You can rewrite your editors,
but not your lawyers.

Cordially,

Bob

Robert Cass

P.S. Here, as you requested, are the requirements
for listing on the American Stock Exchange. Even
with the contemplated new issue of stock, you won't

```
qualify — not enough shares, shareholders or
earnings.  Yourname probably needs more "seasoning"
in the over-the-counter market, and you have eight
houses making a market in the stock.  Pretty good
for such a small issue.
```

American Stock Exchange Inc
86 Trinity Place
New York N Y 10006

Securities Division
212 938-6000

REQUIREMENTS FOR ORIGINAL LISTING APPLICATIONS
STOCKS—LONG TERM WARRANTS—BONDS

Amended to September 27, 1973

This pamphlet contains instructions applicable to applications for original listing of stocks, long-term warrants issues and bonds.

Inquiry should be made to the Securities Division of the Exchange for instructions in connection with applications for special types of issuers or securities as follows: Investment Corporations, Corporations in process of reorganization or recently reorganized, Foreign Corporations—Depositary Receipts, etc.

CRITERIA FOR ORIGINAL LISTING

The approval of an application for the listing of securities on the American Stock Exchange is a matter solely within the discretion of the Exchange. To assist companies interested in applying for listing, the Exchange has established certain guidelines, outlined below, which will be considered in evaluating potential listing applicants. There are, of course, many relevant factors which must be considered in determining whether a company qualifies for listing. Major emphasis is placed on such matters as the nature of a company's business, the market for its products, the reputation of its management, its historical record and pattern of growth, its financial integrity and risk, its demonstrated earning power and its future outlook. The fact that an applicant may meet the guidelines set forth below does not necessarily mean that the Exchange will approve the listing application. Equally, in special situations an application may be approved even though the company does not meet all of the guidelines.

Other than real estate investment trusts or member corporations, a company applying for listing of a common stock issue is, as a general rule, expected to meet the following criteria:

Size (Net Worth):

Net tangible assets of at least $4,000,000.

Earnings:

Net income of at least $400,000 after all charges, including Federal income taxes, in the fiscal year immediately preceding the filing of the listing application, and, except under special circumstances, net income before income taxes and extraordinary charges and credits, of at least $750,000. (In applying these standards, the Exchange may not give consideration to income which is essentially non-recurring, whether or not it is designated as an "extraordinary" item.)

Distribution of Common Stock Issues:

Minimum public distribution of 400,000 shares (exclusive of the holdings of officers, directors, controlling stockholders and other concentrated or family holdings), including at least 150,000 of such shares held in lots of 100 to 500 shares. Minimum of 1,200 public stockholders, including at least 800 holders of lots of 100 shares or more (among which at least 500 holders must hold lots of 100 to 500 shares).

Market Value for Publicly-Held Shares:

$3,000,000 aggregate minimum. In general, the Exchange requires a minimum market price of $5 per share for a common stock issue for a reasonable period of time prior to the filing of the listing application. In certain instances, however, the Exchange may favorably consider for listing an issue selling for less than $5 per share. In this connection, the Exchange will give consideration to all pertinent factors, including market conditions in general, whether the applicant exceeds the Exchange's net tangible assets and earnings standards, whether historically the issue has sold above $5 per share, the applicant's capitalization, the number of outstanding and publicly-held shares of the issue applied for and, in respect of securities of foreign issuers, the general practice in the country of origin of trading in low-selling price issues.

FOR THE FILES

From the Financial Observer (January 8)

YOURNAME PUBLISHING PLACES NOTES

New York—Yourname Publishing Company Inc. said it has received a $1,500,000 loan from Hanseatic Life Insurance Company of New York. The 20-year, 8.5% loan has a sinking fund provision beginning with the fourth year.

Yourname will use the proceeds to pay for the recently acquired Acme Publishing Company, Inc.

FOR THE FILES

From Advertising News (February 10)

George Ryan, vice president of Hanseatic Life Insurance Company of New York, has been elected to the Board of Directors of Yourname Publishing Company, Inc., publishers of magazines and books for the electronics industry. Hanseatic recently loaned Yourname $1,500,000 for 20 years at 8.5% to finance the acquisition of Acme Publishing, publishers of three engineering books.

YOURNAME PUBLISHING

585 Madison Avenue, New York, NY, 10017

July 14

Mr. Robert Cass
Cass, Josephs, Cook
1104 Park Avenue
New York, New York 10017

Dear Bob:

   Things are progressing well, as you know from our Board meetings and monthly reports. We'll be on target with our projected earnings, even though Acme seems a little sluggish.

   I sense a bit of a constriction in the economy, although all the economic reports I read say things are great. The technological industries we service through the Yourname group are steaming ahead, growing at a 25—30% compounded annual rate, just as their industry associations predicted they would when you checked them for our S1.

   But we can see a bit of a tightening in the more mature industries serviced by Acme's four properties. And if this proves to be so it might be a golden opportunity for Yourname to pick up some more properties — perhaps some good young growth companies running into capital problems, or some older books where management would like to take their investment out and retire.

   At any rate it's time for us to be thinking about another issue. Ed and I feel that the market has been unusually good to us — we are selling now, as you know, at $20 per share in a market that is not spectacular. We'd like to do several things: Raise $1,500,000 to add to our own working capital, and sell 50,000 shares for our own account and our in-laws. It's time we had some cash for ourselves.

Would another 125,000 shares of stock from treasury give us enough for a listing on the American Stock Exchange?

Sincerely,

Bill

William Bart

memo   YOURNAME PUBLISHING CO., INC.
        585 Madison Ave , New York, NY
        212 254 3110

from William Bart   date: July 17

to: Ed Frank

      Bob Cass says we're still too small for the
Amex. He's in agreement, however, that we ought
to take advantage of this good stock market to
tidy our house — remember our original plan to
sell whenever the market seems high?

      At any rate I've spoken to the people at the
underwriting house about a combination offering —
50,000 for the two of us, 20,000 for our in-laws
(it's time they lightened up and diversified their
holdings — our stock is the major part of their
estates), about 75,000 shares at current market to
repay Hanseatic and another 50,000 treasury shares
for additional working capital.

      Then let's return to the typewriters at last.

Bill

COMBINATION OFFERING. An underwriting which packages together
shares for the company's account (called "primary") and for some insiders or
management members (called "secondary").

FOR THE FILES

From the Financial Observer (July 13)

KEY ECONOMIC BAROMETER
DECLINED AGAIN LAST MONTH

Washington—Rising concern is being evidenced for the first time by Government economists as a result of the continued decline in leading indicators.

The Commerce Department's composite index of leading economic indicators fell 0.6% in July, the second consecutive monthly decline.

Treasury Secretary John Jones cautioned that "it is premature to interpret an economic slowdown from two modest monthly declines." He said Government economists predict that real Gross National Product—the national output of goods and services adjusted for inflation—should grow at a 6% rate the remainder of the year, creating an overall increase in real GNP of 5% for the full year.

memo   YOURNAME PUBLISHING CO., INC.
585 Madison Ave., New York, NY
212-254-3110

from Edward Frank   date: July 17 P.M.

to:

     I'm in favor, especially to the last part.
Let's go quickly.

     By the way, a friend of mine has mentioned a
publishing company for sale.

     And, if it's not too much trouble, could you
ask Bob what the listing requirements are for the
New York Stock Exchange?

---

memo   YOURNAME PUBLISHING CO., INC.
585 Madison Ave., New York, NY
212-254-3110

from William Bart   date: July 18

to: 'Ed Frank

     No! Let's run the company and forget the
stock market.

CHAPTER THREE

The Ten Key Stories

The financial reporter deals mainly with stories which can be grouped in 10 categories, most of them recurring on a regular basis. They are discussed in the sections following. The groups are:

1. Earnings
2. Dividends
3. Financings
4. Appointments (executive and managerial)
5. Amalgamations (mergers, acquisitions, joint-ventures)
6. Meetings (annual meetings of shareholders, management speeches before various groups of securities analysts)
7. Corporate developments such as contracts, court actions, and price changes
8. Stock-market stories
9. Management interviews
10. Economic reports

With the exception of stock-market stories and management interviews, information relating to each of the other eight basic stories generally comes to the reporter and the news desk by press release from a corporation, or from a brokerage house (in the case of financings) or a communications officer at a Federal agency, such as the Federal Reserve Board or the Securities and Exchange Commission. Whenever numbers are mentioned—such as earnings or dividends—the reporter should telephone the company treasurer or vice president in charge of finance to verify all of the numbers. There have been cases where newspapers have been fed phony press releases by speculators hoping to boost the price of a stock. Remember to check and double-check your thinking, facts, and figures with authoritative sources within the company or industry.

Reporters should never accept numbers or any important information of a financial nature via telephone without calling back to verify that the information came from a duly appointed information source at the company. Even when information is received from reputable public relations personnel, known on a first-name basis by the reporter, he should still recheck with the company.

If the reporter has time to check his library, he might review the previous quarterly or annual reports of the company for information which will permit him to flesh out the figures he is now working on as a result of the press release. If he has a 10-Q or a 10-K available, it will give him even more information.

The Securities and Exchange Commission requires "reporting companies"—if their assets exceed $1,000,000 and their shareholders number 500 or more—to file an unaudited 10-Q form for each of the first three quarters of the fiscal (or calendar) year and an audited report on form 10-K covering the entire year. The 10-Q is due at the Commission within 45 days after the close of the quarter and the 10-K within 90 days after the year-end. Both the Q and K forms require notification and explanations of any change in accounting principles or practices.

Reporting companies must also file monthly 8-K reports of significant changes, a Form 4 reporting the purchase or sale of shares by management, directors and owners of 10% or more of the company's shares (all known as "insiders"), proxy statements, 13-D forms whenever a stockholder acquires as much as 5% of the company's stock—an early warning signal frequently followed by a "tender" offer. Companies which meet all of these requirements are those listed on any national or regional stock exchange (called "12-B" companies), and over-the-counter companies which have at least $1,000,000 in assets and at least 500 shareowners (called "12-G" companies). Any company which has gone public through a "full registration" (an offering of more than $500,000) but does not have $1,000,000 in assets and 500 shareholders (called a "15-D" company) must abide only by the 10-Q, 10-K, and 8-K requirements. It does not even have to issue a proxy statement.

If a company has fewer than 300 shareholders, it can choose not to file reports. In effect, it becomes a private company, and public shareholders are on their own.

When setting up a management interview, the reporter should review all the public documents, as well as documents sent by the company to company shareholders (quarterly and annual reports) and the previous statements made by company officials.

The reporter should also have a subscription to the leading trade journal covering the industry to which he is assigned, and have ready relationships with editors of those publications so that he can call them for background information on trends in the industry. This will enable him to ask intelligent operating questions of the financial and executive officers of the company.

The reporter should also have relationships with working financial analysts at key brokerage houses who are assigned as a specialty to that particular industry, so that if there is a fluctuation in the price of the stock the reporter can quote a knowledgeable Wall Streeter about the reasons.

Although stock-market stories frequently quote respected financial analysts on reasons why the market has gone up or down the previous day—or why a particular stock has fluctuated—the truth is that the analyst knows little more about it than anyone else. He is in a position, however, to make a reasonable guess, since he has a feeling for market attitudes. But the certainty with which Wall Streeters ascribe the behavior of the market to a particular Government action, or Presidential statement, is to be taken with a grain of salt. A reasonable conjecture about what affected the price of a particular stock, however, is more realistic, because frequently specific stocks will move up or down upon the announcement of a change in dividend, an acquisition possibility, or other hard news.

One of the most valuable tools a reporter can develop is a notebook indexing by company name, industry specialty, and individual name all those persons he has met or talked to who have specific knowledge about a particular company, a group of companies, an industry—even the relationships between executives. It is not inappropriate to call a corporate executive of your acquaintance, who sits on the board of a company in a noncompeting industry, to ask him about a third company. He is in a position to give information or insight without injuring his board relationship, or giving away inside information about his own company.

Also, it is wise to keep a glossary of the terms most commonly used in the industries to which you are assigned. The glossary is a living item, and should be continuously expanded to incorporate new phrases and definitions. Nothing is handier to a reporter facing a deadline than a terse description of a complex term.

Here, then, are the ten most frequent stories with which a financial or economic reporter must deal on a consistent basis.

1: EARNINGS

The "full disclosure" edict of the SEC requires reporting companies to immediately release quarterly and annual numbers—along with any other "material" news—to daily newspapers. Public companies comply with this injunction by releasing earnings to the press as soon as the board of directors has been apprised, although the use of such news by publications depends upon available space and its pertinence to the particular audience.

The following elements are found in every earnings report:

1. Revenues (or sales) vs. comparable prior period
2. Net income vs. comparable prior period
3. Earnings per share vs. comparable prior period

Whether in tabular or story form these three items comprise the basic earnings report. They are *always* compared with the comparable period the year before. If second-quarter figures are being presented, they are compared with the second quarter of the prior year; if full-year numbers are being given, the comparison is with the previous full year.

If a record has been established for sales, earnings, or per-share earnings, the letter R normally appears before the figure in tabular form and is generally mentioned in written copy.

Example:

XYZ CORP. (N) The (N) stands for New York Stock Exchange, where XYZ Corp. is traded. If it were listed on the American Stock Exchange, it would read XYZ CORP. (A), and if over the counter, XYZ CORP. (O).

XYZ CORP. (N)
Quarter June 30,

	1977	1976
Revenues.......	R $31,204,000	R $28,742,000
Income.........	1,321,000	R 1,364,000
Share earns.....	1.88	R 1.92

This would indicate that, although record sales were achieved in the June 30 quarter, earnings did not match the record period a year earlier. Either the company spent heavily to achieve higher volume this year, and hurt its profit margins in the process, or something extraordinary occurred in last year's period. If the extraordinary occurrence last year was of a nonoperating nature, such as the sale of a subsidiary or a tax credit, it would be footnoted, either with an asterisk (R 1,364,000 * and R 1.92 *) or by letter (b 1,364,000 and b 1.92), and the footnote would read in either of the two following ways:

* Including $162,000 from the sale of asset.
b Record period included $162,000 from sale of asset.

The table would then read this way:

XYZ CORP. (N)
Quarter June 30,

	1977	*1976*
Revenues.......	R $31,204,000	R $28,742,000
Income.........	1,321,000	R 1,364,000 *
Share earnings ..	1.88	1.92 *

* This amount includes $162,000 from the sale of asset.

A reporter writing copy, instead of just using a table, would lead with "XYZ Corp. earnings declined in 1977, despite record revenues. Earnings fell to $1,321,000 or $1.88 per share from a record $1,364,000 or $1.92 per share earned in 1976. Revenues totalled $31,204,000 against $28,742,000."

This would be followed by an explanation of the reasons for the decline.

Companies report for two periods: the latest quarter and the cumulative period. Therefore, the earnings story or table will contrast the second quarter *and* six months with the comparable periods the year before; the third quarter *and* nine months with the same periods the year earlier; and the fourth quarter *and* full year with the like periods of the previous year. Obviously the first quarter can only be reported alone *and* compared with the first quarter of the previous year.

The three-line tabular earnings report is often expanded in several key ways: through the inclusion of variations in the computation of share earnings and through the use of footnotes to flag the reader that the numbers do not represent the normal course of business. Under the theory that *per-share reporting* gives the investor a better understanding of his entitlement to a proportion of the company's assets in liquidation, and possible dividends during periods of prosperity, accounting regulations require that a company treat possible conversion into common stock as if it had occurred. Therefore, the two ordinary methods of reporting per share earnings are complicated, when warranted, by two additional procedures.

1. Normally, a company reports per-share earnings by dividing earnings by the number of common shares outstanding. Here is an example:

From the *Wall Street Journal,* August, 1977:

```
CARPENTER  TECHNOLOGY  (N)
   Year June 30:    1977        1976
Sales   .........$326,298,000 $266,304,000
Net  income  ..  28,764,000   17,286,000
Shr  earns:
  Net   income         6.80        4.10
    Quarter:
Sales   .........  92,399,000  72,951,000
Net  income  ..     9,000,000   5,973,000
Com  shares  ..     4,229,000   4,212,000
Shr  earns:
  Net   income         2.13        1.41
```

This computational approach is used when there have been no additional common stock sales for the account of the company during the reporting period, and no substantial conversions into common stock by holders of convertible preferred or convertible-bond issues, nor the exercise of such common-stock equivalents as options and warrants which permit investors to purchase treasury shares at a fixed price over a period of time. In other words, the ordinary investor who has not bought additional shares on the open market has the same percentage ownership in the company as at the beginning of the reporting period (if the company had sold new shares, this mythical investor would have ended up with a smaller percentage ownership in the company; or, in the parlance of Wall Street, he would have been "diluted"). If there had been conversions during the year, but the dilutive effect was less than 3% of earnings, per-share earnings are reported on the normal computational basis (as in the case of Carpenter Technology, where the difference in number of shares outstanding was only 17,000, or less than half a percent).

2. If, however, the issuance of new treasury shares affects the per-share earnings by more than 3%, the second approach must be used—the weighted average number of shares outstanding. The dollars paid to the company in exchange for the new shares are not available for management's deployment unless they are paid in on the first day of the fiscal year. Therefore, the weighted average dilutes earnings only by that portion of the year in which the new shares have been outstanding. As an example, a company which on January 1 had 1,000,000 common shares outstanding,

and on October 1 issued another 500,000 common shares, would have its earnings for the year computed on the basis of 1,125,000 weighted (average) shares outstanding and by 1,500,000 for the fourth quarter alone. The computation formula is 1,000,000 shares outstanding for nine months (1,000,000 x 9), plus 1,500,000 shares outstanding for three months (1,500,000 x 3), totaling 13,500,000, divided by 12 months, equalling a weighted average of 1,125,000 for the full year.

An example of a company report computed on a weighted average number of shares:

From the *Wall Street Journal,* August, 1977:

```
IOWA-ILL GAS & ELEC (N)
   Quar June 30:   1977        a1976
Revenues    .... $53,417,880  $44,222,255
Net income  ..    4,321,079    3,164,341
Avg shares  ..    8,107,263    7,268,855
Shr earns:
   Net income         .39          .28
   12 months:
Revenues    .... 235,302,318  192,525,643
Net income  ..   25,093,927   16,581,454
Avg shares  ..    7,669,574    7,162,555
Shr earns:
   Net income        2.67         1.86
   a-Restated.
```

Companies with complex capital structures—having in addition to common shares outstanding a capitalization that includes potentially dilutive convertible securities, options, warrants or other rights that upon conversion could dilute earnings per common share—report on a completely different basis. These companies must use a dual presentation: both *primary,* and *fully diluted.*

1. The *primary* presentation is based on the outstanding common shares, plus those securities which are equivalent to common shares and have a dilutive effect—options and warrants (at all times) and convertible preferred and debentures (sometimes). The determination of whether or not a specific convertible issue meets the test as a common-stock equivalent is based upon its yield, and the decision about classification is generally made by the company's accountants at the time of issue.

2. When a company with a complex financial structure issues its earnings report, it must also calculate earnings on a *fully diluted* basis as if all the common-share equivalents had been outstanding from the beginning of the reporting period *plus* any other

potentially dilutive issue. This would include, for example, common shares to be issued on a contingent basis to the former owners of a business whose payout could be increased by a bonus on higher earnings.

Here is an example of earnings reported on a primary and fully diluted basis:

From the *Wall Street Journal,* August, 1977:

OFFSHORE CO.. (A)		
Quar June 30:	1977	1976
Revenues	$44,794,000	$44,732,000
Net income ..	3,645,000	6,237,000
Shr earns (primary):		
Net income	.53	.91
Shr earns (fully diluted):		
Net income	.49	.83
6 months:		
Revenues	99,318,000	93,558,000
Net income ..	a11,789,000	13,926,000
Shr earns (primary):		
Net income	1.72	2.03
Shr earns (fully diluted):		
Net income	1.57	1.85
a-Includes a gain of $2,253,000 from the sale of non-producing leases in the North Sea.		

The tabular treatment of earnings permits the highlighting of extraordinary events which have distorted the normal operation and results of the business. Witness the earnings statement of Downe Communication in which first-quarter 1977 earnings per share declined to 16¢ from $1.70. Footnote b, however, points out that of the $9,070,000, or $1.70 per share reported in the 1976 first quarter, $8,888,000—equal, by computation, to $1.65—resulted from a profit on the sale of one of the company's properties, *Family Weekly* magazine. *Operating profit,* therefore, was 16¢ versus 5¢ in the first quarter of 1976. And 24¢ against 11¢ for the first half.

DOWNE COMMUNICATIONS (O)		
Quar June 30:	1977	a1976
Revenues	$26,364,000	$30,643,000
Net income ..	c838,000	b9,070,000
Shr earns:		
Net income	.16	1.70
6 months:		
Revenues	51,610,000	63,178,000
Net income ..	c1,280,000	b9,391,000
Shr earns:		
Net income	.24	1.76
a-Includes results of Family Weekly magazine which was sold on June 22, 1976. b-Includes net gain of $8,888,000 on the sale of Family Weekly magazine. c-Includes net gain of approximately $225,000 from the repurchase of 6½% convertible subordinated debentures, also the six months include net gain of approximately $100,000 from the sale of a previously discounted note.		

Given space with which to work, the earnings report becomes one of the more illuminating financial stories a reporter can bring to his readership. Read the *New York Times*'s treatment of Coca-Cola's results for the second quarter and first half of 1977. In addition to sales and earnings, the article notes the importance of the overseas market to Coca-Cola, comments on the undergirding for the higher sales marks and, significantly, points to increased *unit* sales, important in an inflationary period where many companies are attaining record sales by marking up prices, rather than by expanding their market through more units sold. However, the story should compare the 44% contributed by foreign operations with its percentage contribution the year before.

The Coca-Cola Company, the world's largest maker of soft drinks, reported a second-quarter net profit of $95.9 million, or 79 cents a share, up 12.9 percent from $85.5 million, or 70 cents a share, a year ago. This lifted the half-year net by 11.9 percent to $161.6 million, or $1.32 a share, from $144.5 million, or $1.18 a share, for the first six months of 1976.

Foreign operations accounted for about 44 percent of sales. The company continued to set new records in sales and earnings, J. Paul Austin, chairman, reported yesterday following the board meeting, at which the regular quarterly dividend of 38½ cents a share was declared for payment Oct. 1.

Net sales for the quarter were up 11.5 percent to $945.4 million from $847.7 million last year, for a six-month total of $1.731 billion, up 14.8 percent from $1.508 billion a year earlier.

Figures for last year have been restated to include operations of the Taylor Wine Company, acquired last January on a pooling-of-interest basis.

Per-share earnings are also restated to reflect a 2-for-1 stock split effected last May.

Higher Sales of Soft Drinks

Sales reflected higher unit sales of soft drinks and sharply higher prices in the company's coffee and tea operations, which were partly offset by lower domestic syrup prices due to the pass-through of lower sugar costs, the company said.

Coffee and tea operations account for
only a small percentage of the earnings,
Mr. Austin said. Unit-volume gains for
soft drinks were achieved in the United
States, Latin America, Africa and the Far
East. Unit volume in the quarter was up
only moderately in Western Europe, following the upsurge a year ago that
stemmed from a very hot summer.

Commenting on the Food and Drug Administration's proposed ban on saccharin
here, Mr. Austin said that the company's
management had endorsed bills now before the Congress that would stay the
ban in order to allow a thorough review
and evaluation of all scientific evidence.
Management is hopeful of the bills' passage, he added.

2: DIVIDENDS

Historically, mature companies paid dividends equal to some
two-thirds of their earnings, and younger growth companies
established a payout equal to about one-third of profits. Investors
paid little attention to companies which offered no yield and
asked the shareholder to be patient and wait for the price of the
stock to rise. Money paid out in dividends, this management
argument went, could better be put to use by the company so it
would grow faster, causing the stock to rise more quickly as a
reflection of the higher earnings base.

In rejection of this philosophy a Wall Street adage of the time
cautioned companies that investors are sometimes willing "to
discount the future but never the hereafter." In the 1960s the stock
market went berserk. "New issues" were sold to the public on
behalf of just-organized companies, many with no prospect of
earning power, let alone the prospect of dividends. In that hectic
decade the price of many of these unworthy new issues would
nonetheless rise dramatically in a very short period of time,
reinforcing the new notion that earnings, balance-sheet stability,
and dividends were less important than *potential.* The "hereafter"
was being discounted.

By the early 1970s the new issue fad had died, as had many of
the newly-formed companies. Investors were so badly injured that
they moved their funds back into savings accounts and fixed-

income securities. And dividend yield once again became important for companies which wished to coax investors' funds out of the bank and into their equity securities. They had to offer a yield as close to bank interest as possible, while holding out the prospect that increasing earnings would ultimately join a psychologically improved stock market in expanding the company's price-earnings ratio. As a result dividends are again in vogue, and the dividend story—always one of importance to the financial journalist—is a mainstay of the financial pages.

The dividend story has four key elements:

1. Amount (if an increase, compare with old rate)
2. Frequency
3. Payable date (when will check be mailed)
4. Record date (who is entitled to dividend)

As an example, XYZ Corporation declared a 5¢-a-share quarterly dividend, payable November 1 to shareholders of record October 10. The *amount,* 5¢; the *frequency,* quarterly; *payable,* November 1; *to whom,* those who owned the stock at the close of business on October 10.

Cash dividends being paid for the first time are termed "an initial dividend." For example, XYZ Corporation declared an initial quarterly dividend of 5¢ per share.

Reporters must be especially careful of how they classify the *frequency* of the dividend. A dividend can be *quarterly,* which implies management's intention to pay another dividend three months hence; *regular quarterly,* which indicates management is currently committed, though not legally, to a policy of such dividends each three months; *semiannual* or *annual* dividend, which indicates the company only pays dividends each six or 12 months; *extra or year-end extra,* a bonus above the normal dividend rate which shareholders should not expect to see repeated.

As an example; XYZ Corporation declared a 5¢ per share quarterly dividend, plus an extra of 2¢ per share, both payable November 1 to shareholders of record October 10. XYZ said, "the extra dividend reflects the company's unusual profitability in the third quarter and our desire for shareholders to participate."

Generally, companies wishing to declare an extra dividend do so at year end. Such a declaration reads as follows:

XYZ CORPORATION declared a quarterly dividend of 5 cents per share plus a year-end extra of 2 cents.

Let's assume that Yourname Publishing (1) suddenly came upon hard times and had to omit its dividend; (2) after some period of time was able to reinstate the dividend and (3) indeed, at a later date, even raised it. Here's how the story would be handled at different stages:

(1)

YOURNAME PUBLISHING OMITS FISCAL THIRD QUARTER PAYOUT

NEW YORK–Yourname Publishing Co., Inc. said its Board of Directors voted to omit the company's third quarter dividend. The reasons given were a sharp decline in new advertising in three of the company's magazines which service the electronics industry, plus working capital requirements for a new publication, Electronics Age, which is being heavily promoted. The company had paid its usual quarterly of 2 cents per share on June 15.

As reported earlier this week, Yourname Publishing earned $38,000 or 11 cents per share on sales of $230,000 for the third quarter ended September 30, compared with $29,000 or 8 cents per share, on sales of $170,000 in the similar period a year earlier. Nine months results still have not been reported.

(2)

YOURNAME PUBLISHING SETS QUARTERLY PAYOUT OF 2 CENTS

New York–Yourname Publishing Co., Inc., declared a 2-cent dividend payable February 15, to shareholders of record February 5. Yourname, which publishes magazines and books for the electronics industry, last paid a dividend of 2 cents per share in June 19,––. Dividends were omitted last September when the company announced a "sharp slowing in incoming advertising contracts," and said it needed to expend additional dollars on promoting Electronic Age, Yourname's newest publication.

William Bart, President, stated that: "First quarter results are promising enough to reinstate a dividend. The slump in which the electronics industry found itself now seems to be over, and advertising contracts are increasing. Electronic Age is beginning to do well and should soon be at breakeven."

(3)

YOURNAME PUBLISHING RAISES
DIVIDEND 50% TO THREE CENTS

New York—Following a strong earnings advance, Yourname Publishing Co., Inc., a publisher of electronics magazines and books, increased its quarterly dividend to 3 cents a share from 2 cents. The increased cash dividend is payable June 15 to shareholders of record June 5.

The company had recently reported earnings of $70,000 or 20 cents per share on sales of $425,000 in the first quarter ended March 30, a 112 percent increase over the year earlier, when the company earned $32,000 or 9 cents per share on $190,000 in volume.

In addition to cash disbursements, companies sometimes pay stock dividends. The stock dividend is always expressed as a percentage and the story always includes the new number of shares to be outstanding after payment of the stock dividend. A stock dividend or a stock split is like cutting an apple into two: there is no more apple than before, only more *pieces* of apple. And yet there is no denying that most investors *want* stock dividends and think they are receiving a gift. In reality their percentage interest in the company has not changed; they simply have more pieces of paper.

Because of this investor attitude a stock dividend declared in a receptive market climate will frequently bring enough new buying into the stock to raise the price. Realistically the stock price should adjust *down* by the percentage of stock dividend. If one were to pretend that a law existed which fixed the total stock-market value of a corporation (the number of shares multiplied by the closing price of the stock) for 24 hours after the declaration of a stock dividend or split, the price of the shares would have to decline. The increased number of shares would be divided into the fixed price and each share would have a value arithmetically reduced by the percentage of the new stock dividend.

Corporations will often declare stock dividends for the psychological benefit it gives the shareholder as well as in the hope that the shareholder will sell off the stock dividend creating more shares for trading. This is known as trying to increase the "float" in the stock, a device that rarely works since most shareholders keep their stock dividends. Corporations who want an increase in "float" to make it easier for large buyers, such as institutions, to buy and sell the stock without creating volatility generally have to sell a new issue, offering as many new shares as is necessary, to increase the float to the degree desired.

Corporations declaring stock dividends, in addition to their cash policy, generally maintain the going dividend rate on the new shares. When that is done, shareholders do receive some tangible benefit—in effect, a modest increase in payout, although the dividend rate is unchanged. Some companies, however, simply prorate their current cash dividend over the increased number of shares, reducing the dividend rate, but keeping the payout constant.

As we can see from the following illustration, the Medford Corporation declared a 25% stock dividend and gave its shareholders something—by keeping its 30¢ a share dividend constant on the to-be-issued stock dividend. In the next illustration we see that the Lindberg Corporation, in contrast, gave its shareholders nothing—it declared a two for-one split, giving its shareholders a second share for each share owned, but cutting the 25¢ cash dividend in half.

From the *Wall Street Journal*, August, 1977:

Medford Corp. Declares A 25% Stock Dividend

MEDFORD, Ore. — Medford Corp., a maker of lumber, plywood, and fiberboard

products, declared a 25% stock dividend, payable Sept. 30, to stock of record Sept. 9.

Medford said it intends to continue the previous 30-cent-a-share quarterly rate on the increased number of shares "barring any unforeseen changes" in the company's financial condition or capital needs. The move will increase the number of shares outstanding to 1,223,375 from 978,700.

The company also declared a regular quarterly dividend on current shares of 30 cents, payable Sept. 1, to stock of record Aug. 16.

Medford also reported that second quarter sales rose 39% from a year earlier to $28.3 million and earnings increased 129% to $1.3 million, or $1.31 a share.

First half sales jumped 42% to $53.5 million, and earnings rose 103% to $3 million, or $3.06 a share.

From the *Wall Street Journal,* August, 1977:

Lindberg Corp. declared a two-for-one stock split in the form of a 100% share distribution, payable Sept. 1 to stock of record Aug. 10. There will be 2,309,644 shares outstanding after the split. Directors of the metal-processor also declared a dividend of 12½ cents on the new common shares, with the same payable and record dates. That is equivalent to the 25-cent-a-share paid quarterly on presplit shares.

Dividends are also frequently reported in tabular form:

Dividends Reported July 29,30

Company	Period	Amt.	Payable date	Record date
Adobe Oil & Gas Corp ...	Q	.04	9—30—77	9— 2
B.A.T. Indus Ltd ADR ...	G	n	10—18—77	8—30
n-Approximately $.058 per depositary share.				
Binney & Smith Inc new	Q	c.20	9— 9—77	8—10
Blue Bell Inc	Q	.30	9— 1—77	8—16
Koehring Co	Q	.20	8—31—77	8—15
Koehring Co $2.75pfH	Q	.68¾	9—30—77	9—15
Laclede Steel Co			Omitted dividend	
Liberian Iron Ore Ltd		.40	8—26—77	8—11
Lindberg Corp ....Stk		100%	9— 1—77	8—10
Lindberg Corp new	Q	.12½	9— 1—77	8—10

Some newspapers run a tabular column of stocks going ex-dividend (the date after which the new buyer does not receive the most recently declared dividend). For example:

STOCKS EX-DIVIDEND AUGUST 2

Company	Amount
Airborne Freight	.17½
Glenmore	.10

Additionally, if a stock is listed on the New York Stock Exchange or the American Stock Exchange, the fact of its going ex-dividend is flagged in the daily stock market table and foot-noted.

3: FINANCINGS

Companies raise funds through many techniques: selling common or preferred stock (equity) or debentures/bonds (debt). They can sell the shares to a small group of wealthy individuals or institutions (a "private placement"), or use an underwriter to sell the shares or debt (a "public issue").

If the common shares sold to the public are only for the benefit of the company and the money goes into the treasury, the financing is called a "primary" (primary does *not* refer to the first time a company goes public). If the shares are being sold for the account of existing stockholders, the issue is called a "secondary." A "combination" offering couples shares to be sold for the treasury and for selling stockholders.

A coupling of debt and equity is called a "unit offering."

And, lastly, corporations raise additional funds through *borrowing* arrangements with banks, insurance companies, or unnamed groups of "institutional investors," which might include banks, insurance companies, wealthy individuals, university trust funds and mutual funds, among others. A variety of borrowing and debt instruments can be used, including bonds, notes, equipment trust certificates (liens against specific hard assets of the company), and mortgage collateral bonds (using real estate as collateral for bonded debt).

In discussing *equity*, stories should include:

1. The amount of shares to be offered.
2. The anticipated offering price, if this is the company's first offering, or the most recent closing price of the stock if the company is already public.
3. If a combination offering, how many are being sold for existing shareholders.
4. What the company manufactures.
5. How corporate proceeds will be used.
6. Name of underwriter.

From the *Wall Street Journal,* August, 1977:

this story of a combination offering lists:
(1) total amounts of shares
(2) # of shares for
(3) # of shares of insiders company
(4) what company produces
(5) Underwriter

Worthington Industries Issue

COLUMBUS, Ohio—Worthington Industries Inc. said it registered a planned combination public offering of 600,000 common shares with the Securities and Exchange Commission.

Of the total, the producer of specialty steels and other products will sell 420,000 shares. The remaining 180,000 shares will be offered by certain shareholders for their personal accounts.

A syndicate led by Bache Halsey Stuart Shields Inc. and Ohio Co. will underwrite the offering.

But it overlooks 2 essential facts:
(1) What the company will do with the proceeds - frequently that is the real story
(2) the current price for the stock, needed to give dimension to the financing: how much is being raised?

* * *

From the *Wall Street Journal,* August, 1977:

a good story which lists all the necessary facts:
(1) # of selling holders in this "secondary" offering and the amount.

Officials of Celanese to Sell 130,200 of Its Common Shares

NEW YORK—Celanese Corp. said 18 of its officials will sell 130,200 common shares for their personal accounts.

The shares, to be sold by year-end for tax purposes, were bought through the exercise of stock options with funds borrowed from the company early this year. To exercise their options, the officials obtained $4.3 million of four-year loans from Celanese at an annual interest rate of 4%.

The company said the stock sale was keyed to the Tax Reform Act of 1976, under

(2) Reasons for sale, including method of financing the purchase) --
An excellent bit of information for readers facing the same problem

TEN KEY STORIES **99**

(3) Current price of shares

(4) Names some of the individuals doing the selling

which proceeds are taxed at a higher rate unless shares are sold in the same year options are exercised.

The average exercise price was $32.67 a share. The stock slipped $1.125 to close at $47.50 a share yesterday in composite trading on the New York Stock Exchange.

Celanese said it expects the loans will be repaid from the proceeds of the stock sale.

Among the selling stockholders are two Celanese directors and 16 vice presidents. The directors are P. H. Conze, selling 11,000 shares, and A. R. Dragone, selling 10,000.

Celanese recently had about 13.9 million shares outstanding.

(5) Gives perspective to the sale by comparing the # of shares to be sold to the Total outstanding shares — less than 1%. It isn't a "bail out".

In discussing debt, stories should include:

1. Amount.
2. Type of debt—bonds, notes, credit lines.
3. Interest rate and due date.
4. Repayment schedule: sinking fund commitments, if any.
5. Purpose of funds.
6. Lender's name.
7. Any unusual aspect to the loan—restrictions on dividends, convertible features, etc.

Although corporations sometimes do not issue all this information in their announcements, it will all show up in the next SEC filing. The reporter working against deadline, however, does not have the luxury of waiting for an 8-K or 10-Q; he must either telephone management—generally the company treasurer—or go with what he has.

In the announcement from Pantasote, for example, the reporter notes that "neither interest terms nor lenders were disclosed." And in the Documation item interest cost was not given.

Both are from the *Wall Street Journal,* August, 1977:

Pantasote's $12 Million of Notes

GREENWICH, Conn.—Pantasote Co. said it sold $12 million of notes privately to a group of four institutions. Neither interest terms nor lenders were disclosed.

Proceeds will be used to expand manufacturing facilities for this supplier of plastic and rubber products. Dillon, Read & Co. helped arrange the financing, a spokesman said.

* * *

Documation Gets Credit Line

MELBOURNE, Fla. — Documation Inc. said it obtained a $7.5 million credit line from First National Bank of Chicago. Interest cost wasn't given.

The new funds will be used for financing lease contracts to users of Documation's high-speed printer subsystems.

This *Wall Street Journal* item about Weisfield's loan gives much more detail:

Weisfield's Inc.'s Loan Accord

SEATTLE—Weisfield's Inc., a jewelry chain-store operator, said it signed a new $3.9 million five-year loan agreement and a $1 million short-term revolving arrangement with Rainier National Bank of Seattle.

Weisfield's said it will pay $771,000 annually at an interest rate of two percentage points over the prime, or minimum, lending fee. The company said it already has paid $571,000 on the first payment, due next Dec. 31.

"The increased line of credit will give the company added flexibility," Herman Blumenthal, president, said. Weisfield's previous lenders were Seattle First National Bank and Massachusetts Mutual Life Insurance Co.

A proposed unit offering of debt and common shares by City Investing is described in the following fashion (note that the number of common shares to be offered is left uncertain with no explanation).

City Investing Plans Unit Offering of Debt And Common Shares

By a WALL STREET JOURNAL *Staff Reporter*

NEW YORK—City Investing Co. said it is planning a unit offering of debt and equity securities.

How much equity?

> The negotiated public sale, involving 100,000 units, was registered with the Securities and Exchange Commission, the manufacturing and financial services concern said.
>
> The offering will consist of $100 million of debentures, due 1997, plus common stock in amounts to be determined prior to the offering, the company said. Each unit will consist of $1,000 face amount of debentures and shares of the common stock.
>
> Recently the company had about 21.8 million common shares outstanding.
>
> The offering will be made through an investment banking group led by Blyth Eastman Dillon & Co. and Paine Webber Jackson & Curtis Inc.
>
> Proceeds will be used to convert medium-term bank debt to long-term obligations under a program to extend the company's debt maturities, City Investing said.

How much Stock ?

Companies sell debt for many purposes, but one of the most common is simply to refinance earlier obligations. The key feature in a refinancing item is the new interest rate versus what is being paid off.

Prudent financial managers always seek opportunities to refinance debt at an advantage to the corporation. For instance, Centennial Corporation offered to exchange a $500 convertible debenture paying 10¾% interest for a $1000 debenture paying 4%, each due in 1992. By offering holders of this debt an increase of more than 34% in their annual interest, they were able to get 89% to agree to accept a new bond paying them only half of what they were originally owed, a reasonable trade-off for both sides. In the exchange, the corporation reduced its final cost of repaying the 1992 debentures by 18.3% on each swap.

Centennial Corp. Debt Exchange

GRAND RAPIDS, Mich. — Centennial Corp. said it ended its offer yesterday, as scheduled, to exchange $500 principal amount of new 10¾% convertible subordinated debentures, due 1992, for each $1,000 principal amount of its outstanding 4% convertible subordinated debentures, also due 1992.

The company said that about 89% of the 4% debentures were tendered in the exchange. The offer won't be extended, the company said.

Of course, the story could have been improved if the market price of the 4% debentures was included.

4: APPOINTMENTS

Routinely, companies issue announcements regarding the appointment of officers by the board of directors and the election of directors by shareholders at the annual meeting. Although the board elects most senior officers, the president generally announces those key posts immediately below him; and when a board vacancy is to be filled, or the board expanded during the course of the year, the board itself makes the election and shareholders vote for the slate at the next annual meeting.

The basic news is simple:

1. Who got elected?
2. To what?
3. Whose place did he take?
4. If it was unfriendly, why?

Question four transforms the story into a news feature, and this happens more often than one would suppose. For example, a marvelous *New York Times* feature in August, 1977 discussed the replacement of Carl B. Sterzing Jr. as president of the ailing Delaware & Hudson Railway Company and noted industry speculation that he was forced out because he was insistent on competing with Conrail for containerized cargo in the port of New York. The Delaware & Hudson desperately needed a $2,000,000 loan from the United States Railway Association, a government agency supervising the rebuilding of the U. S. rail system—and industry sources claimed U.S.R.A. wanted to protect Conrail.

Some corporate appointments are newsworthy because they signal the advancement of a minority person to a post of great importance, such as GM's recent appointment of black lawyer Otis M. Smith as the corporation's general counsel.

Noncontroversial appointments are simple, and treatment depends upon importance of the individual to the individual to the reading audience. As an example:

(New York)—John Jones, vice president of Amalgamated Steel Industries, was named to the Board of Directors of Bended

Metal Products, Inc. He fills the vacancy left by the death of Roger Jamison, son of a co-founder of the company.

On a local basis this might be an opportunity to recount the growth of an important local company, Bended Metal Products. In Jones' hometown it provides an opportunity for a discussion of Amalgamated, Jones' career and what his expertise can do for Bended Metal Products.

Annual meetings of shareholders normally result in the election of management's slate and, on a local level, permit two news stories—the first tied to management's candidates as listed in the proxy statement sent to all shareholders, and the second, a story of the annual meeting listing the directors elected to serve another term. Some boards now have staggered terms, and not all directors are restricted to one year in office.

The local story derived from the proxy statement can examine salaries, stock ownership (and the current market value), stock options, and other rewards for which management is seeking approval.

5: AMALGAMATIONS

Merger mania continues. Companies continue to grow not only through internal expansion but also through amalgamation with other enterprises. Mostly these are friendly agglomerations of property and people. But sometimes a merger is desired by only one party, and the result is a fight for control of the company, either via tender or proxy.

This generally begins with the quiet purchase of stock in the target company by a raider. New SEC regulations require the acquiror to announce himself once he has assembled 5% of the outstanding common shares of the company. This gives the intended victim an opportunity to marshall his defense; but, if the raider is offering a sharply higher price than the stock is selling for, it is unlikely the raider can be warded off.

Essential to the story are the following:

1. Terms of the offer.
2. Market price and book value of the company under attack.
3. Replacement cost of assets in target company.
4. Number of shares controlled by raider and number by management and friends of target company.
5. Most recent three-year history of sales, earnings, and price action of stock of each company.
6. Acquisition history of raider.

The most aggressively fought tender offers in 1977 included Crane's move against Chemetron, and Anderson, Clayton's battle for Gerber Products Company. Here's the way the Crane story broke in the *Wall Street Journal:*

Crane Seeking To Take Over Chemetron Corp.

Tender Offer of $40 a Share Has $160 Million Value; Suit Filed to Block Move

By a WALL STREET JOURNAL *Staff Reporter*

CHICAGO—Crane Co. offered to buy all of Chemetron Corp.'s outstanding common shares for $40 each. Chemetron filed suit in federal court in an attempt to block the takeover.

New York-based Crane currently owns 175,000 shares, or 4.4%, of Chemetron's four million common shares. The acquisition would have a value of $160 million.

Crane said the offer will begin about Aug. 23, subject to the filing of definitive offering documents with the Securities and Exchange Commission and registration under the tender offer laws of Illinois and Arkansas, if applicable. Until the offer is actually

made, Crane said it may modify, postpone
or abandon it. Salomon Brothers would act
as dealer-manager for the offer, Crane said.

Chemetron, based in Chicago, said it believes the acquisition would violate federal
antitrust laws because it and Crane compete
in several product lines, including welding,
fittings and valves. Chemetron also is a supplier of industrial and medical gases.

Chemetron added that it will bring the
proposed acquisition to the attention of the
Justice Department and the Federal Trade
Commission.

Chemetron stock didn't open for trading
on the New York Stock Exchange yesterday.
It closed Monday at $30.50 a share, up
$1.875. Last year, the stock sold for as high
as $52 a share.

First half earnings slumped due to sluggish capital spending in energy-related markets. Six-month profit was $2.9 million, or 71
cents a share, down sharply from $5.9 mil-
lion, or $1.44 a share. Sales rose to $125.4
million from $116.1 million.

The company has said it expects second
half profit improvement but doesn't expect
1977 net income will match 1976's $13.4 mil-
lion, or $3.40 a share. Revenue in 1976 to-
taled $460.8 million.

Companies under attack bring out their arsenal of weapons
which generally include lawsuits claiming restraint of trade. In the
Gerber story, Gerber contended that an acquisition by Anderson,
Clayton would destroy competition in the salad dressing market,
because Anderson held 12% of that market, while Gerber was
planning to enter the business.

The Anderson strategy added a new wrinkle to proxy tactics,
and received this newsfeature treatment by the *New York Times:*

In a move described by financial ana-
lysts as unprecedented and "very smart,"
Anderson, Clayton & Company Inc. of
Houston yesterday reduced the price of
its proposed tender offer for shares of
Gerber Products Company to $37 from
$40 a share.

This means that Anderson has revised
its offer for the 8.133 million outstanding
Gerber shares from $325.3 million to $299
million.

Yesterday, Gerber said it had no comment "for the moment" on the reduction,

The use of a Wall St. spokesman, Bache Halsey Stuart, reinforces the Anderson tactic. The reporter obviously has excellent Wall St. contacts to be able, under time pres- sure, to determine which brokerage house has a stock- holding position large enough to be a concerned party.

and that it had received no advance warning.

While merger bids have often been raised during negotiations, financial analysts said they could not recall any other cases in which the original tender offer had been lowered. The Anderson Clayton move, they theorized, wsa designed to compel the Gerber board, which has bitterly fought the bid, to take positive action in order to avoid lawsuits from shareholders who would be losing $3 a share under the new terms.

Good Chance of Suit Seen

A spokesman for one brokerage firm, Bache Halsey Stuart, said yesterday there was a good chance that the firm, on behalf of itself and clients who hold about 200,000 Gerber shares, would sue Gerber for the financial loss suffered as a result of the lowered bid.

Anderson, in announcing that it had lowered its tender offer, gave as its reason the 32 percent decline in Gerber earnings for the quarter ended June 30. Anderson noted this was the third consecutive quarter in which earnings per share declined, resulting in a drop in the last nine months of 24 percent under the earnings of the previous year.

Not all acquisition bids are unfriendly. The majority of mergers come by direct negotiation, management to management, and end agreeably. To wit, the Carlisle agreement to acquire Graham Magnetics, and Louisiana & Southern Life Insurance Co. merger discussions with Charter Company, in which it would merge into Charter or one of Charter's subsidiaries. The two following examples are from the *Wall Street Journal,* August, 1977:

— Louisiana & Southern Life Insurance Co. said it is discussing a merger with Charter Co. Louisiana & Southern would become a subsidiary of Charter or one of its affiliates.

Shareholders would receive about $6 cash for each share of Louisiana & Southern. Charter Co. already owns 53% of the 1,152,492 shares outstanding of Louisiana & Southern.

The company said that if a definitive agreement is reached, it will be subject to the approval of directors of both companies,

shareholders of Louisiana & Southern and
the Louisiana insurance commissioner.

Charter Co. is a holding company with interests in oil, communications and life insurance.

——————————

— Carlisle Corp. said it
signed a letter of intent confirming the previously reported agreement to acquire all
the outstanding shares of Graham Magnetics Inc., Graham, Texas, for $18 a share, or
about $16.9 million.

At times a merger bid begins in a more subtle way—the
acquisition, for "investment purposes," of a large block of stock in
the candidate company. Sometimes the block of stock turns out to
be just that, an investment. But this is a classic approach to a full
merger.

And, not all acquisitions are made for cash. A more common
exchange is for stock or debentures. For instance:

Dun & Bradstreet announced that it
had agreed in principal to acquire Technical Publishing Company of Bar-
rington, Ill., through an exchange of
stock on a share-for-share basis. The
transaction involves about 1.520 million
shares of Dun & Bradstreet stock, with
a current market value of about $45.8
million.

And not all proposed mergers work out. For instance, Cardiac
Pacemakers Inc. said that the recent price of its stock had declined
to the point where it had to call off the acquisition of two Buffalo,
N.Y. firms. Cardiac's stock had fallen to 15¼ from 22, probably
arresting more than just the acquisitions!

6: MEETINGS

Annual meetings of shareholders should be monitored carefully. The proxy statement is the starting point. It includes the
issues to be voted on, ranging from the election of directors to
stock options, reappointment of auditors and any important

business of interest to shareholders. Shareholder protectionists, such as Lewis Gilbert and Wilma Soss, or their designees, often announce their intended attendance at selected meetings, and generally raise enough questions at the meeting to result in a news story.

Reporters should make a practice of speaking to the company officials after the annual meeting to clarify any misunderstandings, and to fill in any details. Also, dissidents, if any, should be questioned.

Managements on rare occasions will exclude from a stockholders' meeting all nonshareholders. Should this happen, shareholders in attendance *must* be interviewed, and quoted, if possible. In this unlikely event, look for a dissident shareholder who has a lawyer with him. The attorney is a likely candidate for an accurate description of the meeting, the problems discussed and a good quote or two. Armed with this information, the reporter can speak to management and get its version of the meeting.

If management is still intransigent, a discussion with the company's public relations officer might reinforce the danger of allowing the opposition to appear in print without a rebuttal.

Occasionally an annual meeting is delayed, and the reason creates a news item as this from the *Wall Street Journal,* August, 1977:

American General Convertible

HOUSTON—American General Convertible Securities Inc. said it postponed its annual meeting, which was scheduled for last Friday, until Sept. 8 to allow it to include in the proxy statement details of a $231,000 settlement with a manager it claims made certain improper investments.

Meetings of various securities analysts societies normally provide enough information for a newsstory. There are 48 societies of financial analysts in the United States and Canada and an increasing number of stockbroker clubs. Companies which appear before such groups invite the press and also issue news releases covering their comments. But the alert reporter can generally interview the corporate spokesman before or after the meeting and add substantially to the official pronouncements. As an example, the Dow Jones newsman who covered the Superior Industries talk before the New York Society of Security Analysts extracted an earnings projection from the president that the president apparently did not make to the group. The following example is from the *Wall Street Journal:*

By a WALL STREET JOURNAL *Staff Reporter*

NEW YORK—Superior Industries International Inc. expects 1977 earnings to exceed $1.50 a share, up from $1.9 million, or $1.11 a share, a year earlier. Louis L. Borick, chairman and president, said after a meeting of the New York Society of Security Analysts.

The figures, however, will have to be adjusted for a 10% stock dividend voted recently by directors to take effect Sept. 16.

Mr. Borick also predicted that sales of the maker of automobile accessories will exceed $30 million in the second half. Given sales figures of that level in the first half, this puts sales for the year at more than $60 million, compared with $45.6 million in 1976.

During his speech, Mr. Borick said second half earnings would be a record and would exceed the 77 cents a share earned during the first half.

7: CORPORATE DEVELOPMENTS

It is almost impossible to categorize the variety of news stories which emanate from company headquarters, but a sampling should provide the newsman with some insight. Some of the more common include: announcements of plant expansion; sale of a product line or the liquidation of a line of business; product price reductions or increases; granting of licenses; new contracts; plant closings; listings on various stock exchanges, and a variety of law suits.

For the next week, just review the national financial press and the major local newspapers in your area, and check off the number of truly important stories that fall into this diverse category. In the summer of 1977, as an example, a one-week scanning of the New York, Chicago, Detroit, Dallas, Los Angeles and San Francisco newspapers, plus the *Journal of Commerce* and the *Wall Street Journal,* produced important stories on the following:

1. General Motors said it was expanding its Chevrolet division with the addition of a multi-million dollar casting line being added to its modular iron-casting plant in Saginaw, Michigan; Ford Motor that week said it was expanding its Tulsa, Oklahoma, glass plant by more than 25% in the fall. The GM expansion will add 500 jobs and the Ford expansion some 300.

2. However, Federal-Mogul of Southfield, Michigan, announced that it was selling three plants which make plastic pipes and fittings in Tampa and Ft. Pierce, Florida, and Middleboro, Kentucky. The company said it was selling these factories to former employees because these product lines no longer fit into Federal-Mogul's long-term outlook.

A good story could evolve if one took the trouble to interview the Federal-Mogul management on precisely how they are going to redeploy the funds received from the sale of these factories.

3. At the same time, Esmark, Inc., which once was known as Swift & Co., America's largest meatpacker, announced it was making a major withdrawal from that area of activity. A year earlier, Esmark had announced it was getting out of the soybean milling and leather tanning industries. Now it said it was going to sell or close much of its broiler-chicken operations and at least a third of its carcass-beef capacity, and sharply reduce its fresh-pork operations. Management said that earnings were being injured by its continuation in those businesses. Esmark also said that its processed-meat operations have been doing well because branded products provide higher margins.

An interesting feature article could be developed on the transformation of some of America's basic companies to more diversified enterprises, in large part stepping away from the basic industries with which they had been identified.

4. Stories on new licenses abounded. An announcement that Gulf Oil Chemicals had exercised its option on a license for the manufacturing and marketing of new high-performance polymers fought for space with a Globe Industries story on a new licensing arrangement to use Swiss acoustical technology and manufacturing techniques for the automotive, appliance and construction industries.
5. American Can raised prices 6% and attributed the increase to the higher cost of tin plate; Sanyo Electric of Tokyo said it was raising the price of television sets shipped to the United States by 3.6% because the value of the Japanese yen had risen.

If investigated, there is an additional story in each of these items. What factors are occuring in Bolivia affecting the price of tin plate? Why is the yen so strong against the dollar? Only a short while previous, the yen-exchange rate was 265 to one American dollar, and at the time of the announcement, it had risen to 367 to one American dollar.

6. Shaklee Corp. announced that it would start trading on the American Stock Exchange the following week; Teleprompter asked the Federal Trade Commission to introduce "cease and desist" proceedings against those television broadcast stations which, it said, refused to allow advertising by Teleprompter cable companies operating in their markets. Three nonmanagement directors of Grumman American Aviation Corp., a majority-owned subsidiary of The Grumman Corp., producers of aircraft, said they opposed a merger of their subsidiary into another subsidiary which was wholly owned by Grumman. They said this would freeze out the minority stockholders in *their* subsidiary; and all the elected officers of the Jones & Laughlin Steel Corp., in a move one rarely sees in management, joined 350 top management employees in a 10% salary cut because of low profits.

8: STOCK-MARKET STORIES

The New York and American Stock Exchanges are open for business from 10 A.M. to 4 P.M. (New York time), Monday through Friday, with the exception of New Year's Day, Washington's Birthday, Good Friday, Memorial Day, July 4th, Labor Day, Thanksgiving Day, and Christmas.

At the close of each market day the Associated Press, United Press International, Dow Jones, and Reuters each file a market roundup. Major dailies write their own. The stock-market roundup should include:

1. A reason for the day's price movement or lack of it.
2. Closing price, trend and change from previous day.
3. Market behavior during the day.
4. Issues which showed greatest price movement during day and reasons.

As an example:

DOW AVERAGES DECLINE 2.4,
FOLLOWING PREVIOUS DIVE
OF 8 POINTS

The Dow Jones industrial average, responding to nervousness at a prime rate increase by the Morgan Guaranty Trust Co. and disappointment at a less than anticipated dividend from General Motors, declined another 2.4 points today, finishing at 886. This is the lowest closing price since early January 1976.

General Motors, the most actively traded issue, fell ½ to 67½ after trading as low as 66⅜. It is slightly above its full year low of 66. Wall Street had hoped for an increase in GM's cash payout, but the company instead declared its regular quarterly dividend of 85¢.

Also, Morgan Guaranty yesterday raised its prime lending rate ¼ point to 6¾%. By doing this, Morgan joined other big money center banks which had taken similar action earlier. Inves-

tors' nervousness increased as a result
of what Wall Street reads as a tighter
monetary policy by the Federal Reserve Bank.
   Declining issues on the Big Board
outnumbered gainers almost 9-to-5.

   The Dow Jones Averages are the best known indexes of stock
market performance. Dow Jones & Company, publishers of the
Wall Street Journal, first compiled an average of 12 industrial
stocks to measure market performance and introduced the gauge
on May 26, 1896. The number of issues used in the industrial
index was expanded to 20 in 1916, and to 30 in 1928, where it has
remained since.
   The computation of the average was originally a simple one,
adding the 12 stocks and dividing their closing prices each
evening. Problems arose when companies in the index began
issuing stock dividends or splitting their shares. To compensate for
a split a divisor is used to recreate the presplit shares. Similar
adjustments are made when a new company is substituted in the
average to replace one which has been merged away.
   The divisors used for the 30 industrial stocks, the 20 transportation stocks, and the 15 utilities are listed daily in the *Wall Street
Journal* beneath the stock market chart on the next to the last
page.
   The stocks which comprise the various Dow Jones Averages
are:

Weekly Listing of 65 Stocks

Thirty stocks used in Dow Jones Industrial Average are:

Allied Chemical	Exxon	Owens-Illinois
Aluminum Co	General Electric	Procter & Gamb
Amer Brands	General Foods	Sears Roebuck
Amer Can	General Motors	Std Oil of Calif
Amer Tel & Tel	Goodyear	Texaco
Bethlehem Steel	Inco	Union Carbide
Chrysler	Inter Harvester	United Technologies
Du Pont	Inter Paper	US Steel
Eastman Kodak	Johns-Manville	Westinghouse El
Esmark Inc	Minnesota M&M	Woolworth

Twenty Transportation Stocks used are:

American Air	MoPac Corp	
Burlington North	Norfolk & West'n	Southern Pacific
Canadian Pacific	Northwest Air	Southern Railway
Chessie System	Pan Am World Air	Transway Int'l
Consolid Freight	St. Louis-SanFran	Trans World Air
Eastern Air Lines	Santa Fe Indust	UAL Inc
McLean Trucking	Seaboard Coast	Union Pac Corp

Fifteen Utility Stocks used are:

Am Elec Power	Consol Nat Gas	Panhandle EPL
Cleveland E Ill	Detroit Edison	Peoples Gas
Colum-Gas Sys	Houston Indust	Phila Elec
Comwlth Edison	Niag Mohawk P	Pub Serv E&G
Consol Edison	Pacific Gas & El	Sou Cal Edison

Because the Dow Jones industrial average utilizes only 30 companies, there has been some complaint that it does not truly reflect the movement of the market. Indeed, if IBM, which had been removed from the index, had been left in the Dow Jones would have broken through the psychologically important 1000 mark years earlier.

To rectify this, Standard & Poor's constructed a broader average consisting of 500 stocks—500 industrials, 20 rails, and 55 utilities. Many newspapers quote both the Dow Jones and S & P closing averages.

Reading the stock-market page is simple once one knows the abbreviations. The one-line listing contains the following information:

1. The highest price a single share of the particular stock has sold for during the current year. Prices are listed by ⅛ segments, each ⅛ representing 12½¢.
2. The lowest price a single share of the particular stock has sold for during the current year.
3. The name of the company, generally abbreviated for reasons of space.
4. The total amount of cash (and or stock) dividends paid in the past 12 months.
5. The price/earnings ratio of the stock using the closing price and the most recent 12 months reported earnings.
6. The number of shares traded that day.
7. The highest price paid for the particular stock that day.
8. The lowest price paid for the particular stock that day.
9. The price at which the last transaction of the day was consummated.
10. The change, if any, between today's closing price and the closing price on the last day the stock traded.

There is some pressure to include the computed dividend yield as of the last sale, a most helpful figure. Let's examine ACF, listed first, for alphabetical reasons, in the daily New York Stock Exchange tables.

– 1977 –			Yld	P-E	Sales				Net
High	Low	Stocks	Div. %	Ratio	100s	High	Low	Close	Chg.
39⅜	31⅛	ACF	2	5.8	9	46	35	34½	34½ – ½

1. The highest price for the stock in 1977 was 39⅜.
2. The lowest price for the stock in 1977 was 31⅛
3. The company name: ACF.
4. The company has paid aggregate dividends of $2 per share during the past 12 months.
5. The dividend yield was 5.8% on the day being reported upon.
6. The stock is currently selling at 9 times the earnings of the past 12 months.
7. On December 30, 1977, the day being reported upon, the stock traded 4600 shares.
8. The highest price anyone paid for a share of ACF on that date was $35.
9. The lowest price anyone paid for a share of ACF on that date was $34.50 (34½).
10. The last transaction was completed at $34.50 (34½).
11. The stock declined 50¢ (½) since the previous closing, when it had closed at 35.

Most stock tables include a box with explanatory notes, defining a variety of other data which precedes some of the figures. The *Wall Street Journal* carries this information in this fashion.

EXPLANATORY NOTES
(For New York and American Exchange listed issues)

Sales figures are unofficial.
d—New yearly low. u—New yearly high.
Unless otherwise noted, rates of dividends in the foregoing table are annual disbursements based on the last quarterly or semi-annual declaration. Special or extra dividends or payments not designated as regular are identified in the following footnotes.
a—Also extra or extras. b—Annual rate plus stock dividend. c—Liquidating dividend. e—Declare or paid in preceding 12 months. i—Declared or paid after stock dividend or split up. j—Paid this year, dividend omitted, deferred or no action taken at last dividend meeting. k—Declared or paid this year, an accumulative issue with dividends in arrears. n—New issue. r—Declared or paid in preceding 12 months plus stock dividend. t—Paid in stock in preceding 12 months, estimated cash value on ex-dividend or ex-distribution date.

x—Ex-dividend or ex-rights. y—Ex-dividend and sales in full. z—Sales in full.

cld—Called. wd—When distributed. wi—When issued. ww—With warrants. xw—Without warrants. xdis—Ex-distribution.

vj—In bankruptcy or receivership or being reorganized under the Bankruptcy Act, or securities assumed by such companies.

Year's high and low range does not include changes in latest day's trading.

Where a split or stock dividend amounting to 25 per cent or more has been paid the year's high-low range and dividend are shown for the new stock only.

The over-the-counter tables do not carry nearly as much informa
tion. OTC tables list the stock, its divided payout during the past
12 months, the bid and asked price (the highest price someone
was willing to pay, and the lowest at which someone was willing to
sell), and the net change in the bid and the asked.

Stock & Div.	Sales 100s	Bid	Asked	Net Chg.
--A A--				
Acady Ins Grp	120	1½	1¾	...
AccelratnC .80	26	18	18¾	...
Acceleratr Inc	31	2½	2⅞	...
AcetoChm 5.5i	13	16	17	— ¾
ACMAT Corp	17	1⅝	2⅛	...

9: MANAGEMENT INTERVIEWS

The most widely emulated interviewing technique in financial
journalism is the so-called "Dow Joneser," the in-depth corporate
discussion held between reporter and company official, usually the
president and sometimes the treasurer.

The components of such an interview are:

1. A forecast of earnings and sales for the immediate period
   ahead, and the year, if possible. If full-year predictions are
   not made, a generalized statement about year-end results
   can be used—such as "sales and earnings should be
   somewhat higher than last year" or "earnings for the year
   will again establish records."
2. Reasons for the sales and earnings trends.
3. Comparisons with previous periods.
4. Profit margins, balance sheet items.
5. Competition.
6. Industry statistics and company's performance on a relative basis.

The Applied Data Research article exemplifies the approach:

Applied Data Research Says Operating Profit Rose 80% in 2nd Period

By a WALL STREET JOURNAL *Staff Reporter*

PRINCETON, N.J.—Applied Data Research Inc.'s net income from operations rose nearly 80% in the second quarter to about $400,000, or 30 cents a share, from $223,051, or 18 cents a share, a year earlier, John R. Bennett, president, said.

In the 1976 quarter, the company also had an extraordinary tax credit of $200,000, or 17 cents a share, bringing total net for the period to $423,051, or 35 cents a share. It has used up its tax-loss carry-forwards, so that total net in this year's second quarter will show a decline of more than 5% from a year earlier.

Mr. Bennett estimated that second quarter revenue rose 32% to more than $5.1 million from $3.9 million a year earlier. Applied Data Research provides program products, or software, and professional services for computer users and market communications-management equipment.

First half operating net increased about 88% to about $740,000, or 56 cents a share, from the 1976 period's $392,766, or 32 cents a share, Mr. Bennett continued. A year earlier, the company also had a tax credit of $363,000, or 30 cents a share, bringing total net to $755,766, or 62 cents a share. First half revenue climbed about 33% to $9.6 million from $7.2 million, he said.

First half results were above expectations, Mr. Bennett declared, so the company has increased its forecast of earnings for all 1977 to about $1.5 million, or $1.15 a share, on revenue of about $20 million.

That would be an increase in operating net from 1976 of about 42% on a revenue increase of nearly 27%. In 1976, Applied Data Research had operating net under $1.1 million, or 84 cents a share, plus a tax credit of $384,000, or 30 cents a share, for total net of more than $1.4 million, or $1.14 a share. Revenue last year was $15.8 million.

Earlier this year, Mr. Bennett forecast about a 25% increase in operating earnings and revenue for all 1977.

Mr. Bennett attributed the increased operating earnings primarily to higher revenue from computer software, accompanied by better profit margins. In the first half, software revenue increased about 35% to about $6.3 million from $4.7 million a year earlier, he estimated. Equipment revenue rose about 20% to $1.8 million from $1.5 million, while revenue from services increased about 36% to $1.5 million from $1.1 million.

10: ECONOMIC STORIES

The release by Washington of economic information usually has impact on the stock market and generally translates into confidence or lack of it by the business community. The confidence indicator is more than just a psychological commentator. It is the framework by which many important industrial organizations ultimately make decisions regarding plant expansion and hiring.

Although the most widely reported barometers are the leading indicators, as measured by government economists, other indexes make front-page news as well: productivity, employment, inflation rate, prime-interest rates, help-wanted index. A discussion of economic reporting comprises Chapter 4 of this book, but a review of some of these economic stories is worthwhile.

In one week, newspapers carried stories on the following:

1. Leading indicators fell .6%, but Government economists said they weren't worried.
2. Productivity fell at an annual rate of 1.8% against a 6.1% annual rate in the previous quarter. Government economists said this slump reflected a strong increase in hiring in the second quarter, and that hours worked rose almost at a 10% annual rate. They said they hoped the decline was only temporary.

Confusing the issue further, individual yardsticks continued to gain. The sale of domestic automobiles rose 6% in the last ten-day period of July; big city stores reported a 2.8% rise in sales in July; steel production improved 0.4% in the week ended July 30, reversing eight consecutive weeks of decline; factory orders rose 0.4% in June, and factory shipments jumped 1.4% for that month; and the money supply—a figure watched much too closely—declined $1.5 billion.

Each of these merited and received a major article, some jumping to front page prominence. All the "indicators" of economic growth or decline, and a number not considered by official purposes to be "indicators," are discussed in the next chapter.

GENERAL BUSINESS STORIES

In addition to the ten key stories normally handled in routine fashion, many business stories develop from a review of feature articles in other sections of the newspaper—and, even more frequently nowadays, important *general* news stories evolve from the business pages and move to page one. One excellent example of a business reporter using business techniques to focus in on a major, page-one international story occurred in September, 1975 when forecasters predicted a prospective OPEC price hike of as much as 25%. Political analysts were busy writing heavy columns on what would happen to various nations should oil prices jump more than 10%—with the forecasts incrementally terrible as the 20% mark approached.

On September 17, 1975, *Journal of Commerce* reporter Craig Howard allayed the fears of an extraordinary price jump by stating in a headlined piece:

> The Organization of Petroleum Export-
> ing Countries (OPEC) will increase
> crude oil prices by only 5 percent, or
> possibly not at all, when its oil minis-
> ters meet in Vienna next week. . . .

Howard proved to be closer to the truth than most politically connected journalists who were busy quoting Government sources. (The increase worked out to be about 7.5%, on a total industry basis, taking into account various volume discounts.)

How did he do it? By checking into activity in the tanker freight business. "Tanker market activity is in line with a maximum increase of 5 percent," the story quoted a London shipping broker.

> Freight rates have started to decline, and one VLCC (very large crude carrier) has already signified its willingness to accept worldscale 29.

"Worldscale" is a schedule of nominal freight rates used by shippers as a standard of reference.
The article continued:

> According to the brokers, a price increase of just 5 percent would, after storage costs, etc., leave the majors (such as Exxon, Chevron and Mobil) little economic gain if they had to pay much more than worldscale of 25. Thus, no one is chartering VLCC's.

As you can see, the astute business or financial reporter can put his stethescope to one industry and hear the heartbeat of another. Or, as *Forbes Magazine* puts it, "the world is a giant drum: Tap it in one spot, and it reverberates all over."

Obviously, the business universe is a prism through which a single action fractionates in many directions, affecting people and nations in unexpected ways. A corporate story can frequently be peeled back to reveal other layers, community reaction and the impact on individuals. Conversely, a Government decision ripples out and touches hundreds of companies and often, through their subcontractors, thousands of individuals in towns across the country.

Stories can be parsed and reporters who have the time and interest can bring a news item down many levels, spinning off features and sidebars along the way. For instance, the major economic/political story as of this writing is the cost of petroleum. Of the hundreds of different stories—each with many opportunities for subsidiary articles—here are the headlines from three essentially economic front-page pieces, the first done as a straight front-page news take and the others as politically oriented items:

1.   ALASKA'S FIRST OIL LOADED ON TANKER
              FOR VOYAGE SOUTH

This first headline would also have provided an excellent opportunity to discuss the *types* of companies, many of them public, which stand to benefit or lose from the pipeline. The parallel can be explored in the opening of the American West by the railroads and in the development of international air-cargo shipments.

2.   ENERGY TRENDS SEEN OUTPACING
              PRESIDENT'S GOALS

This fascinating study conducted by A.D. Little Co., one of the nation's leading consulting firms (headed by Gen. James Gavin), stated that existing trends in energy conservation will have a greater effect than President Carter's program. A business story resulted that should have been picked up and questioned by *political* reporters.

3.   END RUN AROUND OPEC WITH TAXES

Here, a politically directed economic approach to lessening the OPEC stranglehold was offered by Senator Church who suggested the reversal of a 22-year-old tax ruling that might tip the balance against the OPEC nations. A thoughtful followup might be an exploration of what political repercussions the United States and its allies might face should such an approach be implemented.

Hidden in economic statistics are sociological and human-interest stories which touch the true spirit of the nation and illuminate our priorities. The *New York Times* front page of August 1, 1977, featured a story titled "Job Gains Made By the Retarded," stating that "despite high unemployment, despite all the other priorities ... the job hunt shows signs of significant success."

No one would deny they retarded their opportunity, at last, for entrance into traditional society. But the contrast is sharpened when, on August 2, 1977 the *New York Times* also front-paged the following: "New York is Lowest In Youth Employment. Survey Shows 86% of Minority Teen-Agers, 74% Whites, Jobless."

An economic story? Surely. Possibilities for human interest stories? For an article probing national priorities? Controversial? You bet!

And how about the feature possibilities in TWA's request that the Civil Aeronautics Board permit it to offer a roundtrip fare of $256 between New York and London? A business story, surely, but a great travel-section piece and one which leads to a discussion of the public utility aspect of mass transportation—the subsidization of foreign airfleets by national governments which consider cheap transportation a responsibility of government. Is our policy correct?

The conflict between ecologists and industrialists has created a new industrial relations specialist: a fellow who persuades air polluters to clean up enough of their emissions so that a new company can locate in the area and add to employment while adding to pollution. A feature was recently done on such a specialist, and it can be redeveloped along local requirements at every paper in the country.

When viewed as the starting point for generalized and localized features financial and economic news is a gold mine.

CHAPTER FOUR

The Interpretation and Meaning of Economic Indicators

No person or activity is unaffected by economics. The "dismal science" is studied by most students with as much joy as sipping castor oil.

Whereas finance is surrounded by a mystique which, stripped away, leaves an easily comprehended logic, economics is theoretical, encased in mathematics and formulations. Reduced to pragmatics, economics still requires an appreciation of abstracts.

Still, the business-news journalist must address himself to this mysterious subject, and write about it with sufficient insight to enlighten his readers about a subject dear to each of them: their pocketbooks.

The repercussions are obvious. Reportage of economic factors is translated into the reader's personal standard of living.

To do justice to his subject, the reporter of economic events must become acquainted with such seemingly arcane subjects as Federal Reserve Banks, the credit system of the United States, leading, coincident, and lagging indicators, and basic statistics released monthly or quarterly by key industries, such as steel, autos, retailing, containers, railroad shipments, and agriculture. The reporter must also monitor employment rates, money supply, inflation (and deflation), plant expenditures and a host of other barometers which are not only news in themselves, but are the basis for interpretive articles and trend analyses.

It is not easy, and when you are through with this chapter, you'll tip your hat to those established by-liners who decipher, report on, and interpret the *economic* news on a consistent basis.

The fragments of data released by the Commerce Department, the Labor Department, the Federal Reserve Board and the Treasury Department have to be woven together into a fabric which represents the economy, and the various signals and semaphores sent up by these four Federal agencies are under constant analysis by those trained observers who comment on the direction of the economy.

Under sharp focus at all times is the Federal Reserve Board and the actions of its Federal Open Market Committee; the money supply (or "stock") as reported in a series known as M-1 through M-7; the indicators—leading, coincident and lagging; and the "heavy hitters," those statistics which are potent enough to crystallize public opinion and, therefore, pack political power. The trinity forming the cornerstone for the latter category is the Unemployment Rate, the Gross National Product and the Consumer Price Index.

THE FED

Perhaps the most logical place to begin is with the Federal Reserve Board, since it is independent of direct politics, and through its control of the banking system, expands or contracts credit, controls the rate of margin on stock market accounts, and engages in international financial transactions, including the trading of foreign currency. It interacts, therefore, with our economic friends and foes every day.

The most visible activity of the Federal Reserve Board is the periodic meeting (one or more Tuesdays each month) of its Federal Open Market Committee. These FOMC meetings are watched not only by business journalists, but also by businessmen, Wall Streeters, bankers, financial analysts, and political leaders throughout the world. And, although this 12-man committee withholds the results of each meeting for one month before making it public, the actions it decides to take become evident in the credit markets within minutes. And the result is felt within hours in Wall Street, the best barometer of economic change.

If the FOMC believe banks are too easily granting credit, and perhaps adding to inflationary pressures, the FOMC mandates the Federal Reserve System (composed of 12 Federal Reserve banks across the nation) to begin *selling government securities.* The actual sales agent is the "Trading Desk" of the New York Federal Reserve Bank.

By *selling* government securities, the Fed acts as a brake on credit. Here's how: All banks which are members of the Federal Reserve System (these include all Federally chartered banks and those state banks which wish to join) must keep on hand *reserves* equal to a percentage of their demand (checking account) and time deposits (savings accounts). Currently, the Federal Reserve requires members with $2,000,000 or less in demand deposits to have reserves equal to 8% of those deposits; the percentage increases to 18% as banks have progressively more deposits. These percentages, of course, change periodically.

If the reserves of a member bank are reduced, the bank must bring in more deposits to bring its ratio in line, build up its reserves by borrowing or by selling investments for cash or reduce its lending activities. When the FOMC orders the New York Fed to sell more government securities, the FOMC is effectively reducing those reserves. In this way, the bank's lending power is curtailed—unless it creates greater reserves, as discussed.

The more the FOMC forces member reserves into government securities, the tighter credit becomes. And the reverse, obviously, is also true—with money becoming easier to borrow.

The Fed has other methods by which it can discourage the easy granting of credit:

1. By raising the discount rate, which is the interest rate it
    charges member banks on loans from the Federal Reserve
    banks (changes in the discount rate must be made sepa-
    rately by each of the Federal Reserve banks for their own
    districts, and as a result there are sometimes variations.
    The initial change, however, is the important one, since the
    other Reserve banks follow);
2. By changes in the reserve requirements and open market
    operations;
3. By changes in the maximum interest rates banks can pay
    on time and savings deposits;
4. By the trading of foreign currencies; and
5. By moral suasion. A telephone call to a bank president
    from a Reserve District official, or a public statement about
    bank responsibilities by the Federal Reserve Board Chair-
    man, can have a substantial impact on commercial bank
    investing or lending policies.

If the *discount rate* is raised, banks are obviously discouraged
from borrowing at the Fed "window" and in turn restrict their
own lending somewhat.

Open-market operations, the Fed's most important credit control, generally focuses on government securities, but also involves
the sale and purchase of bankers' acceptances.

Reserve requirements create the most immediate impact of any
of the Fed's weapons. Within specified parameters, the Fed can
vary the reserve requirements of member banks. Currently, the
guidelines on time deposits range from 3% to 10% for all the
member banks; for demand deposits, they range from 10% to 22%
for city banks and 7% to 14% for country banks.

Margin requirements—the percentage of downpayment when
borrowing to buy securities—are established by the Fed, and can
be used to moderate undue speculation in the stock market.
Regulation T relates to brokers' or dealers' loans to customers;
Regulation U controls commercial-bank loans to brokers, dealers
or other customers; and Regulation G covers loans of other
lenders.

Interest limits on time and savings deposits, established by the
Fed under Regulation Q, can also be a considerable influence on

the flow of funds. The Federal Deposit Insurance Corporation, which sets ceilings on rates paid at nonmember insured banks, must be consulted before action is taken, and must also be coordinated with the Federal Home Loan Bank Board, which sets ceilings on dividend rates payable by its members and other insured savings and loan associations.

Foreign exchange operations, under which the Fed can purchase or swap for dollar credits with foreign central banks, helps the Fed prevent disorderly speculative movement in our currency. Foreign nations or groups with surplus dollars could demand gold, causing speculative dislocations in the foreign holdings of dollars.

The discount rate, open market machinery, and reserve requirements are all termed "quantitative" or general credit controls, whereas margin regulations are considered "qualitative" or selective controls, directed at a particular type of credit. Interest rate ceilings and foreign exchange activities are partly quantitative and partly qualitative.

Though financial leaders often speak of what they perceive to be the Fed's "open market policy," or the Fed's "reserve policy" or "discount policy," the Fed generally has an *overall* monetary policy it is pursuing—and normally coordinates a program encompassing *all* its qualitative and quantitative controls.

The periodic FOMC meetings, as should be expected, are watched carefully by the business and financial community, and by journalists. Movement in the stock market and the credit markets frequently takes place in anticipation of these meetings.

The New York Federal Reserve Bank holds weekly press conferences, at which statistical information is reviewed and which result in the following type of story, quoted from the *Journal of Commerce,* January 7, 1977:

Fed Report Issued

Nation's Money Supply Rises

By KAREN PENNAR
Journal of Commerce Staff
M1, the nation's basic
money supply consisting of

Defines M1

currency plus demand deposits, increased by half a billion dollars to $312.4 billion in the week ended Dec. 29, pushing that aggregate's seasonally adjusted annual rate of increase for the latest quarter to 7.3 per cent, according to figures released by the Federal Reserve Board Thursday.

Points out M1 is rising faster than target

This rate of increase is above the Fed's own targeted range of increase for the aggregate of 4.5 to 6.5 per cent, and in recent weeks, M1 has increased at a rate well within the range.

Reports on impact of news in first 2 grafs

Credit markets didn't greet the news happily, since it fueled a growing market feeling that earlier expectations of further ease by the Fed were unfounded. The Fed funds rate probably has been targeted at 4⅝ per cent rather than 4½ per cent by the Fed, some analysts now believe.

Further, this week's economic indicators have signalled greater health in the economy than had been projected, and the credit markets are now awaiting next week's indicators to see if this trend continues.

Now she explains M2

The nation's broader monetary measure, M2, consisting of M1 plus time deposits at commercial banks other than large time certificates of deposits, rose by $600 million to $740.3 billion in the week ended Dec. 29, the Fed also reported.

Which is also above target

That aggregate's seasonally adjusted annual rate of increase for the latest quarter now stands at 12.8 per cent, well above the upper end of the Fed's target

all of this leads to a logical comment on effect on money market

range.

Meanwhile, money market rates showed a mixed picture in the week ended Jan. 5. The federal funds rate fell 19 basis points to average 4.47 per cent on the week, chiefly because of a particularly low effective rate prevailing on Dec. 31, 1975 — 4.17 per cent. This low rate is understandable, a Federal Reserve spokesman explained, in light of most banks, desire to show n o borrowings on their books on the last day of the year. Thus, the low demand for funds pushed the rate down on New Year's eve.

O t h e r money market r a t e s were either unchanged or up on the week. The three month Treasury bill rate gained eight basis points to average 4.41 per cent for the week ended Jan. 5, while the three month certificate of deposit rate offered in the secondary market gained five basis points to 4.68 per cent.

Citibank's prime rate formula is closely followed, and this indicates nothing will immediately happen to change CB's prime rate

The 90-119 day dealer placed commercial paper rate, however, was unchanged at 4.63 per cent. Although this rate, averaged into Citibank's prime rate formula, does bring the f o r m u l a result down a notch, the result is still closer to Citibank's current 6¼ per cent than the 6 per cent which a few major banks now offer their corporate customers.

Commercial and industrial loans granted by New York City's ten major reporting banks fell $101 million in the week ended Jan. 5, the New York Fed reported Thursday. Loans would actually have gained during

Now she discusses general loans

the week had it not been for a large decline of $250 million in holdings of bankers acceptances. These holdings accounted virtually entirely for the gain in business loan demand at New York's banks in the past four months, and a run off of this build-up was expected to begin with the new year.

The money watchers—particularly those who consider themselves "monetarists"—place great emphasis on the rise or fall of the money supply, known as "money stock." Money supply or stock is measured seven different ways, and there is much disagreement among economists and the financial community as to which of the series has the most application. Known as the "M series," the money supply figures are released by the New York Federal Reserve Bank each Thursday afternoon.

M-1 represents currency outside banks, plus commercial bank checking accounts.
M-2 consists of M-1, plus savings accounts at commercial banks, excluding certificates of deposits in denominations of $100,000 or more.
M-3 includes M-2 and savings accounts at savings and loan associations and savings banks.
M-4 is M-2 plus large negotiable certificates of deposits.
M-5 is M-3 plus large certificates of deposits.
M-6 is M-5 plus short-term marketable U.S. Government securities.
M-7 is M-6 plus commercial paper.

Everyone agrees that too much emphasis is placed on the weekly release of these figures, and that they should be viewed in a longer-term perspective. But the weekly release, nonetheless, has immediate impact, and generally is noted in the Friday evening roundup of factors which affected that day's trading in the stock market.

The close attention given these figures reflects the increasing recognition paid to those economists who practice monetarist theories—one of which holds that an inordinate increase in money supply leads to a rise in prices.

Recent economic research tends to support the view that changes in money supply affect demand for goods and services (GNP). In the 1920-1973 period, each business recession or depression was preceded by monetary growth.

Keynesians, whose economic theories have guided the Western world since the mid-1930s, argue that fiscal factors—changes in the full-employment budget and investment—are the major factors in recession and growth. The Government's policy on spending and taxes plays the major role in the Keynesian framework.

Both philosophies have as spokesmen and disciples leading figures in the economic establishment, and their comments ricochet from business page to front page.

Economists, financial analysts, businessmen, business journalists, and other perceptive observers of the national scene spend much time trying to fray statistical reports, pulling from them those strings which they hope will prove to be an economic trendline. Ultimately, great social movements and sometimes important international political decisions circle back to a nation's economic health, and the ability to determine *where you are now* is of enormous help in predicting *where you are going,* and deciding how best to get there.

The use of economic models—econometrics—has created a new specialty within the economics profession, and the computer-oriented econometricians are becoming an important force in government and business. By the use of complicated formulations—some including as many as several hundred equations—these specialists game-play alternative scenarios—changing employment, inflation, interest rates, tax structures—and try to model the various types of end results.

The latest sophistication of what was until recently termed "business-cycle forecasting" tries to correlate economic theory with reality, moving it closer to a pragmatic science. Some businessmen focus on one particular index or formula which has particular application to trends in their own industry, and influences their buying and spending judgements. For them, modeling can present alternative business choices with which they can move quickly once events parallel the models.

One businessman in the apparel field considers the sale of men's suits to be a true indicator of the health of the nation, reasoning that when family finances become tight, the male head of the family cuts back on his own personal spending before reducing the family's standard of living. Using this personal index, this businessman has twice successfully forecast a severe decline in the economy—in 1928 and 1971—and in 1928 sold his manufacturing business as a result.

Iben Browning, a leading climatologist, uses as a leading indicator the rise and fall of the water level in Lake Michigan, which he says over an extended period has demonstrated an uncanny relationship to the rise and fall of the American economy. He reasons that a decline in the water level of Lake Michigan means a decrease of rainfall in the Corn Belt and in the Great Plains, presaging a drought, agricultural panic, and ultimate recession. He claims the reverse is also true. Whether one can rely on "The Lake Michigan Leading Indicator" or not, amateur and professional readers of the economic tea leaves are forever looking for signs.

Since 1873 the United States economy has experienced 23 business cycles. Economic historians spend much time looking for indicators which—as in the case of the prescient apparel manufacturer—will warn them of impending changes. Of the many which have been devised, 26 indicators have been singled out by economists as the most important to watch. The object of this intensive focus, the business cycle, was best defined in 1946 by Wesley C. Mitchell and Arthur F. Burns in *Measuring Business Cycles,* published by the National Bureau of Economic Research.

Burns and Mitchell defined business cycles as a "type of fluctuation found in the aggregate economic activity of nations that organize their work mainly in business enterprises; a cycle consists of expansions occuring at about the same time in many economic activities, followed by similarly general recessions, contractions and revivals which merge into the expansion phase of the next cycle. This sequence of changes is recurrent but not periodic; in duration business cycles may last from more than one year to ten or 12 years; they are not divisible into shorter cycles of similar character with amplitudes approximating their own."

The 26 key indicators which economic forecasters use to evaluate and predict the business cycle include 12 leading indicators, which are used as a guide to the future course of the economy; eight coincident indicators, which show what is happening now in the economy; and six lagging indicators, which measure imbalances which occur during prosperity and may have to be corrected during recessions. From time to time substitutions are made.

The Leading Indicators are:

1. *Average Work Week of Production Workers, Manufacturing.* Focusing on the average number of hours worked per week in manufacturing jobs, this sensitive barometer anticipates turning points in the business cycle by about four months. An increase obviously points to greater production, a decrease to declining manufacturing activity.

2. *Contracts and Orders for Plant and Equipment, 1972 Dollars.* This is is also a significant barometer, reflecting optimism about the future. Do not confuse this indicator with the less valuable "Business Expenditures, New Plant and Equipment," a lagging indicator which relates to *past* contracts and orders, currently being fulfilled, and tells nothing about the future.

3. *Index of Net Business Formation.* This calculates the net number of new businesses formed each month, an increase being a harbinger of improving profit opportunities and greater business activity in the future. A decline signals the reverse.

4. *Index of Stock Prices, 500 Common Stocks.* For those who believe in group intelligence, the stock market is one of the more accurate bellweathers of economic activity. The market quickly reflects corporate profits and interest rates. There have been few sustained movements in stock prices that have not been paralleled by related moves in the business cycle. (Indeed, a study by Edmund A. Mennis showed common stock prices forecast business cycles 80% of the time. However, there was no consistency to the number of months by which the stock market led the cycle.) The bond market is also sensitive to the business cycle. Interest

rates on bonds and savings normally rise during the late stages of upward business cycles and fall during the downswings, with bond prices doing just the opposite. Generally, prosperity is good for common stocks, whereas depression is good for bond prices.

5. *Index of New Housing Permits, Private Housing Units.* A measurement of anticipated building (excluding mobile homes), this index counts the number of permits issued to construct private housing. An increase in the number of permits should translate into increased construction—affecting many industries and jobs. There is a lag of several months between permit and construction, and this is sometimes distorted by weather factors and occasional labor and building shortages.

6. *Layoff Rate, Manufacturing.* This one is self-explanatory. At times when people are being laid off by manufacturing companies, the economy is generally lagging; the converse is true as well.

7. *New Orders, Consumer Goods and Materials, 1972 Dollars.* Manufacturing companies produce goods in relation to the amount of demand, and maintain only enough inventory to keep the pipelines filled to their distributors and retailers. Therefore, when consumers stop buying for any reason—fear, or an actual decline in their income levels—the new orders for consumer goods declines and manufacturers follow. When consumers begin to buy, retailers and distributors generally turn to the manufacturers and order new goods for inventory so they can supply on an immediate basis those customers who walk in the door. This is a pretty sensitive indicator.

8. *Net Change in Inventories On Hand and On Order, 1972 Dollars (Smoothed).* As in "New Orders, Consumer Goods and Materials" (Indicator 7), this indicator is sensitive to consumer demand. Retailers and distributors build up their inventories when they see consumer demand increasing. Naturally, they want to consummate a sale as quickly as possible and prefer to have the product on hand or in a nearby warehouse for immediate delivery. The greater the confidence of the retailer and distributor, the more this index moves up in anticipation of expanding consumer demand, forecasting an upturn in the economy. The reverse is true as well.

9. *Percent Change in Sensitive Prices, WPI of Crude Materials, Excluding Foods and Feeds (Smoothed).* Certain commodities, such as ferrous metals, are highly cyclical and over an extended period have been harbingers of economic growth or decline. Since manufacturers using ferrous metals do not like to build up bulky inventory, new orders for such materials reflect a most immediate need by the buyers. The buyer, in turn, is generally manufacturing a product in which the ferrous metal is an integral component, so that he is responding to a newly emerging consumer demand. All of this happens very quickly, and the wholesale price index (WPI) of crude materials is an important barometer of future economic activity. "Smoothed" refers to the averaging of prices over a period of time to even out weekly or monthly distortions.

10. *Vendor Performance, Percent of Companies Reporting Slower Deliveries.* This index, an indicator of lesser importance, measures how rapidly goods are delivered to customers. Supposedly, a forthcoming expansion of economic activity is presaged by an increase in the percentage of companies reporting slower deliveries. A drop in the percentage—indicating that companies are receiving their ordered materials more rapidly—forecasts a slowdown in the economy.

11. *Money Balance (M-1), 1972 Dollars.* Monetarists, such as followers of economist Milton Friedman of the University of Chicago, believe that this is one of the most important statistics. M-1 includes cash in circulation and all the money in our checking accounts. The Federal Reserve Board sets its own target for M-1 (see *Journal of Commerce* story on page——), and there is much controversy over whether or not the target figure it has selected is appropriate to maintain a reasonable growth for the economy. Monetarists believe that excessive money growth will force up prices by pushing the economy forward too quickly, causing inflation. Conversely, they feel that a declining money supply—or growth of M-1 at a rate less than they believe necessary—causes recession and price cutting.

12. *Percent Change in Total Liquid Assets (Smoothed).* A measurement of how much money individuals have on hand in cash or equivalents, this indicator foretells consumer spending patterns. When the total rises, consumers are expected to begin

spending more heavily; the reverse is also true. The "Total Liquid Asset" figure in this index includes eight items: currency, demand deposits, time deposits in commercial banks, time deposits in non-bank thrift institutions, savings bonds, short-term marketable securities, negotiable certificates of deposit, and other private money market instruments. "Smoothed" refers to the averaging of prices over a period of time to even out weekly or monthly distortions.

The Coincident Indicators are:

1. *Employees on Nonagricultural Payrolls.* A good barometer of short-term current economic moves, this index generally increases during good business times, and decreases when times are bad.

2. *Unemployment Rate.* One of the most closely watched indicators (for political and sociological reasons, as well as economic), it generally expands and contracts with the business cycle. Though highly publicized, it is not a forecasting tool.

3. *Gross National Product in Current Dollars.* The total business done by the nation in market value of goods and services produced. Another well-publicized indicator, but useful only in measuring contemporary business activity.

4. *Gross National Product in 1972 Dollars.* Measuring the GNP in constant dollars, this points out what the nation's Gross National Product would be if prices were the same as in 1972 and purchasing power was unchanged. It is probably a better index of changing standards of living than the GNP since it reflects the real physical volume of output.

5. *Industrial Production.* Widely publicized on a monthly basis, this index measures industrial production on a current basis but is not used to forecast.

6. *Personal Income (less transfer payments).* This is a useful indication of what is really happening on a current basis in the nation, since it measures the total income received by all in the country and therefore reflects employment, wage rates and even production.

7. *Manufacturing and Trade Sales, 1972 Dollars.* The monthly

volume, in dollars, of sales made by manufacturing, wholesale and trade businesses. This index also reflects current business conditions.

8. *Retail Sales, 1972 Dollars.* This is the monthly volume of merchandise sold, plus receipts for repairs and similar services.

The Lagging Indicators are:

1. *Average Duration of Unemployment.* A measure of long-term unemployment, this index, when at low levels, points to shortages developing in the labor market. Do not confuse this with the total unemployment rate, which is a coincident indicator, or with the average weekly claims for unemployment, which is a leading indicator.

2. *Labor Cost per Unit of Output, Manufacturing.* Changes in unit labor cost affect profit margins, and therefore comprise an important component of the ratio of price to unit labor cost, a leading indicator. On its own, however, this index simply measures the cost of labor involved in manufacturing production.

3. *Manufacturing and Trade Inventories, 1972 Dollars.* The total inventory on hand at the end of each month in manufacturing, wholesale, and retail establishments, this measurement highlights imbalances which might be developing, and those that are being adjusted.

4. *Commercial and Industrial Loans Outstanding.* This indicator measures borrowings by businesses, and lags the business cycle. Of greater interest, and forecasting value, would be an index which measured the rate of change of loans outstanding.

5. *Ratio, Consumer Instalment Debt to Personal Income.* This is an indication of how much of current earning power consumers must put aside to repay instalment debt, thus reducing their available cash for new purchases. It is also a measure of how far in debt consumers are willing to go to supplement their earning power, and therefore a measure of their own confidence—which could be mistaken.

6. *Average Prime Rate Charged by Banks.* When high in terms of recent rates, business borrowings are generally throttled, with a resulting reduction in business expansion; the reverse is

also true. At times, however, a hike in the prime rate simply indicates good business for funds demand and business confidence.

The U.S. Department of Commerce summarizes the indicators in Composite Indexes, putting the leading indicators in one series, five of the eight coincident indicators in another and six lagging indicators in a third series. Here's how the Commerce Department treated one monthly release of leading indicator figures:

Key Indicators Index Dips Again; June 0.6% Decrease Is Discounted

2d Consecutive Drop of Little Significance, U.S. Officials Say

By EDWARD COWAN
Special to The New York Times

WASHINGTON, July 29—The Commerce Department reported today that its index of leading economic indicators, which is designed to show which way the economy is headed, declined in June for the second consecutive month.

The decrease was dismissed by the department and by the Treasury Secretary W. Michael Blumenthal as a fluctuation without apparent significance.

"I don't think that what we've se in two months means there is a serious weakening of the economy," said Maynard Comiez, deputy chief economist of the department.

At a news conference in St. Louis, Mr. Blumenthal said, "I don't think it's a cause for real concern."

The department reported that the index of leading indicators decreased in June by six-tenths of 1 percent, following a May dip of two-tenths of 1 percent. However, the June decline was particularly unpersuasive as a harbinger of economic weakness because it was due entirely to softness in wholesale prices of crude materials, notably natural gas and scrap steel.

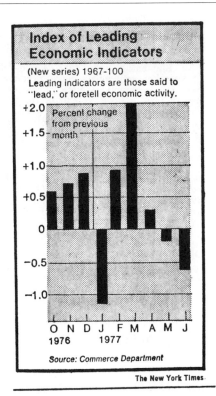

Index of Leading
Economic Indicators

(New series) 1967-100
Leading indicators are those said to
"lead," or foretell economic activity.

Percent change
from previous
month

O N D J F M A M J
1976   1977

Source: Commerce Department

The New York Times

Without a decline of 0.62 percent for this component of the index, changes in the other components were just offsetting.

A Slowing in the Price Trend

The index stood at 129.4 for June compared with 130.2 for May. The base period, 100 on the index, is 1967.

"One should not consider as unfavorable news that we've had a slowing down in the rate of increase in prices," Mr. Comiez said. He suggested that such a slowdown would have been worrisome had it occurred amidst widespread signs of economic softness.

Of the 12 components of the composite index of leading indicators, six moved in the direction of economic weakness in June, four pointed to a stronger economy and two were unreported as of today. Apart from the change for materials prices, all of the changes were very small, on the order of one-tenth of 1 percent or less.

Mr. Comiez said there would have to

be "several more months of weakening
before we could say there's some trouble."

Mr. Blumenthal noted that he and Administration economists have predicted
that the economy's brisk 7 percent
growth rate in the first half of the year
would slow to 5 percent in the second
half. Five percent, he said, "will allow
us to reduce unemployment and is about
the right speed to show us that inflation
can be reduced as well."

Mr. Blumenthal commented that a long
period of economic expansion usually
unfolds with some irregularity. "There's
always a slowdown and a speedup, slowdown and a speedup," he told reporters.

As information becomes available on each of the components, a
news story develops.

In addition to highlighting economic stories, one must not
overlook statistics which come forth from various trade associations, especially those reporting for basic industries, such as steel,
paperboard, food, retail operations. Since these raw figures are
direct, and do not have to be fed into indexes, they often present
quicker insight into the business cycle.

THE "HEAVY HITTERS"

As we have seen, the actions of the Fed, the money supply, and
each of the indicators represents hard news. Some of these items,
however, are of such impact that they move off the business pages
and onto the front pages. Watch for them. They include the
following:

1. *The Overall Unemployment Rate* is issued monthly by the
Bureau of Labor Statistics, and it is broken down by category:
adult men, women, teenagers, married men, blacks, white collar
and blue collar and so forth. The rate is also available by
geographic region. Bear in mind that *employment* can rise at the
same time *unemployment* rises, because of the increased number
of persons seeking work. Unemployment statistics, by the way, are
gathered in a surprisingly simplistic fashion: 60,000 households

are telephoned by pollsters, who in their canvas ask how many in the household are seeking work. The results of this poll, conducted by the Census Bureau of the Commerce Department, is extrapolated into the headline figures in the newspapers. In economic terms, unemployment at the rate of 10% or more signals a depression. During the 1930s, unemployment rose to 25%.

2. *The Gross National Product* is issued quarterly by the Commerce Department. This figure is not stable, for it is continually revised as other factors become known, sometimes years after being reported, and the revisions help give economists a better historic picture. The estimated GNP for 1978 is about $2 trillion.

The GNP, which measures the economic performance of the entire economy, has four components.

(a) *Consumer Spending* (which accounts for two-thirds of the Gross National Product), composed of durables, nondurables, and services.

(b) *Nongovernmental Investment Spending* (about 10% of the Gross National Product), which includes outlays for plant and equipment, changes in inventories, and residential housing.

(c) *Government Expenditures* (about 25% of the Gross National Product), including defense spending, plus state and local government expenditures.

(d) *Exports and Imports of Goods and Services* summarize our international transactions and tell us how goods from the United States are measuring up to our overseas competitors. In recent years complications arising from massive imports of oil have tended to surround this statistic with a good deal of uncertainty. The Balance of Payments and the Balance of Trade are extracted from these statistics. Some economists and businessmen think that of the two, the Balance of Trade figure—the relationship between exports and imports—is the more important, and that it more accurately signals the trend of the economy: up when the balance is in our favor, down when in favor of our trading partners. The difference between our exports and imports is added or subtracted from the reported Gross National Product.

The Gross National Product can often be a misleading figure because the total of goods and services increases through inflation. Therefore, the economy may seem to be robust because of a GNP expansion, while the gain is made up entirely of price increases rather than the sale of more units.

To overcome this, the Commerce Department also issues on a quarterly basis a figure representing the *Gross National Product Deflator,* which is the difference between the GNP and what is termed the "Real GNP" (a figure adjusted to take into account inflation at all levels of transaction). By dividing the Gross National Product by the "Real" GNP, a Deflator figure is arrived at which moves up or down, almost but not exactly, with the Consumer Price Index and informs us of how prices are doing.

3. *The Consumer Price Index* is issued monthly by the Bureau of Labor Statistics. This key index is composed of three major groupings:

(a) *Food,* including prices of everything from meat through cereals.
(b) *Other commodities,* including durables (washing machines, toasters, etc.), nondurable goods, and nondurables other than clothing.
(c) *Services,* including everything from rent and medical costs through transportation expenses.

The Consumer Price Index is worthy of front-page treatment. Almost half of the population of the United States is tied to the CPI by escalator clauses which increase their salaries or benefits each time it rises. A 1% increase in the Consumer Price Index adds approximately $1 billion in wages and other payments.

The CPI is based on prices of approximately 400 items chosen by analysts at the Bureau of Labor Statistics and checked monthly by the BLS shoppers who purchase the 400 items at some 18,000 establishments around the country. The relative weighted importance of each of these 400 items in the CPI formula is based upon a study, conducted about once a decade, of the spending habits of 10,000 families. The current formula is weighted 25% for food, 39% for nonfood commodities and 36% for services.

The CPI is now reported on a dual basis to more clearly reveal its impact on different types of households. First, the CPI reports on its traditional basis—covering urban wage earners and clerical workers. This, however, does not include the spending habits of such groups as wealthy people, impoverished groups, and professionals who do not have a wage but receive fees of varying amounts. To rectify this, the second report—the "Consumer Price Index for all Urban Households"—has been constructed, taking all of these groups into account and covering some 80% of the population.

The monthly Consumer Price Index is based upon prices in 1967, a base year used for many economic indexes.

The Consumer Price Index and the Gross National Product Deflator are the two main indicators which allow the observer to keep up with the movement of prices.

"UNDERCURRENT INDICATORS"

Ten lesser-known indexes represent a silent undercurrent riding beneath these three well-publicized ratios, (the Unemployment Rate, the Gross National Product, and the Consumer Price Index) and provide important trend stories for reporters who follow them up. They include the following:

1. *The Wholesale Price Index* is a monthly statistic issued by the Bureau of Labor Statistics. This is an extensive list of specific items ranging from farm products through industrial commodities, which tends to forecast trends that ultimately show up in the CPI and the GNP.

2. *Average Price of Small, Specially Selected Industrial Raw Materials* is a weekly indicator, compiled by the Bureau of Labor

Statistics. It is composed of 13 raw material items, and has proven to be one of the best forecasters of trends which later are magnified in the Wholesale Price Index, the Consumer Price Index and the Gross National Product Deflator.

3. *Standard of Living* is not measured by any composite index, but the reporter can fit pieces together with data and quotes from leading economists. The data bank includes two key series issued monthly by the Bureau of Labor Statistics. One is on purchasing power, and the other relates to earnings.

The first, purchasing power, is watched closely by union leaders and used in their arguments with management and government. Issued monthly by the BLS, it carries the forbidding title "Spendable Average Weekly Earnings per Production Worker on Payrolls of Private Non-Agricultural Establishments, Expressed in Constant Dollars." This index adjusts gross weekly paychecks to conform with price increases, thereby coming up with "constant dollars." However, it does not take into account fringe benefits, an item which has become increasingly important in the standard of living of wage earners in the United States. A recent study of 1800 large corporations by The Conference Board, a nonprofit business and economic research organization, indicated that fringe benefits now account for almost 33¢ of every payroll dollar, compared with less than 20¢ a decade ago.

The second BLS monthly statistic, which can be used to postulate the Standard of Living, is the "Per Capita Income Series," which covers the entire population of the United States and totes up all sources of income, including dividends, welfare payments and social security benefits.

4. *The Discomfort Index* is an informal yardstick used by some economists and economic writers. This hybrid adds together the overall rate of unemployment and the rate of increase of the Consumer Price Index to come up with a figure at which people feel distress. Arthur Okun, prominent economist and advisor to several Presidents, has half-seriously suggested that a discomfort index reading of 9% is a level at which people become "quite unhappy." The index is now runnning 13% or worse (about 6% inflation, 7% unemployment). Since this is not a formal economic index, it is largely overlooked.

5. *The Productivity Index* is expressed in two quarterly indexes issued by the Bureau of Labor Statistics. They add a further measure to the standard of living since most economists agree that the standard of living cannot increase without improvements in the rate of productivity. The two indexes measure output per man hour in private businesses, one including agricultural workers and one without. These indexes eliminate productivity gains created by rising prices, and use the 1967 "Real" GNP as the base. When they rise, the standard of living generally improves; and the converse is also true.

6. *The Capacity Utilization Rate,* or operating rate, measures the efficiency of United States manufacturing, locking into the indexes on productivity and therefore the standard of living. Since the end of World War II this ratio has ranged from 70% to 95%, with the preferred rate of plant operation being about 85%. A rate higher than 85% begins to bring about inefficiencies, due to bottlenecks, shipping delays and related problems. This ratio is available through various independent surveys, the most important of which is the one conducted by McGraw-Hill.

7. *FRB Index of Industrial Production* is a monthly series that measures the output of American industry. It is a useful gauge in appraising current production levels. The best overall index of current production patterns.

Two other indexes which have proven to be quite useful in determining consumer confidence, but are not used for forecasting, are consumer sentiment (#8) and the quit rate (#9).

8. *The Survey Research Center of the University of Michigan* each quarter releases its *Index of Consumer Sentiment.* Although the Commerce Department cautions against using any unofficial index—such as Michigan's or the one produced by The Conference Board—as true indicators of business cycles, these measures have proved to be quite useful as *"undercurrent indicators."*

9. *The Quit Rate,* an obscure index compiled by the BLS, computes the number of people who quit their jobs as a percentage of those employed. This is as dramatic a confidence indicator as is available.

10. *The* Journal of Commerce Daily Index *of Sensitive Spot Commodity Prices* is widely used by business and financial

interests as an indicator of economic and price trends. Use of spot rather than futures prices reflects their value as a more realistic consistent barometer. Each commodity is weighted in relation to its importance in the overall picture. Thirty commodity prices are involved in compilation of the index with individual calculations including totals for grains, foods, textiles, metals and miscellaneous data. The current index was initiated in 1954 with a 1947-1949 base as 100. Formerly the index in use had been based on August, 1939. Subsequent revisions have been made in the index to reflect changing conditions but these have had minimal impact insofar as affecting the calculations. The index is compiled each afternoon after markets have closed—thus assuring current data are used and that the compilation has no time lag.

These "front page" indicators, the "heavy hitters," and their "undercurrent" relatives, are worthy of news coverage.

CHAPTER FIVE

The Interpretation and Meaning of Financial Statements

Although capitalism has worked well for the United States, it does not seem to be an exportable philosophy. After more than 200 years of demonstration there is today only one other large, free-market capitalistic nation—West Germany. Because of the construction of capitalism—its reliance on pooled capital from individual investors (publicly owned companies), short-term bank financings and long-term insurance-company loans, three highly regulated industries—Government policy is highly visible. The moment a Government decision is made about defense, housing, welfare, foreign aid, national medical insurance, or schooling, some segment of American industry begins to tool up or shut down. This same visibility does not exist in most other governments.

By focusing on the universe of publicly owned corporations the trained observer can generally gain substantial insight into important changes in industry, society, and government. There is hardly an industry which does not have some member whose shares are owned by the public and who, therefore, must report to the Securities and Exchange Commission on a quarterly or annual basis. The range of documents available is impressive and includes 10-Qs (quarterly filings); 10-K's (annual filings); 8-K's (significant changes, such as acquisitions, as they occur); proxy statements, S-1's and S-2's (registration forms for the sale of new securities) and others. The nation's 15,000 professional securities analysts, working for the research departments of brokerage houses, banks, and funds, pour over these documents as they become available—*and so should the financial journalist.* There are approximately 40,000 publicly owned companies in the United States representing the hopes of more than 25,000,000 individual investors. Some 1575 public companies are listed on the New York Stock Exchange; 1140 on the American Stock Exchange, and about 16,000 over the counter, of which some 2500 are traded actively enough to be listed in those daily newspapers which devote space to closing prices. Some 20,000 more trade so infrequently that markets are not made in their stocks at all.

Of the documents which are in the public domain the most easily accessible is the annual report to shareholders, a copy of which is included in the 10-K filed with the SEC. The 10-K, however, contains much more information of use to the journalist and should be read along with the annual report.

A great mystique has grown up around the subject of finance and financial statements. Many persons believe a study of the subject requires a great knowledge of mathematics. This is not so; more important is an ability to grasp abstract concepts. The only mathematics that enter financial analysis are basics taught in elementary school. A good many adults, of course, have difficulty with elementary math and, for them, the inexpensive pocket calculator is a lifesaver.

The language of finance is much easier to master than any of the foreign languages studied in school. Every financial journalist comes in daily contact with corporations and their balance sheets and income statements and, when one understands their meanings, stories leap out.

The analysis of financial statements is a *comparative* art. It requires the *comparison* of this year's figures with those reported by the same company last year, to see if data reported last year have been restated and to note both the absolute dollar *differences* of each line item and the *trends* in every financial category. By reducing key comparisons to percentages the financial journalist can easily view several companies in the same field and notice the *differences* in operation. But he *must check* his observations and conclusions with authoritative company sources.

As an example, if ABC Supermarkets sells and repurchases its merchandise stock ("termed inventory turnover") 12 times a year and XYZ Supermarkets turns its inventory 18 times a year, the journalist can pick up several stories, each starting with the question "why?" What type of promotion is XYZ using? Have they changed their hours? Or their mix of products? Does ABC have financial problems? ABC certainly has to rely more heavily on bank financing than a competitor whose inventory is turning into cash 50% more quickly.

The possibilities are endless and exist in every category of the balance sheet and profit and loss statement. What a field day for the reporter who enjoys being a financial detective!

A complete presentation of financial statements contains several major parts: an income statement, a balance sheet, a statement of retained earnings, and a statement of changes in financial position, each with several related *explanatory notes.* The income statement shows revenues, costs, and resultant income or loss for the period being reported upon. The balance sheet shows what the company owns, what it owes, and the difference between them (its net worth, or stockholders' equity). The balance sheet is a photograph of the company at a single moment in time—every statement is dated—and therefore does not reflect the health of the company the day before or the day after. That is why it is important to compare the recent year's income statement and balance sheet with those issued for the previous year.

The statement of changes in financial position explains the differences between the balance sheets at the end and the beginning of the period being reported upon. This statement acts as a bridge between balance sheets.

Most balance sheets list assets (what the company "owns") on the left page and the liabilities (what it "owes") on the right-hand page. The assets include money in the bank; monies due from others; inventories; and property and related items, each of which will be described. Liabilities include the debts of the corporation.

The difference between the assets and liabilities of the corporation represents the ownership interests of the stockholders and is called corporate capital or net worth. Legally, a corporation is an entity to itself. It has a legal life with rights which allow it to do business and incur and pay its obligations. Almost all financial statements are prepared on a "going-concern" basis which assumes the continued existance of the corporation. The net-worth section of the balance sheet, reflecting, in summary, the difference between corporate assets and liabilities, is classified to show both the amounts stockholders have paid to the corporation for their interests and undistributed accumulated earnings of the corporation. Amounts paid to the corporation (not other stockholders) by owners is shown on the lines "capital stock" and "capital surplus." Undistributed accumulated earnings are called "retained earnings" (or, less frequently, "earned surplus.")

Pretend for a moment that the fictional company we are about to create bears your name and is engaged in the publishing business. Here is the balance sheet:

YOURNAME PUBLISHING COMPANY, INC.
Comparative Balance Sheets
As of December 31

	1978 (000)	1977 (000)
ASSETS		
(2) Current Assets:		
(a) Cash . . . . $		
United States Government Securities		

      (b) Receivables. . . . .

      (c) Inventories . . . .

      (d) Prepaid Expenses . . . .

           Total Current Assets. . . . . .   _____

(3) Long-term Receivables. . . . .

FIXED ASSETS

(4) Property, Plant and Equipment (at cost, less accumulated depreciation and amortization: 1978, \$_____; 1977, \$_____) . . . .

(5) Sundry Assets and Investments. . . . .   _____

(1)   Total Assets . . . . \$ _____

LIABILITIES and

STOCKHOLDERS' EQUITY

(6) Current Liabilities. . . . . \$

      (a) Accounts Payable . . . .

      (b) Long-term Debt Due within One Year . . . .

      (c) Accrued Taxes. . . . .

      (d) Dividends Payable . . . .

           Total Current Liabilities. . .   _____

                                       \$

(7) Long-term Debt, Due in 198_, Interest Payable Annually. . . . .

(8) STOCKHOLDERS' EQUITY. . . . . .

      (a) Common Stock (1,000,000 common shares authorized, 400,000 issued, no par, \$1 stated value). . . . .

      (b) Capital Surplus . . . .

      (c) Retained Earnings. . . . .   _____

           Total Stockholders' Equity. \$

                               _____

           Total Liabilities and Stockholders' Equity . . . . \$ _____

WHAT IT ALL MEANS

(1) Total Assets and Net Sales.

A company's size can be measured in many ways but the two most common are by size of its assets or of its sales. One must remember that in analyzing financial statements every conclusion is based on *relative* positions. Therefore one must measure the asset size or sales volume of a company against others in the same industry.

Generally the more sizeable the asset base and/or sales volume, the stronger the company. Investors seeking safety look to many measurements, relative size being one, since a company with a dominant position in an industry is less likely to be shaken out in bad times.

Lack of size does not imply unworthiness. Companies with unusual products or concepts can exhibit dazzling growth. For example, Intel, a producer of advanced semiconductor circuits had volume in 1971 of $9,200,000 and six years later had grown to $226,000,000; Data General Corporation of Massachusetts, entering the highly competitive computer industry, brought sales to $161,000,000 in 1976, only eight years after going into business, by concentrating on the minicomputer market.

(2) Current Assets.

These are assets which can be *immediately* converted into cash or which normally turn into cash in less than a year. Because of their rather liquid nature this asset category is sometimes called liquid or quick or floating assets.

Three groups of assets fall into this category: cash and its equivalents, such as government notes or bonds or certificates of commercial deposits (CD's), purchased by corporate treasurers who want the company's temporarily idle funds to be earning interest; receivables, representing money due from customers to whom finished goods were sold, or services rendered; and inventories of raw materials being held for conversion into finished goods, inventories of goods in process, and finished goods being held for sale.

Current assets are usually listed in the order of their liquidity. As you will note, Yourname Publishing lists cash, securities, receivables, and inventories in that order. Any portion of the company's receivables due to be received in a period beyond 12 months is excluded from current assets and placed in the long-term receivables account. Inventory, however, includes *all* inventory, even of slow moving merchandise, on the theory that, at some distress price, finished goods can be sold. Inventory on the balance sheet should represent some reasonable relationship to current market conditions for those goods. This is a corporate responsibility and testing inventory valuation is a major part of the company's independent auditors' field work. Explanations of unusual inventory adjustments (found in the footnotes) may lead to good stories.

If Yourname Publishing were in the newspaper publishing business and its inventories included $100,000 worth of *yesterday's* newspaper, at manufactured cost (including reporters' salaries), the figure would obviously be suspect. If, however, Yourname was also in book publishing and the inventory figure included $100,000, at manufactured cost, of a book which in each of the past three years had brought in some $10,000, the company might be able to argue the case that, although slow moving, the book had market life and should be considered a current asset easily convertible into cash.

(a) *Cash.* Watch the cash account from year to year, especially during economic recessions. Some companies under stress build up cash by liquidating other assets, particularly inventories and receivables, which may solve short range problems but obviously curtails future possibilities. Other companies show a sharp loss of cash, or a big buildup in bank loans, again pointing to the possibility of problems and, therefore, to story leads. Of course, the conversion of inventories to cash may simply be a good business judgment at the moment, presenting the company with other business possibilities—and the reporter with another story.

Good corporate cash management calls for keeping on hand

only enough cash and equivalents to cover usual business needs and a reasonable reserve for emergencies. Where the cash and equivalent accounts are unusually high in relation to current liabilities there is the potential for an increase in the dividend policy, the acquisition of other companies, or the expansion of facilities—each a story possibility worth probing.

(b) Receivables. Generally these vary with overall economic conditions and the availability of bank credit, going up when bank credit is hard to get and the company must extend more generous terms to customers. *Measure receivables in relation to historic sales: an unusual increase in receivables as a percentage of sales frequently points to a management decision to fight to hold sales at the current level,* or an inability to collect old accounts, or new markets entered with different payment characteristics. Story possibilities: Is the company facing a challenge to its present market position? Or is management fighting to take market position from a competitor by offering a more liberal—and perhaps riskier—credit policy?

Special scrutiny must be given companies which sell their products on a long-term payment basis, such as department stores, mail-order firms, or manufacturers of office equipment and farm implements. This type of business is frequently conducted through finance companies which pay the manufacturer and collect from the buyer. They generally demand, however, a repurchase agreement from the manufacturer so that if the buyer defaults the finance company has recourse. *The manufacturer does not carry on his books the receivable due from the buyer, nor does he carry on his balance sheet the contingent liability to the finance company. These can be found in the footnotes to the balance sheet. Discounted receivables should be watched to see if there is a large percentage change in the relationship between the discounted receivables sold to the finance company and the amount of recourse the finance company has to the manufacturer.* If increasing amounts of product are being sold to less credit worthy clients, the *quality* of the company's reported sales and earnings is obviously declining, and with the decline stockholder's assets are at greater risk. A good story for the persistent reporter.

(c) Inventories. Normally this is the largest item under current assets. *The soundness of the inventory is determined by dividing average inventory into cost of sales to see how many times it turned over during the year.* This too, is a relative figure and must be measured against others in the same industry. There is always a story attached to any company whose inventory turnover varies sharply from the industry average.

A major problem in comparing inventory turnover among companies relates to the two main ways of calculating inventory value—each a generally accepted method. The methods are termed "first-in, first-out" (FIFO) and "last-in, first-out" (LIFO).

The common illustration of the differences in the two methods is to visualize a coal pile. If newly purchased coal is piled on top and coal being used is taken from the bottom we have the traditional case of "first-in, first-out." The old coal at the bottom is used up first. If the old coal had been purchased at $1 a pound and new coal costs $5 a pound, because of a rapid inflation, the user of coal is going to mark up the end product by $4 per pound of coal used to reflect the going market. He therefore will be making an additional profit of $4 per pound of old coal used—an "inventory" profit if you will.

Now take the case of a competitor who is identical in every way to the first company—with one exception. The competitor uses the "last-in, first-out" (LIFO) method of inventory valuation. He uses coal taken from the top of the pile—coal that he just purchased at $5 per pound. He sells his product at a price competitive with the company in our first illustration and makes only his normal profit margin—nowhere near the profit being reported by the first company.

What has happened here? The FIFO company, in a period of rising prices, is showing better earnings than its LIFO competitor simply by *evaluating* its inventory to reflect the current market price. It chose to match older (lower) costs of merchandise with current (high) sales prices. It has to pay increased taxes on this windfall profit but some publicly owned companies, striving to show big earnings gains, elect this method. When prices begin to decline, the FIFO company shows inventory losses and lower earnings.

LIFO, introduced at the beginning of World War II to avoid marking up inventories in scarce products, matches current costs with current revenues and saves the payment of taxes in a period of rising prices. One cannot quarrel with either method but, as you can see, what appears to be a comparison between apples and apples is sometimes a comparison between apples and oranges.

(d) Prepaid expenses. Insurance premiums, or real estate taxes, or interest portion of any expense applicable to the year following the balance sheet is shown here, representing an allocation of costs among the periods benefitted. It is considered a current asset because if the company were liquidated, the monies would have to be returned to the company.

Deferred charges, similar to prepaid expenses, are sometimes found under "other assets." These are dollars the company has paid for a benefit that accrues to the company for several years but where a liquidating company can expect no repayment even in part. An example would be the cost of relocating a plant, the expense for which might properly be written off over five years. One-fifth of the cost would be charged to annual expense of doing business and the remainder would be carried as an asset under deferred charges.

(3) Long-Term Receivables.

These are items which are owed to the company and will be paid beginning 12 months from the date of the statement or later. These would include such items as a loan to a subsidiary or affiliate, to be repaid in, for example, five annual instalments. That portion to be received in the current year would appear under "current receivables," with the balance listed as "long-term receivables."

(4) Fixed Assets.

Property, plant, and equipment owned by the company comprise the fixed assets. Despite the fact that they fall under this category on the financial statement, many of these items, such as tools and trucks, are movable.

The Internal Revenue Service provides a schedule of the expected useful life of every conceivable "fixed" item and the corporation is permitted an annual deduction, equal to one year in the supposed life cycle of the product. With this money the company is supposed to ultimately replace the plant or piece of equipment so that America's industrial base will always be in top condition.

Most companies carry their fixed assets at conservative figures, generally at cost minus the cumulative writedown for depreciation and amortization—these being the formidable sounding terms accountants use to describe a simple process, the wear and tear on an asset until it theoretically becomes useless and has to be replaced.

The SEC now requires the larger corporations to report, in their 10-K's, on the *replacement cost* of their property (fixed asset) accounts and this is sometimes a truer reflection of the real worth of this asset category although, if the asset is costly and useful for a single purpose only, it might not be replaced when worn out, or purchased by another company if put up for sale. In that case, "replacement value" would be meaningless. (In years past, some corporations—even those of great prominence such as United States Steel—marked up their property accounts by great amounts giving a very high and fictitious value to the assets of the company. The term "watered stock" was applied to this tactic. Fortunately, accounting regulations are much stricter today and, if anything, asset values are generally understated.)

(5) Sundry Assets and Investments.

Balance sheets eliminate the holdings a company has in wholly owned subsidiaries but place in this "sundry" category the interest in *partly* owned or affiliated companies. This can frequently point to a new direction the company is taking and the reporter should ask management to explain the purpose of each of these investments.

(6) Current Liabilities.

This grouping corresponds to "current assets." It includes all debts due to be paid within 12 months.

(a) Accounts payable. Generally, these comprise the cost of running the company on a day-to-day basis, covering the invoices from suppliers.

(b) Long-term debt due in one year or less. This category represents the current portion of long-term obligations.

(c) Accrued taxes. These include the unpaid portion of income taxes due at various times the following year. On your *personal* balance sheet the monies you owe the government from January 1 through April 15 *on last year's income* are your accrued taxes.

(d) Dividends payable. If, towards the closing of the calendar or fiscal year, the company declares a dividend payable early next year, the obligation is short-term and falls within this category.

(7) Long-term Debt.

This represents that portion of a company's debt which will not be repaid in the 12 months following the date of the balance sheet.

(8) Stockholders' Equity.

This represents both capital (paid in) and the earned (undistributed profits) surplus. Founders and investors beginning a new company pay cash and, in some instances, services for stock in the new enterprise, their percentage stockholding interest varying according to their contribution. Generally, the stock issued is "common" shares but, at times, there may be other designations to connote differences in dividend policy or voting rights, such as class A or class B stock, or preferential rights in liquidation such as preferred stock.

The common stock may or may not have a definite par value. The par value traditionally indicated how much capital was paid in for each share by the original investors. A company with 100,000 shares outstanding, $10 par, would have been capitalized with $1,000,000 of investors' money. However, because of increasing incorporation fees and transfer taxes—frequently based on the par value—many companies now list nominal value or no par at all.

If one accepts a corporation as a living entity, the balance sheet being its ownership and obligations, then the surplus account is still another obligation to be distributed to the investors upon liquidation.

INCOME STATEMENT (Profit and Loss)

The income statement, also known as the profit-and-loss-statement, is the second major part of the financial report. Publicly owned companies with 300 or more shareholders issue an income statement quarterly; those with fewer than 300 shareholders are termed nonreporting companies and issue such statements on an annual basis only.

Companies were fearful, in years past, of revealing too much competitive information and many would issue earnings without any comment regarding sales volume. It was impossible, therefore, to judge the relationship between companies in an industry. Today, sales must be reported. Also, companies now must report all phases of revenue and costs, including various segments of income, rather than one "pooled" number.

The Securities and Exchange Commission, responsible for virtually all the improvements in reporting procedures, requires "reporting" companies to issue their financial statements within 45 days after the close of the quarter and 90 days after the end of the year. The New York Stock Exchange and the American Stock Exchange have their own requirements for companies whose stock is traded on their floors—the *year-end financial statements* must be in the hands of shareholders within 90 days after the close of the fiscal period, or 15 days before the annual meeting of shareholders, whichever is sooner, and quarterly results must be issued within 45 days after the close of the period.

Furthermore, there are reporting regulations concerning dividends. An announcement must be made to the press immediately upon declaration of a dividend by the board of directors of a company and at least ten days must elapse between the declaration date and the "record" date—the date by which the newest shareholders have their names put on the company's stockholder list in time to receive the just-declared dividend. During this period of time purchasers of the stock are entitled to receive the dividend. The stock goes "ex-dividend" four days before the "record" date, selling after that without the right to the recently declared dividend.

YOURNAME PUBLISHING COMPANY, INC.
Comparative Statements of Earnings
for the years ended December 31

	1978	1977
	(000)	(000)

CURRENT EARNINGS
- (1) Income:
  - (a) Net Sales . . . .
  - (b) Other Income (expense),
    - Net . . . .
- (2) Costs and Expenses:
  - (a) Cost of Goods Sold . . . .
  - (b) Selling and Administrative .
  - (c) Depreciation and
    - Amortization . . . .

Balance at Beginning of Year . . . . .
Add—Net Income for the Year . . . .
- (3) OPERATING PROFIT . . . .
- (4) INTEREST CHARGES . . . .
- (5) EARNINGS BEFORE INCOME
  - TAXES . . . .

(6) PROVISION FOR FEDERAL
    AND STATE TAXES ON
    INCOME . . . .
(7) NET INCOME FOR THE YEAR .
(8) DIVIDEND ON PREFERRED
    STOCK. . . . .
(9) NET EARNINGS (available for
    common stock). . . . .
(10) NET EARNINGS PER SHARE
    OF COMMON STOCK. . . . .
(11) RETAINED EARNINGS (Also
    known as statement of earned
    surplus. This is sometimes shown
    as a separate statement.). . . . .
    Balance at Beginning of Year . . . . .
    Add - Net income for the year . . . .
    Less Dividends Paid On
        Preferred Stock . . . .
        Common Stock . . . .
    Balance at End of Year . . . .

Unlike the balance sheet, which refers only to a specific date, the income statement covers an extended period which could be several days, three months, six months, nine months, or a full year. As shown on the statement following, for the 12 months ended December 31, YOURNAME Publishing had income derived from sales (a) and other sources (b).

(1) Income.

(a) Net sales. Yourname Publishing Company sold a certain quantity of newspapers, magazines (including advertising and circulation income), books, and so forth. This includes amounts still receivable from customers in the next 12 months (land companies and others specializing in instalment sales used to report the remaining balance due, even if over 20 years, as part of the current sales). Companies generally report to shareholders on

an *accrual* basis—taking into current sales those amounts due shortly—recognizing revenue when the sale is made and title passes, regardless of when the receivable is paid. Remember that a company's reports to shareholders are not identical with its reports to the Internal Revenue Service. The differences (clues to which can be found in the balance sheet and the 10-K) are often the source of a good story idea. They report, however, to the Internal Revenue Service on a *cash* basis listing as sales only that amount which has been paid to them by customers as of the close of the fiscal or calendar period. If the companies did otherwise, they would have to pay taxes on monies not yet received.

If proper accounting procedure is followed, and inventories are properly evaluated and reserves are prudent, the accrual basis gives shareholders a fair presentation into the on-going nature of the business.

(b) Other income (expense). This refers to income derived from activities other than the sale of the company's product or principal services. Examples are the profit from the sale of machinery no longer needed by the company; rent received from unused space which the company has sublet; interest earned from government securities; or shares held in other companies which paid dividends. Expenses incurred in like transactions—loss on the sale of equipment—are included here and "netted out" to a final figure.

(2) Costs and Expenses.

(a) Cost of goods sold. This includes the cost of raw materials, direct labor, and manufacturing, as well as the overhead for the items sold during the period.

(b) Selling, general and administrative expenses. These involve officers' salaries, salesmen's commissions, advertising and promotion, and similar general expenses.

(c) Depreciation and amortization. Depreciation, as explained earlier, is the cost to a company of using up certain assets over a period of time. The government permits pre-tax income to be

reduced by an annual amount prorated (in any of several different permitted ways) over the expected life of the asset, in the expectation that the management will put this fund aside to replace the asset when it no longer functions. Two oversimplifications are at work here: Most fixed assets last longer than the depreciation schedule and do not have to be replaced at the end of that arbitrary IRS period, and when an asset finally does wear out, the replacement cost is inevitably much higher and the depreciation does not cover it. (Can you replace a truck purchased five years ago at the same price?)

Amortization, as also mentioned earlier, is the concept of depreciation applied to the company's intangible purchases. These include patents and licenses which, over a period of time, lose their value as newer products are invented to make them obsolete.

(3) Operating Profit.

This figure is arrived at after deducting costs from sales.

(4) Interest Expense.

Most companies borrow to supplement their capital. The size of the borrowings is generally related to the size of the capital base—just as your personal ability to borrow is based on your current unpledged assets as collateral. Earning power of your current business is also taken into effect, plus the earning power of any business you intend to purchase, if that is the reason for the borrowing. The company can borrow from a bank or it can issue bonds. In either case interest must be paid and is treated as a cost of doing business.

(5) Earnings before Income Taxes.

This figure is important in judging comparative results of companies in the same industry. The tax impact might vary from state to state, tax abatements might be offered in certain localities (such as Puerto Rico), or tax-carryforward losses might temporarily reduce the taxes a company has to pay. The pre-tax figure, therefore, is as important in judging a company's progress as its after-tax earnings.

(6) Provision for Federal and State Taxes.

Check to ascertain not only the current tax rate but the anticipated tax rate for the forthcoming year. Earnings could leap because of any of the previously mentioned tax benefits.

(7) Net Income for the Year.

Check the percentage growth or decline versus the previous year's growth or decline. If the percentage change is significantly broadened, or narrowed, a good story can generally be had.

(8) Dividend on Preferred Stock.

Many companies do not have preferred stock, although they may have the right to issue it.(It is introduced here as an illustration.) Most people are familiar with common stock since no public company can be organized without it. Preferred stock differs from common in that it has a prior claim on earnings or assets, or both. Common dividends cannot be paid unless the dividend claims of the preferred class are met and, in liquidation, preferred shareholders may have a claim to the remaining assets after all debts have been paid, but before common shareholders receive any cash from liquidated assets. The preferred shareholder, generally, gets a fixed dividend. Some preferred shares also carry the right to convert into common stock at a predetermined price, a privilege extended by the company to make the sale of that issue easier.

(9) Net Earnings (Available for Common Stock).

This is the income theoretically available for disbursement to the holders of common stock, after the payment of taxes and dividends to preferred shareholders (if any). If no dividends are paid to common shareholders, the entire net earnings after taxes is placed in the earned surplus account, from which it is then disbursed for other purposes and into other accounts—cash, inventory, fixed assets.

(10) Net Earnings Per Share of Common Stock.

This is a shorthand method of showing how well each owner of common shares fared in the company. Arrived at by dividing the number of common shares outstanding into the net after-tax earnings.

This is the single figure most closely followed by the average investor in stocks. It is the denominator of the price/earnings ratio, i.e.: (price of a share of stock ÷ earnings per share) = price/earnings ratio.

(11) Retained Earnings.

Retained earnings, or net income after taxes and preferred dividends, can be distributed in full, or part, to the holders of the company's common stock. *Any portion not distributed in this fashion is transferred to the earned surplus account.* These earnings are retained in the business to finance the expansion of the company and end up on the asset side of the balance sheet as cash, marketable securities, inventories, or new plant and equipment. In any event, should the company liquidate, the surplus account gives a reasonable picture of what will be left for the common shareholders providing the inventories and plant and equipment can be liquidated at the value stated on the balance sheet. Frequently, both inventories and equipment lose value when buyers know the company is going out of business and has a liquidating deadline. However, land and machinery are sometimes so depreciated on the account statements as to be unrealistic, and the liquidation brings a great deal more than the surplus statement would lead one to believe.

ANNUAL REPORT TO SHAREHOLDERS

The annual report to shareholders now contains a plethora of information not available even a few years ago. As recently as the 1930s, major companies would report their full-year activities on a single sheet of paper, at times not listing sales volume or any of the other items we now consider important, except for earnings. In another context, but illustrative of the then disdainful attitude of many earlier managements towards labor *and* stockholders, the president of the Philadelphia & Reading Coal and Iron Company offered this observation in 1902: "The rights and interests of the laboring man will be protected and cared for not by the labor agitators but by the Christian gentlemen to whom God has given control of the property rights of the country and upon the successful management on which so much depends."

This attitude led to the formation of the Securities and Exchange Commission in 1933 with Joseph Kennedy, Sr. as its first chairman. And in the ensuing 40 or more years, the SEC has consistently introduced more demanding regulations regarding reporting and accounting, leaning forcefully toward the doctrine of "full disclosure." Included in contemporary financial statements is the Consolidated Statement of Changes in Financial Position (called the "cash-flow" statement since it lists the flow of cash through the business in the period being reported) and the recently introduced "management's analysis of operations."

Management's analysis of operations, included in the annual report form since 1975, delves into the specific reasons behind the trends in the latest year and does so on a comparative basis for the past three years. Management historically covered this information in the President's Message found at the beginning of the annual report.

Other important sections of the annual report to shareholders are the notes to the balance sheets, without which the balance sheet is not complete, and the accountants' letter in which the auditor certifies as to his procedures and any exceptions he wishes to make.

Professional investors always read the accountants' letter before getting into the financial statements or reading the president's letter. This can't be stressed enough: always check the accountants' letter to see if they are flagging any danger spots. Accountant's letters follow a strict procedure: A "clean" letter, with no reservations or qualifications, explains in two paragraphs the scope and opinion. The first paragraph—the scope—states what financial statements were examined and how the examination was performed. The second paragraph—the opinion—states the CPA's opinion on the presentation of the statements (be aware that anyone—even a bookkeeper—can call himself an accountant; the only accountant who can audit books, offering the "attest" function, is a certified public accountant).

The key phrases in a "clean" report are "generally accepted auditing standards," "auditing procedures," "present fairly," "generally accepted accounting principles," and "applied on a consistent basis."

Here is a typical "clean" certificate. (italics mine):

APPLES, PEARS & PLUMS & CO.
Certified Public Accountants
1500 Baltic Street
Escondido, California 21006

The Board of Directors and Stockholders,
Yourname Publishing Company, Inc.:

We have examined the balance sheets of Yourname Publishing Company and subsidiaries as of December 31, 1977 and 1976 and the related statements of earnings and changes in financial position for the years then ended. Our examination was made in accordance with *generally accepted auditing standards* and accordingly included such tests of the accounting records and such other *auditing procedures* as we considered necessary in the circumstances.

In our opinion, the aforementioned financial statements *present fairly* the financial position of Yourname Publishing Company and subsidiaries at December 31, 1977 and 1976, and the results of their operations and the changes in financial position, in conformity with *generally accepted accounting principles* which have been *applied on a consistent basis.*

Apples, Pears & Plums & Co.

February 18, 1978

Any deviation from this form is of concern and offers a story possibility. There are five other types of opinion the auditor can offer, each involving the inclusion of a third paragraph to his opinion. These are unqualified, subject to, except for, disclaimer and adverse. No need to illustrate each; just check the accountants' letter first to see if its "clean."

FINDING STORIES BY RATIO ANALYSIS

The balance sheet and income statement are less forbidding than they seem. Their construction is logical and represents the conversion of commonsense concepts into formulae. The easiest method for spotting stories in the financial statement is to convert into simple formulations these concepts where a *sharp variation* immediately alerts the reporter/businessman/investor/financial analyst that something is happening. The following are 19 key barometers to monitor the health of a public company. Each of them can yield numerous story ideas. These ratios can help you focus on significant relationships in the financial statements.

(1) Pre-tax Profit Margin.

This ratio is used to determine the operating efficiency of the company. It is computed by dividing operating income before taxes by net sales. Yourname Publishing profit margin: $ income ÷ $ net sales = pre-tax profit margin.

When measured against others in the publishing industry the pre-tax margin will tell you if the company is in the high or low end of the business and whether it is being operated in the most efficacious manner.

(2) Current Ratio (also called Working-Capital Ratio).

This is probably the most used ratio for industrial companies and is the ratio of current assets to current liabilities. It is a fast method of telling if the company is in position to meet its immediate obligations or if it might have to refinance. A two-to-one ratio is accepted as standard, but there are many exceptions and, depending upon the industry, current ratios as low as 1.5-to one are acceptable. A gradual increase in the current ratio is considered a sign of financial strength but bear in mind that a very high current ratio, compared to others in the industry, might mean that assets are not being properly used and the management is too conservative. Financial analysis is a *comparative* art, as stressed before, and exposure to as many companies as possible is the best teacher.

This ratio is computed by dividing current assets by current liabilities: current assets ÷ current liabilities = current ratio.

(3) Quick-Assets Ratio.

This ratio known as "the acid test," formulates the most stringent standard of fiscal strength by suggesting that a truly conservative company be able to pay *all current liabilities* out of cash, securities and receivables. It does not include inventories. A one-to-one quick-asset ratio should provide great comfort. Also termed the "liquidity ratio," because only the most liquid current assets are used in the measurement, this ratio often falls during a period of expansion and rising prices because of heavier capital expenditures and larger accounts payable. This should be watched as a clue to financing. If the decline continues more capital will be needed.

To determine the quick ratio, the current assets less inventory, are divided by current liabilities: cash and securities ÷ current liabilities = quick ratio.

(4) Capitalization Ratios.

The capitalization of a company consists of its outstanding bonds (if any), preferred stock (if any), common stock and surplus (capital and earned). The greater the percentage of common stock and surplus, the better the position of the common shareholder and the safer he is. Public utilities, and other mature companies in stable industries, can safely carry a higher proportion of bond debt than an industrial company which generally should not have more than one-third of its capitalization in bond debt. For the most part industrial companies should have at least half of their capitalization in common stock and surplus. In computing the value of the common stock for this purpose, use shareholder's equity as shown on the balance sheet, not the current market price of the shares.

The ratio of funded debt to total capitalization measures the relationship between long-term borrowed capital and permanent capital. If the long-term debt is too heavy, the fixed charges against earnings can become unbearable and, with a sharp decline in earnings, cause insolvency.

Bond ratio is arrived at by dividing the amount of bonds outstanding by the total of the bonds, preferred stock, common stock, capital surplus, and retained earnings: face amount of bonds ÷ bonds plus preferred stock plus common stock plus capital surplus plus retained earnings = bond ratio.

Preferred-stock ratio is determined by dividing the face value of the preferred by the total of the bonds, preferred stock, common stock, and all surplus. In this fashion: face amount of preferred stock ÷ bonds + preferred stock + common stock + capital surplus + retained earnings = preferred-stock ratio.

Common-stock ratio is determined by dividing the common stock by the total of bonds, preferred stock, common stock, and surplus (both capital surplus and retained earnings): common stock ÷ bonds + preferred stock + common stock + capital surplus + retained earnings = common-stock ratio.

(5) Sales-to-Fixed Assets Ratio.

This is an important ratio, because it helps one easily see if funds spent on plant expansion have been invested wisely. If not, sales policies may be altered. A major investment in plant should, in a reasonable period of time, produce a sizable sales growth. This ratio is computed by dividing annual sales by value—*before depreciation and amortization*—of plant, equipment and land at the end of the year. A low ratio (1.1 or 1.2 to one) indicates that the company is in an industry which demands heavy investment. The ratio is computed this way: annual sales ÷ plant, equipment and land (at year end) before depreciation and amortization.

(6) Sales-to-Inventories (The Inventory Turnover) Ratio.

The greater the turnover, the greater the profit and the less capital required. Even if the margin of profit per unit sold is less, the company with a higher inventory turnover will generate more profit. Additionally, merchandise will generally be more current. There are good merchandising stories to be found in companies whose inventory turnover ratio is greater than the industry average. This ratio is computed by dividing the cost of goods sold by the average inventories: cost of goods sold ÷ average inventories.

(7) Net Income to Net Worth. (Return on Stockholders' Investment).

This is one of the most significant ratios and is increasingly used as a major yardstick by bankers and investment analysts. It focuses on the efficiency of the operation (margin of profit) plus the way in which the company was capitalized. This ratio is derived by dividing net income plus fixed charges by the total of preferred stock, common stock, and surplus: net income plus fixed charges ÷ total preferred stock + common-stock + surplus = return on stockholders' investment.

By adding bonds to the formula, another increasingly important ratio, one can quickly determine return on invested capital: net income plus fixed charges ÷ bonds + preferred stock + common stock + surplus accounts = return on invested capital.

(8) Interest Coverage.

These are safety tests, and if the company in question falls below accepted averages, it would do well for the reporter to begin questioning bankers and creditors. One must be discreet, however, and not cause credit problems by the asking. Normally, a manufacturing company's interest charges should be covered five times, public utilities three times. The more conservative financial organizations, however, recommend that fixed charges be covered seven times for the most recent seven-year period and at least five times in the poorest of the last seven years: total income ÷ fixed charges.

(9) Preferred Dividend Coverage.

The requirements are the same as in the Interest Coverage Test. To compute this ratio divide total income by total of fixed charges and twice the preferred dividends: total income ÷ fixed charges + 2 × preferred dividends.

(10) Combined or Overall Coverage Ratio.

A preferred stock is considered well protected if the average of common-stock dividends over a five-year period is three or four times greater than the preferred requirements. But some companies with preferred stock outstanding do not pay common-share dividends. In this case, earnings after taxes, but before fixed charges of four times the combined interest and preferred dividend requirement is considered acceptable. The conservative financier wants to see this as a five-year average.

To compute this, divide after-tax profit before interest charges by the total of interest and preferred dividends: after-tax profit, before interest ÷ interest and preferred dividends.

(11) Earnings Per Share on Preferred Stock.

To compute this ratio divide the net income by the number of shares of preferred stock: net income ÷ number of preferred shares outstanding.

(12) Earnings Per Share on Common Stock.

This is one of the primary yardsticks used in determining the growth of a company. Wall Streeters consider a company a growth stock if per share earnings expand at a compounded annual rate of 15% or more. Stocks normally sell at a ratio of after-tax earnings, depending upon many variables, such as dividend rate, balance sheet stability, industry growth prospects, and management's capability, as demonstrated by return on net worth and invested capital.

To compute earnings per share divide after-tax earnings, (after deducting preferred dividends if any), by the number of common shares outstanding. If a stock dividend or a stock split has occurred during the year, earnings per share are adjusted to reflect the dividend or split. For example, if the company has earned $1,000,000 net after taxes, and there are 1,000,000 common shares outstanding (but no preferred) each common share has earned $1. If the board of directors declared a 10% stock dividend, the reported earnings would be adjusted to 91¢ per common share.

Although earnings are adjusted to reflect a stock split or stock dividend, they are never adjusted to reflect the issuance of *new* shares in a *new* financing. When *new* company shares are issued, per-share earnings for the period are computed on a weighted average basis. If, for instance, a company with 1,000,000 common shares outstanding issued an additional 500,000 on July 1st, the per-share earnings at December 31st year-end would be computed on the basis of 1,000,000 shares outstanding for all 12 months, 500,000 shares outstanding for six months (on the theory that the company did not have the benefit of the funds for the full year): $1,000,000 \times 12 + 500,000 \times 6 \div 12 = 1,250,000$ average shares.

Occasionally a company will report earnings per share on two bases—primary E.P.S and fully diluted E.P.S. Primary E.P.S is the amount of earnings attributable to each share of common stock outstanding, including common-stock equivalents (C.S.E.), such as convertible bonds or convertible preferred stock, options and warrants, contingent and participating shares. Fully diluted earnings per share reflects the maximum potential decrease in per share earnings as a result of the conversion of such equivalents. To compute this, after-tax earnings minus preferred dividends ÷ common shares outstanding.

(13) Dividends Per Common Share.

Divide the dividends paid on the common shares by the number of shares outstanding. For instance, $200,000 of dividends disbursed to holders of 1,000,000 common shares will give them 20¢ for each share owned.

To get the *yield* on the stock divide the dividend by the current stock price. If the stock were selling at $5, and the dividend were 20¢, the yield would be 4% (.20 ÷ 5 = .04).

(14) Dividend Payout.

Traditionally, mature companies have paid out 50% to 66 2/3% of earnings. Growth companies, which have to reinvest in new plants, have paid out one-third of their earnings or less— sometimes nothing at all. A new tradition of no payout by young growth companies developed in the soaring sixties, but stockholder interest in yield seems to have returned in the sagging seventies. By reviewing the payout ratio on an historic basis, both for the company and the industry in which it competes, one can sometimes anticipate a dividend increase. Although it is the prerogative of the board of directors to determine dividend policy, a comment regarding historic payout ratio versus a currently reduced ratio sometimes elicits a story—either about a recommendation to the board for a dividend increase or the reason for management's desire to hold onto a greater percentage of the earnings than in the past.

To determine the payout ratio: dividends paid on the common stock ÷ the net income minus preferred dividends (if any).

(15) Book Value Per Share on the Common Stock.

This is the liquidating value per share. When the common stock of the company is selling much below this figure, the company becomes inviting to a raider. Surprise tender offers to shareholders are always major news stories.

To arrive at the book value per share divide the stockholder's equity (capital stock, capital surplus, and retained earnings) by the number of common shares outstanding.

(16) Price/Earnings Multiple.

This is the multiple of last year's per-share earnings which the public is willing to pay to own the company's common shares. If a multiple is much higher than others in the industry, it indicates the company has some unusual product or the potential to make extraordinary leaps in earning power. At times the market is wrong in its supposition, and the high-flying stock has a sharp decline. The price/earnings multiples of companies vary not only with the company's potential but with investors' perception of the nation's economic future. It is a highly psychological ratio.

The price/earnings ratio is computed by dividing the market price of the stock by earnings per share.

(17) Depreciation as a Percentage of Cost of Plant.

This ratio translates the average life of all items in the property account to a percentage and permits one to compare the age of a company's assets with its competitors who may have newer equipment and higher productivity. If the company's ratio is much higher than its competitors it might foretell increased spending. To determine this ratio: depreciation, depletion, and amortization ÷ property, plant, and equipment account.

(18) Depreciation as a Percentage of Net Sales.

This is sometimes called the "service" or "usage" test. Increased sales resulting from heavier use of the plant could result in increased depreciation without additional investment in plant, creating greater cash flow, a stronger earnings base and perhaps a greater dividend payout.

To get this ratio: depreciation, depletion, and amortization ÷ net sales.

(19) Days Average Account Receivable Is Outstanding.

This will give you an insight to the credit policy of the company as compared with others in the same industry.

Using 360 days as the basis of the "collection ratio": receivables ÷ net sales × 360.

The financial reporter obviously does not have the time to analyze in such depth every company to come across his desk, and each of its competitors. But a mastery of these ratios will provide the journalist with a significant number of story leads.

CHAPTER SIX

Analyses of Specialized Industries

As stressed time and again, financial analysis is a comparative art. Frequently companies seem comparable, but are not. The use by one company of LIFO inventory evaluation and the adoption by a competitor of FIFO results in widely divergent earnings as reported by the two companies, even when each have the same volume, the same expenses and charge the same amount for the product.

Comparisons are even more difficult when companies are in different industries. Although *basic* financial analysis can be applied to all companies, the ratios used to determine whether a company is doing well or poorly as compared to its direct competitors change from industry to industry. A ratio which is good in one industry may be awful in another.

Because of this, financial analysts tend to specialize in one or two related industries. To give some perspective to the variation in analytical techniques, eight of America's foremost financial analysts have contributed commentary about their specialties—what particular trends they look for within an industry, what particular ratios signal improvement or decline, and what publications they use to keep abreast of their specialty.

There are 39 specialties to which analysts are assigned, but we have selected only eight—each a basic industry, some (such as banking) more complex than others. To have included all 39 specialties would have required a separate text, and would have diverted from the purpose of producing a book for journalists.

The reporter assigned to any of the specialties covered by financial analysts would be wise to have his name added to the mailing list for all industry and company studies ("market letters"). He also ought to become acquainted with some of the analysts.

The membership directory of the Financial Analysts Federation, (219 East 42nd St., New York, N.Y. 10017) lists the following industry specialties: aerospace, advertising, amusements, automobile and accessories, brewing and distilling, banks, building materials, chemicals, conglomerates, communications, containers, drugs and cosmetics, education, electronics and electrical, foreign securities, finance companies, food, natural gas, hospital supply, insurance, investment companies, leisure-time, machinery, metals (nonferrous), oil, office equipment, paper, publications, pollution control, real estate, retail trade, rubber, steel, service, transportation, textiles, and utilities.

Ten functional specialties are also listed: bonds, director of research, economist, generalist, investment counsellor, portfolio manager, special situations, technicians (stock market), underwriter, and venture capital.

The illustrations in this chapter are:

- Banking, by David C. Cates.
- Life Insurance, by Michael Frinquelli.
- Property-Casualty Insurance, by Michael Frinquelli.
- Conglomerates, by Harriet L. West.
- Office Equipment, by Frederic H. Cohen.
- Utilities, by Ernest Kiehne.
- Building Materials, by George Einsfield.
- Chemicals, by John Thies.
- Broadcasting, by William Suter.

* * *

BANKING
BY DAVID C. CATES

David C. Cates, a principal of Cates, Lyons & Co., Inc., is one of the country's leading banking industry analysts. Mr. Cates received his B.A. degree from Harvard College in 1950, followed by an M.A. in Linguistic Anthropology from the University of Chicago in 1957. He joined Hanover Bank of New York that year, serving until 1961 as an Assistant Secretary of the bank. From 1961 through 1969 he served as an officer of several leading investment banking firms. In 1969 he formed his own firm, David C. Cates & Co., Inc., as a consultant specializing in the analysis of banks and bank holding companies for a clientele of bank managements, lenders, and investors. In February, 1977, John Lyons joined him as a partner. Mr. Cates has served as founder and first chairman of the Bank and Financial Industries Subcommittee of the Financial Analysts Federation, from 1972 to 1976, and is presently serving on the F.A.F.'s Corporate Information Committee. He has also served as contributing editor of the *Financial Analyst's Handbook,* published by Dow Jones-Irwin, Inc., 1975, covering the banking industry. In 1975 he wrote a monograph, *Bank Investor Relations,* published by the Bank Marketing Association, and in 1976 coauthored with Samuel B. Chase, Jr., *The Payment of Interest On Checking Accounts,* published by the South Carolina Banker's Association.

I. HOLDING COMPANY STRUCTURE

Virtually all larger banks are comprised within holding companies, a movement that took place between 1970 and 1972 as bank managements recognized the flexibility of this corporate vehicle. Unlike banks, holding companies can issue commercial paper, diversify into closely related industries such as sales finance, and operate nonbank affiliates across state lines.

This movement, however, brought with it certain penalties and responsibilities from which banks alone had been free. The three most important are: (a) registration of bank holding company securities with the SEC, and subjection to the disclosure requirements which the SEC staff specifically developed for bank holding companies (Guides G1 and 3, published October, 1976); (b) scrutiny by the two major rating agencies (Moody's and Standard & Poor's) of the long-term debt and commercial paper of these companies; and (c) an awareness, first by managements and later by investors, that the cash-flow dynamics of a parent of the bank-holding company are entirely different from the cash flow resources of a bank.

To illustrate, a typical parent must meet its own financial obligations to shareholders and lenders by relying principally on the ability of its bank subsidiaries to pay dividends to the parent. These bank subsidiaries, in turn, are regulated by bank examiners whose primary concern is with the safety of deposits and the power of banks to finance their own growth internally. Thus there is a *de facto* regulatory supervision of bank dividends, which limits the payout of bank earnings to a sustainable range of 50% to 70% of those earnings.

Though it would be an overstatement to say that parent companies are obliged to live on a diet of 60% of bank subsidiary earnings, many professional lenders and investors act as though this were true. By contrast, a bank may convert any available asset into cash in order to meet its financial obligations!

Financial journalists, therefore, need to keep in mind that a bank holding company is a complex corporate organism. The "fully consolidated" statements of bank-holding companies mask this complexity. Beneath the mask lie the parent, the "lead" or principal bank (from which much of the overall management is often conducted), the other bank affiliates (if any), and the nonbank affiliates (if any). Source documents include the annual report to shareholders, the 10-K report to the SEC (note particularly the affiliate displays in Schedule III of each 10-K), and the statutory financial statements (or "call reports") which each bank is obliged to file with a federal agency (Federal Reserve, Comptroller, or FDIC), and which are in the public domain.

II. RATIO ANALYSIS

There are some key diagnostic ratios, all based on "fully consolidated" disclosure.

1. Profitability Ratios.

To begin, bank earnings are reported two ways: income *before* securities transactions, and income *after,* called "net income." Professional analysts consider that securities transactions (which are the net gain or loss, during an accounting period, on the multitudinous sales and purchases in a bank's investment portfolio) blur the quarterly and annual trend of basic earning power. Assuming, therefore, that the difference between the two earnings figures is not greater than 5% of either, it is more indicative of earning power to base analysis (and reporting) on income *before,* often called "net operating income."

(a) Earnings to assets is a very basic measure of profitability (distinguish between "daily average" assets and "end-of-period" assets, the latter being less reliable as a performance guide). A very high ratio would be, say, 1.2%, whereas a very low ratio of earnings to assets would be, say .35%.

(b) Earnings to net worth (or, synonymously, stockholders' equity) is a secondary profit ratio, often blurred by the level of capital itself to assets. A very high ratio would be 18%, a very low ratio would be 7%.

2. Capital Ratios.

The level of capital supporting possible risk inherent in assets is measured by:

(a) Net worth to assets, which ranges in practice from a very high level of, say, 10% to a very low level of 4%.

(b) Capital formation rate is a ratio measuring the ability of a bank (and/or bank holding company) to "grow its own" equity. It is computed by dividing retained net operating income (or, if you choose, net income, but in either case *after* dividends to shareholders) by net worth.

3. Asset Quality and Loan Losses.

The quality of a bank's assets is the most important—and by far the least measurable—of its characteristics.

(a) Nonperforming loans to total loans. The SEC now requires the annual disclosure of "non-performing" loans, defined as non-accruing loans (but excludes consumer and residential mortgage delinquencies, unless very high); loans renegotiated to a lower rate of interest due to borrower difficulty, and "other problem loans" not yet charged off. Closely related to nonperforming loans are delinquent and/or renegotiated leases and foreclosed properties (usually construction loan collateral, often called "other real estate owned"). Because of vague SEC definitions, management discretion toward "conservatism" or its opposite, and intrinsic uncertainty of measuring the collectibility of loans, interpretation of these figures should be very cautious. Nonetheless, a ratio of 1% is very low and a ratio of 10% is very high.

(b) Net charge-offs to loans. This barometer of loan loss experience should be read on a five-year basis, because of the year-to-year volatility in *gross* charge-offs and *recoveries* (between which the net is computed). A ratio of .25% is very low and a ratio of 1% is very high.

(c) Loan valuation reserve to loans. This is an important protective cushion between loan losses and net worth, the other being earnings (see just below). A ratio of 0.8% is very low *if* net charge-offs are .5% or higher, and a ratio of 1.5% is very high *if* net charge-offs are 0.75% or lower.

(d) Earnings coverage of loan losses. A bank whose earning power can cover its loan losses is in better condition than one that can not. The ratio is computed by dividing net charge-offs by pretax net operating income to which the loss provision has been added back. A coverage of one time is very low and a coverage of eight times is very high.

4. Overhead Ratios.

Operating expense other than interest expense and loan loss provision (these two may be thought of as the "cost of goods sold" in banking) take a large bite out of the income stream available to cover overhead. This "available" income is often called adjusted operating income and is computed by subtracting interest expense from total revenue (to get a rough equivalent of "gross profit").

(a) Overhead to adjusted operating income. A ratio of 40% is very low, and a ratio of 75% is very high. If the ratio is high, its year-to-year trend should be watched to see if the level is rising (bad) or falling (good). The largest segment of overhead, of course, is staff expense. The next largest segment is a catchall or miscellaneous, which sometimes includes property write-downs and other asset losses, which may occasionally be detected by year-to-year volatility in the numbers.

III. SOURCES

Good articles about banking are to be found in *The American Banker* (a daily), *The Bankers Magazine* (a quarterly), and the monthly publications of the Federal Reserve Board and many of the 12 regional banks. Also, M.A. Schapiro & Co., Inc., New York City, publishes a valuable *Bank Stock Quarterly,* and the firm of which this author is a principal, Cates, Lyons & Co., Inc., publishes a biweekly letter *The Informed Bank Director.* Finally, for further background, this author's contribution on "Banking" is included in the *Financial Analysts Handbook* (Dow-Jones Irwin,

1976), his book *Bank Investor Relations* is published by Bank Marketing Association, 1976, and his coauthorship (with Samuel B. Chase, Jr.) of *The Payment of Interest on Checking Accounts* was published by the South Carolina Bankers Association in 1976.

LIFE INSURANCE
By Michael Frinquelli

A. Michael Frinquelli is acknowledged as one of the premier financial analysts following the insurance industry. A C.F.A., Mr. Frinquelli received his Bachelor of Science Degree in Economics in 1963 from City College of New York and followed with an M.B.A. in Finance and Investments from the Baruch School in 1970. He joined Standard & Poor's in 1964 as an analyst following the insurance and banking fields and is now vice president-insurance stock research department at Salomon Brothers, a prominent New York Stock Exchange firm.

The life insurance industry plays a vital role in the functioning of the American economy, representing, along with pension funds, the largest suppliers of long-term capital to American industry. Because of that role, along with its obvious responsibilities to policyholders, if there is a key word to the operations of a life insurer that word is stability. Put another way, the earnings of a mature standard life insurer should be expected to progress at a moderate, steady pace year in and year out and, indeed, even on a quarterly basis. To the extent that this does not occur, it could reflect a serious problem, or, in the more likely case, random items such as an adverse mortality fluctuation, costs of new office space, etc.

Industry structure and regulations are two additional factors which should be understood. While the industry appears to be highly fragmented in terms of the number of companies, structurally, there exists significant concentration. Specifically, while there are some 1700 companies in the country selling some form of life insurance, five control almost half of the industry's assets. Furthermore, those five are all *mutual* in form (Prudential,

Metropolitan, etc.) rather than *capital* stock. Mutual companies are owned by policyholders rather than shareholders.

The industry is heavily regulated and monitored, principally by state insurance commissions. In some respects such relation can vary materially state by state, but essentially all regulators focus principally on solvency considerations rather than growth or earnings considerations.

Insurance is very much a "numbers" business and, as such, is conducive to numerous statistical benchmarks and tests. To begin with, of course, there are the standard investment measures of earnings growth record, profit margins, return on equity, etc. In addition, there are a number of specialized items. These include:

1. Breakdown of and growth in life insurance in force.
2. Breakdown of growth in premium income.
3. Growth in first year ordinary premiums (a measure of new sales).
4. Growth in investment income.
5. Ratio of net investment income to mean assets.
6. Ratio of expenses to premiums.
7. Ordinary life lapse ratio.
8. Accident and health insurance (if any) loss ratio.
9. Percentage distribution of assets.
10. Ratio of assets to liabilities.

It is most vital to understand that stock life insurers operate with at least two sets of books, one using accounting prescribed by regulatory authorities ("statutory accounting"), and the other using generally accepted accounting principles. It is the latter that shareholders typically consider more appropriate for their long-term purposes.

There are a number of publications that may be used by interested observers of the life insurance industry. Key company generated literature includes annual regulatory filings (usually referred to as "convention statements"), SEC for 10-K and company annual and iterim reports to shareholders. The acknowledged statistical authority on the insurance industry is A. M. Best Company which puts out a great many insurance industry publications. These include *Best's Insurance Reports, Life Health*

Edition, Best's Insurance Securities Research Service, Best's Review (a monthly magazine) and *Best's Insurance News Digest,* a weekly report. Other recognized publications include the *National Underwriter and Business Insurance.* In addition, the Life Insurance Marketing and Research Association (LIMRA) publishes monthly and quarterly surveys of life insurance sales as well as an annual Life Insurance Fact Book. Of more academic interest, the American Risk and Insurance Association publishes a monthly *Journal of Risk and Insurance.* Finally, in recent years, the public accounting firm of Ernst & Ernst has published several books on accounting and Federal Income taxation for life insurance companies.

PROPERTY-CASUALTY INSURANCE
By Michael Frinquelli

Unlike life insurance the property-casualty industry is highlighted by volatile year-to-year results. This, in turn, principally is a function of cyclicality in underwriting results. This cyclicality reflects such factors as changes in overall inflation patterns, price competition, and catastrophe losses (e.g., hurricanes, tornados). Secular growth in property-casualty insurance is greater than that in life insurance, but year-to-year earnings swings are also much greater.

Also, unlike life insurance, the property-casualty industry is primarily stockholder-owned in nature, although the largest company in the business—State Farm—is a mutual company. Regulation of the industry is pervasive, principally at the state level. Regulation is especially important in the premium rate (pricing) process, with some 34 jurisdictions requiring prior approval of rates in personal lines, such as auto insurance and homeowners multiperil coverages.

Probably the single most important and most well-known ratio in property-casualty insurance is the "combined" or underwriting ratio; this represents the sum of the following: the ratio of underwriting expenses to net premiums written, plus the ratio of losses to net premiums earned. When this sum is at 100%, underwriting results (excluding investment income) are at about breakeven; over 100% indicates underwriting losses; under 100%, underwriting profits.

Another increasingly important benchmark is the ratio of net premiums written to statutory policyholders surplus. This is a key regulatory tool for assessing financial health. A ratio of three to one here is considered a norm and over three to one might suggest further inquiry. It must be emphasized that this ratio provides only a rough guide rather than a strict rule.

Other useful industry statistical measures include:

1. Breakdown of and growth in premiums by major line of coverage.
2. Breakdown of and growth in premiums by major state.
3. Breakdown of assets.
4. Ratio of loss reserves to statutory surplus.
5. Ratio of loss reserves to premiums earned.
6. Rates of growth in total premiums, investment income and earnings.
7. Ratio of stocks owned in portfolio to statutory surplus.

Literature and publications particularly helpful in property-casualty insurance include the following:

1. Company annual statements to insurance commissions ("convention statements").
2. SEC Form 10-K.
3. Shareholders annual and interim reports (sometimes including statistical supplements).
4. A.M. Best Company publications such as:
   a. *Best's Insurance Reports, Property-Liability Edition.*
   b. *Best's Review* (monthly).
   c. *Best's Insurance News Digest* (weekly).
   d. *Best's Insurance Securities Research Service.*
5. The *National Underwriter* (weekly).
6. *Business Insurance* (bi-weekly).
7. *Insurance Facts* (published annually by the Insurance Information Institute).
8. *Property-Liability Insurance Accounting* (a text published for the Insurance Accounting and Statistical Association by the Merritt Company).

CONGLOMERATES
By Harriet L. West

Harriett L. West is one of the nation's leading financial analysts specializing in conglomerates, electronics, and aerospace companies. A graduate of the University of California at Berkeley, with a B.S. degree in Business Administration, her majors were accounting and finance. She entered the securities field in 1961, joining a San Francisco brokerage house and following companies in high technology areas. In 1973, she joined a money management company and became a member of an investment management team handling some $350 million of funds. A Certified Financial Analyst, Ms. West has written for Barron's magazine, and is the author of a chapter in a well-known book, *Stock Market Techniques.* She is listed in *Who's Who of American Women.*

> "n. A composite mass or mixture;
> ... a widely diversified company
> ... v. ... to collect or form into a
> mass or coherent whole."
> --- Webster's Dictionary

INDUSTRY BACKGROUND

What do Swingline, The Andrew Jergens Company, Sunshine Biscuits, and Acushnet Company have in common? They are all part of a modern-day "conglomerate" known as American Brands, Inc. The conglomerate form of corporation is not new. Throughout history of the financial markets there have been companies that have grown externally through the merger and acquisition of other businesses. Yet financial analysts today tend to think of conglomerate companies as those which came into prominence during the "Soaring Sixties" stock market. Most of these are included in the Standard & Poor's index of conglomerates:

City Investing
Gulf & Western
Kidde (Walter)
LTV Corporation
Litton Industries
Teledyne, Inc.
Tenneco, Inc.
Textron
United Brands
U. S. Industries

Other companies that popped into the spotlight during that era were: International Telephone & Telegraph, ATO, Colt Industries, Whittaker, Fuqua Industries, Signal Companies and Norton Simon.

Typically, each company took on the characteristics of its chief executive officer who was usually a combination of an accounting genius and graduate of one of the nationally acclaimed business schools during the fifties. Dr. Duke, the engineer behind Whittaker, coined a term called "synergism" to describe the company he was building. The analytical community of the sixties "bought the act" that these men espoused and the upside potential for their stocks was limited *only* by how fast analysts such as myself could come up with an earnings estimate, following a new acquisition announcement.

Sounds wild, versus the seventies? Well, it was. Conglomerate analysts (who were also business school graduates and, therefore, could understand the conglomerate form of organization) abounded. No one questioned the *internal* growth rates of the acquired companies (usually well below that of the externally generated growth of the acquiring company). The creative accounting of some of the managements caused the S.E.C. to put pressure on the accounting board, resulting in APB# 16. This bulletin defined purchase versus pooling of interests in accounting for acquisitions.

With the economic downturn of 1970 the companies, where management structure and financial controls had not grown in line with acquisitions, began to experience difficulties. This resulted in severe stock price attrition for *all* of the companies (well and poorly managed alike) into the market bottom of 1974. By that time there were few experienced conglomerate analysts. These companies had been assigned secondary status to analysts following other industries.

The drastic decline in these stocks, however, did not mean an end to the conglomerate form of corporation. What I call "modern-day" conglomerates of the seventies include some of the best-managed, diversified companies in the U.S.:

> General Electric
> United Technologies
> Pepsico, Inc.
> Northwest Industries
> Esmark
> Atlantic Richfield
> Heublein
> Pillsbury
> Mobil
> TRW, Inc.

All of the above have had part of their recent growth from acquired businesses.

I have covered industry background because it is *key* to analyzing and reporting on this type of company. First of all, one must understand management's growth objectives; what can be generated internally *(real* growth), and why management has chosen to invest in external sources of growth rather than spending money in areas it is already in. This further explains accounting "caveats" that one must watch for.

THE SIXTIES VERSUS THE SEVENTIES

In the past twenty years (since 1958), the stock market—as measured by the Dow Jones and Standard & Poor's indices—has sold below stated book value in only three periods: 1974, 1976, and 1977. Thus, the acquisition craze of the sixties was not based purely upon value, but rather earnings growth (real and created) of the acquiring company. In addition, buy-out candidates during the sixties were a mixture of public and privately owned corporations.

The poor stock market environment of the seventies has provided cash-rich companies with huge, publicly owned acquisition opportunities. The equities of the target companies usually have been selling at or below stated book value—which, if one considers replacement cost of facilities in an inflationary environment—could be substantially understated. Some old-line, public companies that have disappeared in the seventies include: Anaconda, Otis Elevator, and Utah International. To illustrate all of the accounting questions that arise from a takeover bid, I have chosen the battle for control of Babcock & Wilcox in 1977.

In the spring of 1977, J. Ray McDermott amicably acquired 1,200,000 shares of Babcock & Wilcox in the low to mid-thirties a share. In August, 1977, United Technologies made a surprise tender offer for any and all BAW shares at $58.50 in cash a share. At that time, BAW's common stock was selling at $34.75, or at book value of $34.18 (1976). Babcock & Wilcox is a fine company in energy-generating equipment. BAW made business sense for *both* companies; UTX is in generating equipment (power plants) and controls; MDE is an offshore oil equipment and service company.

McDermott, owner of 1,200,000 shares of BAW, immediately counter-offered with cash of $62.50 a share for 4,300,000 more shares which would have raised its position to 45% of BAW shares outstanding. (Subsequently, this was raised to 4,800,000 shares.) A package of securities was intended to be offered for the balance of 12,100,000 shares. The target company's management made it very clear that the UTX tender was not appreciated. In a move to turn the tide toward MDE's offer, BAW directors voted an extra $2.50 a share dividend on their already $1.50 a share annual rate.

On August 25, UTX terminated its cash offer, following a turbulent two weeks of jockeying for control. As background, Chairman Harry Grey of UTX is a "graduate" of Litton Industries. Since joining UTX in 1972, he has masterminded the takeover of Otis Elevator (at book value) and Essex International. To analyze what managements of UTX and MDE were looking for in a merger with BAW, the following accounting factors will be considered and described:

1. The *book value* of Babcock;
2. The *liquidating value* (book value less long-term debt per share) of the company;
3. The *cash and debt position* of BAW (i.e., the ability of the company to pay for its own acquisition);
4. *Goodwill* created on the acquiring company's balance sheet;
5. *Pooling versus* accounting for mergers; and
6. The *equity method of accounting.*

According to 1976 annual figures, book value of BAW was $34.18, and the liquidating value was $26.00 a share. The common stock had sold at a slight premium to book in most years except those of 1975, 1976, and 1977. The last time the stock sold at $58.75 a share was in 1967. The balance sheet was strong, with $5.80 a share in cash and only $7.61 a share in long-term debt. Working capital was $11.40 a share.

Knowing what the entrepreneurs of the sixties, like Mr. Grey, look at, and considering the above facts, I do not believe that his intent was to use Babcock's liquid assets to acquire itself. Rather, he was interested in the impact of BAW's earning power upon the UTX results. Mr. Grey was willing to pay $711,000,000 in cash, or 171% of stated book value, for BAW. If one pays more than book value for a company, *goodwill* is created on the asset side of the acquiring company's balance sheet. Goodwill is amortized over a 40-year period, *but might result in a one-time write-off* at some future time if management's judgment of the acquired company's assets is erroneous. (This was the error made by the conglomerates in the sixties—paying too much for cyclical companies.) Similarly, liquidating value provides a rough "feel" for what BAW assets would be worth if it were put "on the block" tomorrow.

However, BAW's business is capital intensive and replacement value in an inflationary environment might be much higher than stated book value. (Companies are required to report replacement value of assets in current annual reports.) In addition, the Company's business is long leadtime contracts represented in a healthy backlog which is not reflected in book value.

According to United Technologies management at the time that their tender offer for BAW was terminated, the acquiring company had $350,000,000 in cash flow and could have borrowed $600,000,000 from its banks to finance the $711,000,000 acquisition. Since I believe that the earning power of BAW was of interest to Mr. Grey, let us consider the following. According to the September 30,1977 quarterly report of McDermott, BAW had net income of over $28,000,000 for the six months ended September 30. The company's tax rate is 47%. Working backward and annualizing BAW's earnings, produces estimated pretax income of $106,000,000 a year.

If UTX were to borrow $361,000,000 (or the balance to add to cash flow of $350,000,000, for a total cash price of $711,000,000), its annual interest cost would be just over $25,000,000. (Interest is figured at the going rate for the prime of 7% in August, 1977.) The tax rate of UTX is 50% and—since the acquisition would be treated as a purchase for accounting purposes—there would be no addition to the Company's 26 million shares outstanding. The following would be the incremental impact of BAW on earnings per share alone of UTX:

HYPOTHETICAL BAW CONTRIBUTION TO UTX

	($ mil.)
Pretax income of BAW	$106
UTX interest on the acquisition	25
Pretax after interest on debt	81
less 50% tax rate	41
Net income accruing to UTX	$ 40
÷ 26,000,000 share outstdg.	+$1.54 a share

The cash offer brings up another accounting question: *pooling versus purchase.* Outright purchase (as in the case of UTX's offer) would have impacted the income statement immediately as of the date the deal is consummated. Hence, there is a "one-shot" impact upon sales, expenses and earnings of the conglomerate for 12 months following the acquisition. No previous figures are restated. Therefore, one must report on the extraordinary impact of the acquisition all during the year of occurrence. The balance sheet is consolidated only for the current year; no restatement of prior years takes place. (An interesting exercise is to do a pro forma combination of the two companies prior to a final merger to check for strengths and weaknesses in the balance sheet and income statement. This is possible if both are public companies.)

Turning to the winning offer of McDermott, the September 30, 1977 quarterly report indicates that, as of that date, MDE owned 49% (6,000,000 shares) of Babcock & Wilcox. Since 51% (a controlling interest) had not been attained for full consolidation, MDE used the *equity method of accounting*. This method is commonly used when a business is far afield from the conglomerate's basic business, i.e., Sears and Allstate, or when under a 51% interest in an affiliate is held. The income statement shows equity in the after-tax income of the unconsolidated subsidiary. The balance sheet carries the investment in the subsidiary under fixed assets. The subsidiary's own balance sheet and income statement usually can be found in the footnotes to the annual report or the 10-K statement. Holdings in a regulated industry, such as the railroads and insurance, commonly would be reported in this manner.

The quarterly report further reveals that MDE's carrying value for BAW's 6,000,000 shares is $351,600,000 ($58.60 a share), which—in turn—is $146,500,000 less than its cost. Management states: "At the present time, the Company is unable to relate this difference to specific accounts of the Babcock & Wilcox Company. It is therefore considered to be *goodwill* (writer's emphasis) and is being amortized over 40 years." Negotiating committees from both companies currently are studying various forms of combination for the remaining 6,000,000 or more shares of BAW. A package of securities worth $62.50 a share have been discussed in the past. Hypothetically, *pooling of interest* accounting would be used if securities are exchanged for the 51% (majority) interest. In this method of accounting, the prior ten-year financial statements are restated *to show the two companies as if they always operated as one.* There is no "one-shot" impact on earnings. However, in this case one must watch and report on *dilution* caused by the increase in new securities of the conglomerate possibly being greater than the earnings contribution of the acquired company.

In summary, the conglomerates formed in the sixties or the seventies do not differ in the top managements that built them. Things are a little more sane and usually based upon *value* in this decade of high interest rates and capital shortage. Today's conglomerates acquire businesses because (1) the cost of entry and becoming a major factor in an industry are greater internally than buying a company outright; (2) cash flow from the company's basic business is greater than its capital needs, yet growth is starting to slow (like McDermott and American Brands); and/or (3) vertical or horizontal integration of the company's basic businesses make sense (as with the Utah International-General Electric combination).

TRADE SOURCES, KEY RATIOS

There are no trade sources, per se, for analyzing conglomerates. Since 1971, the SEC has required companies to report sales and profit breakdowns of their basic businesses. While these are broad breakdowns, it shows what economic statistics provided by the U.S. Government are most applicable to analyzing a particular company. For instance, in analyzing Teledyne, I have used the Aerospace Industries Association (for Ryan and Continental Motors) and the U.S. Atomic Energy Commission Division of Industrial Participation (for Wah-Chang.)

As I mentioned previously, the sixties taught us that tight financial controls and planning are a "must" in analyzing conglomerates. Also previously touched upon are stated goals of management which govern the company's internal, external, and total growth rates.

Other than these—which partially can be ascertained from standard ratios of return on equity, profitability, cash flow/capital expenditures, earnings and dividend growth—the only other factor to watch is whether the company has been buying its own stock.

Teledyne had 34,300,000 shares outstanding in 1972. Recently, through purchase of its own stock, shares outstanding have been reduced to 12,000,000. Net income since 1971 has risen 140%, while the number of shares is down 65%. You can imagine what has happened to earnings per share!

Also, since 1972, Teledyne "took its lumps" in the write-offs of goodwill and closing down of Packard-Bell and the semiconductor division (formerly Continental Devices) which were designated "problems" at that time.

OFFICE EQUIPMENT
By Frederic H. Cohen

Frederic H. Cohen is acknowledged to be one of the most incisive analysts of computer and electronic companies, with a broadening specialty in office equipment. An Iraq-born French citizen, Mr. Cohen received his Degree in Electrical Engineering from the Federal Institute of Technology in Zurich, Switzerland, in 1958, and a Certificat de Aptitude à L'Administration des Enterprises (equivalent of an M.B.A.) from the Sorbonne in Paris in 1962. Assigned as project manager for two French government projects being developed in association with Scientific Data Systems of California, Mr. Cohen was fascinated by the price rise in SDS stock and began to study financial analysis and the stock market. He joined the corporate finance department of Oppenheimer & Co., a New York investment banking firm in 1968, and then moved to Legg Mason Wood Walker, another major brokerage firm. He is currently Chairman of the Program Committee of the Computer Industry Analyst Group.

Many of the criteria used to analyze office-equipment companies are applicable to companies in other industries and owe a great deal to Graham and Dodd. In most cases analysts focus on management's track record, on the quality of earnings (adequacy of the reserves, depreciation life of fixed assets, etc.), as well as on the strength and liquidity of the balance sheet. Financial ratios such as gross margin, pre-tax margin, current ratio, receivables turnover, inventory turnover, return on assets, and return on equity are carefully scrutinized and monitored over time. The benchmark numbers are often those of IBM, in computers, and of Xerox, in office products.

What sets office-equipment companies apart from most others is, first, the rapid pace of technological change. To keep up, companies have to have a sizable research budget. Research and development expenditures exceeding 5% of revenues are a plus. These companies, however, are not labor intensive, and a high ratio of revenue dollars per employee (of 50,000, say) is viewed favorably.

Office-equipment companies, historically, tend to be highly capital intensive. This is partly due to the fact that IBM and Xerox, which dominate their respective markets, were emphasizing rentals. The ability to finance a base of equipment on rental was thus a requirement for effective competition, if not survival. To examine how well this fixed asset is managed, analysts monitor its "yield." This is defined as rental revenues per dollar of investment in the rental base of equipment. More recently, due to increased customer sophistication and willingness to make longer-term commitments, the emphasis on rentals has diminished. This, in turn, has benefited cash flow. Capital, however, remains an attractive commodity, and earnings are mostly reinvested rather than paid out in the form of dividends.

Most office equipment companies market and often manufacture their products on a worldwide basis. IBM and Xerox, for example, derive only about 50% of their revenues and earnings from the United States, with substantially most of their product requirements for foreign markets manufactured abroad, oftentimes in the same marketing region. This large percentage of foreign revenues, earnings, and assets results in a significant impact on the income statement and the balance sheet of these companies as foreign currencies fluctuate relative to the United States dollar. Like most multinational companies in other industries, the large vendors attempt to minimize this impact by careful hedging operations.

Accounting practices vary. Because the trend in selling prices is generally down, the more conservative companies price their inventories on a FIFO, rather than LIFO, basis. Tax rates vary also, depending on whether or not investment tax credits are amortized (conservative), and Domestic International Sales Corporation benefits are deferred (conservative) and also, where available, on the relative contribution to profits from tax-sheltered manufacturing operations in domiciles such as Puerto Rico and Ireland.

The relative size of both IBM and Xerox has raised antitrust questions. The office equipment analyst must thus monitor Supreme Court rulings and congressional proceedings for clues to a possible structural change in this industry.

UTILITIES
By Ernest Kiehne

Ernest Kiehne turned to financial analysis after 26 years as an executive with American Telephone & Telegraph, the last portion of which was spent working on the computerization of the Bell System. A 1940 graduate of Johns Hopkins University with a B. S. in Business, he joined the Chesapeake and Potomac Telephone Company as a lineman. During World War II, he served as a communications officer aboard destroyers, returning to American Telephone & Telegraph after service in the South Pacific. In 1967 his interest in investing drew him to the stock market, and he started a new career at age 49 as director of research of Legg Mason Wood Walker Incorporated.

The first thing I look at is the fuel mix. I prefer no natural gas and little oil—both have to go. Thus coal and nuclear are the best. Next, the regulatory climate is very important. This is political and, in some parts of the country, it is always bad. After that I look for conservative accounting and a strong cash flow per share to give good coverage of the dividend. These stocks sell on yield so the dividend must be very safe. I don't want a utility to be growing too fast since a rapid rate means they will need new plants, and that can be brutally expensive.

While it may appear surprising, I like to see a high tax rate because it means the earnings are of high quality; and, if they get into trouble, the Government will be paying a large part of the bill through lower taxes.

Earnings, what with changes in regulatory climate, in the short term can go all over the place. I look at the longer-term trends of earnings. Basically, a growth rate of 3% to 4% a year in earnings and in dividends also is good. You should get a dividend yield of something like 8%, giving a total return of around 11%, which is good for any field. Since these stocks sell on a yield basis, these are the important factors.

The quarterly and annual reports of the companies are about all I need along with Standard & Poor's and Value Line material. These are not the dynamic day-to-day changing types of situations that require sifting through piles of newspapers and trade magazines.

BUILDING MATERIALS
By George Einsfield

Prominent building materials analyst George Einsfield first became interested in that particular industry by working in the construction field to earn his college tuition.

He worked for a variety of contractors, doing everything from carpentry to bricklaying and laying tiles. By the time he graduated from Hofstra University with a B.B.A. in Finance in 1956, he was a skilled building trades artisan, and subsequently built his own home. He took advance graduate work in finance at Hofstra University and joined the Home Insurance Company in 1957 as a junior analyst assigned to utilities and rails. By 1960, he had made the switch to covering the building trades industry for W.E. Hutton & Co., members of the New York Stock Exchange, where he ultimately rose to a vice-presidency in the research department and a seat on the board of directors. He currently is the building materials analyst for U.S. Trust Company. Mr. Einsfield is past-president and founder of the Building Analysts Group, a splinter group of the New York Society of Security Analysts.

The prime concern is talking with the companies and keeping

close to their situations as well as their observations of the industry—demand situations, pricing, and capacity ratios. Along with the demand outlook for the upcoming months, other vital factors are pricing structure, volume, and why the outlook, up or down, is as it is. The price/earnings ratio of each stock must be related to the Standard & Poor's 500. Of special concern to this industry is the relation of the 90-day Treasury bill rate to the S & P composite of building stocks. There is an inverse relationship. When the Treasury bill rate approaches 6%, the stocks tend to go down the drain.

Trends must be watched closely, along with such standard items as ROE and ROI, tax rates, liquidity, protectivity, sales to assets, employees and plant, and how all these factors relate one company to another. A ten-year growth rate calculated on a "least squares" growth method, not compounded growth rate, is best in order to avoid cyclical distortions.

Government statistics are important, particularly from the Commerce Department and the Bureau of the Census, along with *House and Home, Professional Builder, Engineering News Record, Pit and Quarry, Stone Products, Home Furnishings Daily, Hardware Age, Floor Covering Weekly, Retail Building Products* and publications from the Association of the Furniture Manufacturers. In recent years various colleges and universities have done significant work on housing from a variety of aspects that can be used in analysis.

CHEMICALS
By John Thies

John Thies, a 1953 graduate of Antioch College (B. A. in Economics), and a 1972 Graduate of Fairleigh Dickinson University (M.B.A.), spent the better part of a decade with the Celanese Corporation as a specialist in marketing and market research. In 1969, he came to Wall Street and worked as a securities analyst, institutional research, for W. E. Hutton & Co., an investment banking/brokerage firm. His specialty was chemicals, as it is today. Mr. Thies joined Fidelity Management and Research, one of the most-respected and largest mutual fund organizations in America, in 1974. Mr. Thies is acknowledged to be one of the most astute observers and analysts of the chemical industry.

Chemical companies are usually huge affairs with large geographic, market and product mixes. A DuPont catalog, for example, had over 3000 major product group headings—the combinations ran over a million. A typical chemical company has several thousand products at any given time. That makes analysis an all-encompassing job. While an analyst in most industries can get by with only one or two company contact people, I need a half-dozen or so in order to get the full story: worldwide, product, competition, financial, etc.

Despite that, or perhaps because of it, I find that only one set of figures are vital as indicators of what is happening in a company: that consists of the various margin figures—gross margin, pre-tax, after-tax on a trend basis for say ten years and quarter-by-quarter. They indicate if a company has control of its destiny. A secondary gauge is return on equity. The other standard ratios come afterward. Once you see how the key margins are holding up, or what pressures are on them, you have a pretty fair picture of how a company is doing.

Absolutely required reading, for my work, includes the chemical and plastics page of the *Journal of Commerce, Chemical Market Reporter, Chemical Week* and *Chemical and Engineering News. Textile Organon* is a necessary tool also. These publications provide everyday news items on such things as construction projects, products and markets, pricing, competitive factors—and a most import area now—regulatory factors.

Secondary publications include *European Chemical News, Modern Plastics,* and *Daily News Record.*

A key government publication is the *Synthetic and Organic Chemical Report* published monthly by the U. S. International Trade Commission. It reports monthly figures on production of key chemicals. The Bureau of Mines has a mineral industry survey which is also helpful, particularly for work in fertilizers.

BROADCASTING

By William Suter

Financial analyst William Suter, vice president and research analyst at Merrill Lynch, Pierce, Fenner & Smith, became enamored of broadcasting when he worked as a radio announcer for his college radio station. He graduated from Brown University in 1959 with a B.A. in Political Science, and from Harvard Business School with an M.B.A. in 1961. He joined Donaldson, Lufkin & Jenrette as an assistant vice president in research, and moved on to a partnership in Jessup & Lamont, another New York Stock Exchange firm, where he took on administrative duties. His earlier interest in broadcasting remained with him and in the early 1970s he began to specialize in the field. As one of the most influential and respected broadcasting analysts, he is responsible for "Broadcasting Basics," an annual publication issued by Merrill Lynch, and the highly respected "Broadcasting Monthly," a 20 to 25 page bimonthly (despite its "monthly" title), also issued by Merrill Lynch.

Broadcasting, particularly television, is a supply-and-demand business. There is no room for growth in the number of hours of the day advertising can be sold and little room for creation of new prime-time hours. The audience grows about 3% annually, and you have to decide how much can be charged for the advertising time by looking at ratings and potential ratings—figuring cost per thousand exposures of the commercial time for the advertiser. It is a tremendous cash-flow business. Furthermore, since any one company is limited to owning seven AM radio stations, seven FM Stations, five VHF television stations and two UHF television stations (something many of the large group broadcasters are now beginning to look at because of improving profitability), the companies feel they must diversify into such areas as publishing, records, musical instruments. Thus you must be adept at getting a feel for those areas and their potential pluses and minuses. In analyzing the companies there are no unique ratios of particular importance. *Broadcast Magazine* is an important source of information, as is *Radio and TV Age, Variety, TV Digest, Advertising Age* and the *Television Bureau of Advertising.*

CHAPTER SEVEN

The Securities and Exchange Commission

The indifference to stockholders' rights displayed by many corporate managements in the earlier years of this century gradually brought about a government resolve that the public interest called for protection of the innocent investor. The principle of *full disclosure* was behind the earliest legislation. This concept has evolved, in less than half a century, into a complex, sophisticated entaglement of regulations embracing corporations, management, advisors (lawyers, accountants, and public relations counselors), journalists, financial analysts, investment bankers, underwriters, and brokers—all interface with *information* before it gets to the public, and therefore have an opportunity to use it, or shape it, to their own benefit first.

As new statutes extended the disclosure requirements, a new leading edge entered securities legislation—the matter of "materiality." SEC regulations define it this way:

The term "material," when used to qualify a requirement for the furnishing of information as to any subject, limits the information required to those matters as to which an average prudent investor ought reasonably to be informed before purchasing the security registered.

An early definition, still valid today, is that a material fact is "a fact which, if it had been correctly stated or disclosed, would have deterred or tended to deter the average prudent investor from purchasing the securities in question."

A good part of the enforcement actions taken by the SEC is to reinforce the objectives of full disclosure and materiality. (Section 10b-5 of the regulations pertains to fraud and is cited most frequently in the news items regarding SEC indictments.)

Formed in 1933 as one of President Roosevelt's new administrative groups, the Securities and Exchange Commission had as its first chairman Joseph Kennedy, father of the late president, at that time known as one of the more sophisticated Wall Streeters-turned-industrialist. Seven securities acts were passed in the period between 1933 and 1940, each further extending the loop to cover new groups—underwriters, brokers, through investment advisors (1940).

The two initial acts are the most prominent. The Securities Act of 1933 is aimed at the *distribution* of securities and binds all those involved in the process (from corporate officials and advisors through the underwriter) to the truthful presentation of information about the corporation so that the purchaser is not misled. He is, however, entitled to be stupid. The Commission does not pass on the merits of the securities. The purchaser, however, should be able to rely upon the accuracy of the *prospectus,* the document which purports to give all the information—negative and positive—about the company. It is the end result of forms S-1 (which requires "full" registration of established domestic and foreign private issuers), or S-2 (registration statement for a company of a speculative or promotional nature, in its initial developmental phase) or a Regulation A (which permits certain United States and Canadian companies to make offerings, exempt from full registration, not to exceed $500,000), and the intervening "Red Herrings," which respond to and update the filing with changes to meet the SEC comments, until the final document is approved and securities sold. Each prospective investor who receives a "Red Herring" must receive all followups, through the final prospectus, and each purchaser of a new issue must get a final prospectus.

The Securities Act of 1934 is aimed at the *retailer* of securities—the broker (also known as a registered representative or salesman). This act requires publicly owned companies to make continuing, complete and truthful disclosures to the *investing public*—a much broader universe than its own shareholders—and prohibits anyone from either defrauding another person or manipulating the price of securities.

Several landmark securities cases have advanced the purview of the SEC and the sharp bite the Commission has developed has transformed it into one of the most effective consumer-advocate agencies. Its viewpoint on more technical questions, such as negotiated commission rates and a central marketplace, is more questionable and there are many reputable and distinguished opponents of the Commission's attitudes and decisions in this sphere.

The most notable test of the Securities Act of 1933—the heart of which is *full disclosure of all material facts in the issuance of new securities*—came in the BarChris case, decided in 1968 (Escott v. BarChris Construction Corp., United States District Court, S.D.N.Y. 1968, 283 F. Supp. 643, McLean, District Judge). The plaintiffs brought action in 1962, under Section 11 of the Securities Act of 1933, alleging material false statements and material omissions in a registration statement of 5½% convertible subordinated 15-year debentures of BarChris Construction Corporation.

BarChris, primarily engaged in the construction of bowling alleys, was founded as a New York partnership in 1946. The introduction of automatic pin-setting machines in 1952 sparked a boom in bowling alleys and BarChris' business took off. In 1960 BarChris installed about 3% of all lanes built in the United States and had become an important factor in the bowling industry.

The company, growing rapidly, was chronically short of capital. Sales, according to the company's first prospectus issued in 1959, were about $800,000 in 1956, rose to $1,300,000 in 1957, and to

$1,700,000 in 1958. In 1959 volume jumped to more than $3,300,000 and in 1960 the company reported sales of more than $9,165,000.

An initial public offering of common stock was made in December, 1959, through the underwriting firm of Peter Morgan and Company, selling 560,000 shares of common stock to the public at $3 per share.

By early 1961 BarChris again needed funds and an underwriting syndicate led by Drexel Co. raised $3,500,000 through the sale of debentures. BarChris received the net proceeds of this offering on May 16, 1961.

By May, 1962, the company was hopelessly overextended. A registration statement was filed with the SEC for another stock issue and withdrawn. And on October 29, 1962, the company filed for an arrangement under Chapter XI of the Bankruptcy Act.

What happened?

The ensuing investigation by the court revealed that at the time of the debenture offering the company was already experiencing difficulties in collecting receivables from some of its customers; the bowling boom had burst. Debenture holders claimed that important information of this nature was withheld from the prospectus and that sales, earnings, and other figures were overstated.

A thorough review of Judge McLean's findings would be helpful to all journalists who would like an insight as to how numbers can be misrepresented so as to obscure alarming facts. Judge McLean found that misrepresentations had occurred; information had been omitted; certain corporate transactions had been improperly classified, and that the directors and underwriters had not exercised "due diligence" in either their investigations of the company's actions or in their relationship to the company. As a result of this finding, the burdens of corporate directors expanded dramatically to the point where smaller corporations today have a difficult time getting outside directors. The premium cost of Directors Liability Insurance, in fact, has risen sharply in the past five years, and some smaller companies can't get any at all.

1968 was the year for major SEC legislative victories. Perhaps the raging bull market of the 1960s provided corporations with a screen for misbehavior or, more likely, the extraordinary stock activity created an environment where morality became lax.

At any rate 1968 was also the year of the Texas Gulf Sulphur case which tested the tenet that public companies had to make *continuous and truthful disclosure* of information which a prudent investor might use in buying or selling a security (Securities and Exchange Commission v. Texas Gulf Sulphur Co., United States Court of Appeals, Second Circuit, 1958. 401 F.2d 833, Cert. denied 394 U.S. 976 (1969), Before Lumbard, Chief Judge, and Waterman, Moore, Friendly, Smith, Kaufman, Hays, Anderson and Feinberg, Circuit Judges).

Geologists of Texas Gulf in October, 1963, made an extraordinary copper strike near Timmins, Ontario, in eastern Canada. On orders of the company president, the information was withheld from the public, and even from other members of management, so that the company could conclude the purchase of nearby properties in which Texas Gulf had an interest.

The information was not released to the public until six months later, April 16, 1964 (although the *New York Herald Tribune* on April 11 had carried a story about a rumored major strike by Texas Gulf in eastern Canada, and Texas Gulf had officially denied the article via a press release on April 12. The *Northern Miner,* a Canadian mining industry publication, ran an article April 15 reporting a 10,000,000 ton ore strike and, on April 15th, Texas Gulf presented the Ontario Minister of Mines with a press release confirming a 25,000,000-ton strike).

The common stock of Texas Gulf rose from 17⅜ on November 8, 1963, the day when drilling began, to 37 on April 16, 1964, the day of the announcement. The stock hit 58¼ by May 15, less than a month after the official announcement, an increase of 57%—a good indication that the market considered the information "material" to its judgment regarding the increased value of the company. During the November-April period, several insiders purchased common stock on the open market; some advised friends the stock was a good buy (making the friends, in the new

SEC language, "tippees"), and a few accepted stock options awarded by Texas Gulf's Stock Option Committee whose members were not privy to information about the strike.

The SEC sued under Rule 10b-5, which provides:

> It shall be unlawful for any person, directly or indirectly, by the use of any means or instrumentality of interstate commerce, or of the mails, or of any facility of any national securities exchange,
>
> (1) to employ any device, scheme or artifice to defraud,
>
> (2) to make any untrue statement of a material fact or to omit to state a material fact necessary in order to make the statements make, in the light of the circumstances under which they were made, not misleading, or
>
> (3) to engage in any act, practice, or course of business which operates or would operate as a fraud or deceit upon any person, in connection with the purchase or sale of any security.

The SEC action made it clear that it now considered noncompany investors who received inside information as culpable in its use as insiders—a major extension of the 1934 Act.

Judge Waterman's commentary included the following:

> The core of rule 10b-5 is the implementation of the Congressional purpose that all investors should have equal access to the rewards of participation in securities transactions. It was the intent of Congress that all members of the investing public should be subject to identical market risks—which market risks include, of course, the risk that one's evaluative capacity or one's capital available to put at risk, may exceed another's capacity of capital. The insiders here were not trading on an equal footing with the outside investors. They alone were in a position to evaluate the probability and magnitude of what seemed from the outset to be a major ore strike; they alone could invest safely, secure in the expectation that the price of TGS stock would rise substantially in the event such a major strike should materialize, but would decline little, if at all, in the event of failure, for the public, ignorant at the outset of the

favorable probabilities would likewise be unaware of the unproductive exploration, and the additional exploration costs would not significantly affect TGS market prices. Such inequities based upon unequal access to knowledge should not be shrugged off as inevitable in our way of life, or, in view of the congressional concern in the area, remain uncorrected. We hold, therefore, that all transactions in TGS stock or calls by individuals apprised of the drilling results of K-55-1 were made in violation of Rule 10b-5.

In 1968, the SEC also moved against Merrill Lynch, Pierce, Fenner & Smith, the nation's largest brokerage house, and for the first time officially held a "tippee" in violation of Rule 10b-5. As prospective underwriters of an issue for Douglas Aircraft some Merrill Lynch employees came into possession of some negative information about Douglas and passed it along to others who used it for trading purposes. The Commission held that the "tippees" should have known the information was inside, nonpublic information since it came from the underwriter.

All of the 10b-5 actions stem from a 1961 precedent law case, Cady Roberts & Company. A partner in that brokerage firm had received information about a pending dividend cut from a company director, and had telephoned the news to his office, precipitating selling in the stock.

One of the most spectacular frauds in recent securities history—the Equity Funding case—is an example of a 10b-5 violation. One of the most dazzling high-flyers of the 1960s, the Equity Funding Corporation of America was revealed to have "manufactured" most of the growth it had been reporting. Through a subsidiary, Equity wrote more than 60,000 fake insurance policies, sold them to re-insurers for cash, created phony death claims and carried on its books some $120 million in assets that did not exist.

All of this was achieved through a computer fraud with senior management of Equity feeding false information to its computers. Among many other things, this case proved that it is virtually impossible for an auditor to prevent a fraud from taking place if a clever crook is operating against him.

This case has unusual ramifications. Securities Analyst Raymond L. Dirks, acting on information from a former Equity Funding employee, conducted his own investigation and, despite conflicting reports from management, decided there were undisclosed problems at Equity. He told his clients, who sold their holdings—before the general public received similar warnings.

Was Mr. Dirks a "tippee"? Or, simply an analyst fullfilling his obligation of investigation, interpretation and analysis? It is a question the courts will have to resolve.

But it also points to dangers for journalists. Many publications have stringent regulations regarding the use of information for personal investment, and the best advice is to follow the "prudent man" rule. Don't buy stock in a company the moment you have come into possession of information which a "prudent man" would think should affect the price of the company's securities; if already a shareholder, hold securities in a company you have just written up if the story can affect the stock price, until the effect has diminished.

The SEC has not held journalists to be inviolate of investigation. The SEC has a number of times sought a link between reporters' investments and the timing of the stories they wrote; financial journalists of prominence at major daily newspapers and magazines have been publicly mentioned in probes of their investment habits.

Obviously, handling financial and business information carries an obligation of investment ethics, and the journalist is closer to this problem than most other professonals.

The seven SEC Acts are compiled in Appendix A of the supplement and should be perused.

PUBLIC DOCUMENTS

As we have seen, the publicly owned corporation is an information machine, and the adept journalist will quickly learn to push all the buttons. The company files reports with the Securities and Exchange Commission, sends reports to shareholders and issues press releases to the media so as not to be in violation of any SEC edicts on full disclosure and materiality.

Additionally, if the company is listed on a national or regional stock exchange, it must file periodic reports with that exchange.

All of this information is available to the journalist who requests it.

Of the documents filed with the Securities and Exchange Commission, the most important to the journalist are the 10-K, 10-Q and the 8-K. These guidelines are revised from time to time, and the journalist should keep abreast of changes by having himself put on the mailing list of the local SEC office. These offices are listed in Chapter 9 (Reference Sources).

The 10-K, as previously noted, includes a copy of the annual report to shareholders, but it is much broader than the Annual Report. It must be filed within 90 days after the end of the fiscal year covered by the reports.

Journalists reviewing the 10-K can uncover such valuable information as the following:

1. Operation of foreign subsidiaries (with the caveat that the company may omit information "to the extent that the required disclosure would be detrimental to the registrant").

2. Information on employee stock purchases, savings, and similar plans.

3. Material changes in the company's business since the beginning of the fiscal year, including trends at subsidiaries.

4. Competitive conditions in the industry, with separate consideration given to principal products or services or classes of products.

5. The names of customers whose loss would have a material adverse affect on the company's business.

6. The dollar amount of backlog of orders, and a characterization as to how much of it is firm and how much is going to be worked off within the current fiscal year. Also it's seasonality.

7. Sources and availability of raw materials essential to the company.

8. Importance of the company's patents, trademarks, licences, franchises, and concessions.

9. Expenditures being devoted to research and development for new products or to improve existing products.

10. Description of any new products in the planning stage or in prototype.

11. Industry practices and conditions and how they impact the working capital of the company.

12. If the company is engaged in more than one line of business, the approximate volume and income for each product line.

13. A five-year history, in tabular form, of the company's operations.

14. Description of company properties, such as factories.

15. Legal proceedings.

16. Securities transactions.

17. Number of shareholders, by class.

18. Executives by name, age, and family relationship by marriage or adoption to the controlling persons in the company.

19. Indemnification provisions to hold directors or officers free of liabilities.

20. Directors by name, age, and shareholding as well as renumeration.

21. Stock options to management by name, number of shares, and price.

22. Transactions between members of management and the company or any of its subsidiaries.

23. Debt owed to the corporation by any member of management or the board of directors.

24. Specific financial information including the collateralization of any assets to banks or insurance companies.

The 10-Q is a quarterly statement, broader than and including the quarterly report to shareholders, which, for "reporting" companies, must be filed within 45 days after the close of the quarter. If the public company has more than 300 shareholders, it must file such a report in each of the first three fiscal quarters of the year. In addition to covering much of the ground discussed in the 10-K, the 10-Q specifically requests additional information on:

1. Any consolidation or combination of subsidiaries, or sale of a

subsidiary. The effect on revenues and income must be disclosed.

2. Any change in accounting practices and the reasons for it must be discussed. Any arrangements made for bonus and profit sharing arrangements normally determined at year end must be included in the 10-Q.

3. Any material adjustment in a prior financial report must be listed and discussed.

4. A special form must list the sales of unregistered equity securities as well as all debt securities in amounts over $100,000 and with terms of maturity exceeding one year.

The 8-K, filed only when significant changes have occurred, must be at the Commission within 15 days after the unusual event has occurred. The types of information which a reporter can glean from an 8-K include:

1. Change in control of the company, giving the name of the new controlling person or persons, a description of the transaction and the percentage of voting securities the new control person has.

2. The acquisition or the disposition of corporate assets in an amount significant enough to be material. The identity of the persons from whom the assets were acquired or to whom they were sold, as well as the nature of any material relationships between them and the company and its officers. The term "acquisition" is used broadly here and includes every purchase, acquisition by lease, exchange, merger, consolidation, or any other technique. The converse is true for "disposition" of assets.

3. Legal proceedings, if any, must be given in detail.

4. Any change in the rights of holders of any class of registered securities must be defined, especially if the rights have been modified or limited by the issuance of any other new security.

5. Defaults in the payment of principal, interest, a sinking or purchase fund in installment, or any other material default not cured within 30 days.

6. Any 5% increase or decrease in the number of shares outstanding in any category—common stock, preferred stock, debentures—and the details of the transactions.

7. The granting or extension of options, including their exercise price and the market value of the securities underlying the options.

8. Extraordinary charges or credits, material provisions for loss, or any restatement of the surplus account.

9. Any change in auditor, including commentary as to whether or not there was a disagreement with the former auditor, and if so, the reason for it.

10. The financial statements of any newly acquired business.

Companies which are regulated by the Federal Power Commission, the Interstate Commerce Commission, or the Federal Communications Commission file a 12-K report with the SEC. The 12-K is similar in format to the 10-K.

Journalists assigned to an industry should keep a complete dossier of the various filings including "Red Herrings" and final prospectuses. Occasionally, a comment will be made in a "Red Herring" and removed from the final prospectus. The financial journalist should always be on the lookout for *changes, adjustments,* and *eliminations* of previously reported material.

The S-1 standard registration form and S-2 (for development companies) are filed whenever a company is going to issue more stock either as a primary offering for the company treasury, a secondary for insiders, or a combination for both. The guidelines for each of these filings is available from the SEC and should be secured for the files.

CHAPTER EIGHT

Glossary

Over a period of years a financial reporter will be shifted from industry to industry. In doing so he will tune in to the special language of that industry, and will add to his lexicography those phrases and definitions peculiar to that specialty. The following glossary will give the journalist a broad dictionary of financial terms, and his own persistence will add to it as the years pass.

Remember that under a deadline nothing is more helpful than a precise definition of a difficult term. Keep your glossary alive by adding to it new definitions in finance and industry as you learn them.

"A" 1. Bond rating bestowed by the two recognized independent services, Moody's and Standard & Poor's. Highest S & P rating is AAA and top Moody's rating is Aaa. Lowest by either is C.

2. Class A Stock sometimes issued by a company to differentiate it from Class B which might have limited voting or dividend rights. Rarely done.

ABOVE PAR. A price higher than the par, or face, value of the security.

ACCELERATED AMORTIZATION. Very-rapid depreciation granted for the write-off of facilities (generally five years). Usually permitted when the government wants to encourage industry to build new defense or war plants.

ACCELERATION CLAUSE. Bond indenture provision which permits

the principal to be declared due earlier than maturity date, usually because of default in interest payment.

ACCOUNT AND RISK. Stockbrokers execute customer orders for the account and at the risk of the client.

ACCOUNT EXECUTIVE. Security salesman, also known as registered representative, broker, investment broker.

ACCOUNTS PAYABLE. Monies due others in payment of goods or services purchased from them. Carried on balance sheet under current liabilities.

ACCOUNTS RECEIVABLE. Monies due from customers in payment of goods sold to them or services rendered. Carried on balance sheet under current assets.

ACCRUALS. Expenses charged against current operations but to be paid at a later date. *Accrued dividends* refers to that portion of regular dividend not yet payable but accumulated since last dividend paid; *accrued interest* is the interest accrued on the company's books each month, but which may not be payable for some time; *accrued liabilities* includes the total of wages, taxes and insurance incurred but not yet payable.

ACCUMULATED DIVIDENDS. Unpaid as of the due date. *Accumulated interest* refers to past due interest payments; *accumulated surplus* is the undistributed profit carried on a cumulative basis in the surplus statement.

ACTIVE MARKET. Refers to stock trading greater than normal and must be compared to the current

norm. In the early 1960s, daily average trading on the New York Stock (1978) average daily trading is about 27,000,000 shares. Most active trading day in New York Stock Exchange history occurred on August 3, 1978 when 66,370,000 shares traded on the Big Board alone.

ACTIVE PARTNER. Partner in brokerage firm (or officer, if a corporation) active in the day-to-day operations, as opposed to other forms of brokerage partnership: general partner, limited partner, special partner. An *allied partner* (or voting stockholder) cannot transact business on the floor of an exchange, but is bound by the same rules as exchange members.

ADJUSTMENT BOND. Known also as income bond, interest on this type of security is payable only when earned. Usually results from a reorganization.

ADMITTED TO TRADING (or admitted to dealings). Refers to a stock which previously had been *approved* for trading on an exchange, but now starts trading.

ADVANCE-DECLINE LINE (or index). A technical barometer which conforms the general market condition to the Dow Jones Industrial Stock Average by subtracting the daily declines on the New York Stock Exchange from the daily advances and adding them to a base figure. When plotted on a chart against the Dow Jones, it indicates if the general market is indeed being reflected by the prominent DJI.

AFFILIATED COMPANY. SEC definition is a company which "directly or indirectly, through one or more intermediaries, controls, or is controlled by, or is under common control with another." Control, according to the SEC, is "the power to direct, or cause the direction of, the management and policies ... (of a corporation) whether through the ownership of voting securities, by contract, or otherwise."

AFTERMARKET. The market for a security which automatically develops after it has been initially sold to the public.

AIR POCKET. Sudden sharp decline in price of a stock, out of proportion to behavior that day of the entire list.

ALLOTMENT. Amount of stock in new issue alloted to prospective buyer who has responded to prospectus. If issue is "hot" (in demand), subscriber may receive smaller allotment than requested.

AMERICAN DEPOSITORY RECEIPTS. Also known as ADR's. Came into being in the 1920s, to facilitate trading in the United States of securities of foreign corporations. The transfers of actual certificates to the United States owner and back again when sold to overseas buyer slowed transactions. With ADR's, the foreign certificates are deposited abroad, and the *depository receipt* is issued to the United States buyer. In future transactions here, the ADR changes hands.

AMORTIZATION. The gradual reduction of a liability, deferred charge or capital expenditure. Fixed assets are amortized by charges for depreciation, depletion and obsolescence.

ANALYST. A professional trained to investigate and analyze facts about securities, companies and industriess. Chartered Financial Analyst (C.F.A.) is a relatively new designation awarded those who have passed three increasingly rigid exams.

ARBITRAGE. The simultaneous purchase and sale of securities, or commodities, with the profit being made on the spread in two different markets. Very sophisticated technique. A few brokerage houses have arbitrage desks or departments, and some arbitrage stocks are listed on more than one exchange in the United States and overseas.

ASSET VALUE (or Book Value). The total tangibles owned by a corporation, including amounts owed it, after deducting debts.

ARREARS. Overdue debt. Before paying dividends on common stocks, company must pay off arrearages on preferred and, in some cases, on bonds.

AUDIT. Examination of the financial operations of a company. A year-end audit should result in a certified statement from the auditor (or certified public accountant).

ASKED PRICE. The lowest price a seller will take for his security is the "Asked" price. The "Bid" price is the highest price a buyer will offer.

AT A DISCOUNT. Selling below par.

AT A PREMIUM. A security selling above its par value.

AT THE CLOSE. Security to be sold at the best price obtainable at close of market, or closest to it. Some exchanges forbid the practice.

AT THE MARKET. An order to sell a security at the current market price, whatever it is.

AT THE OPENING. An order to be executed, or cancelled, at the market opening.

AUCTION MARKET. A market where goods are freely sold to the highest bidder. The various stock exchanges are auction markets for securities. A broker who has a buy order goes to a location on the exchange floor where a specialist maintains an orderly market of requests to buy and sell a particular security. The broker can then bid for the amount he wishes to buy—or, conversely, to sell. The specialist acts as an auctioneer. The over-the-counter market, on the other hand, is a *dealer* market—where everything is done by negotiation.

AUTEX BLOCK INFORMATION SYSTEM. An automated trading system for *blocks* of stock where subscribers can indicate interest through computers. Transaction is generally consummated on an exchange, or through an over-the-counter dealer.

AVERAGING. The purchase or sale of additional shares of stock in a particular company at successively lower or higher prices, to average out the price of the transaction. Averaging Up or Averaging Down.

BABY BOND. A bond issued in denominations less than $1000. Generally sold at discounts because of their limited marketability.

BALANCE SHEET. A financial picture of a company on a particular date. Lists all assets in left column, and all liabilities in right column, and columns are always equal in total amount.

BACKDOOR LISTING. The listing on an exchange of a company which originally did not meet listing requirements but, through the merger into, or acquisition of, an already listed company, is now traded on the exchange.

BACK-OFFICE. Generally refers to the operations end of a brokerage house, where customers' accounts are updated.

BARRON'S CONFIDENCE INDEX. Compiled and published weekly by *Barron's Magazine*, it allegedly reflects changes in the attitudes of sophisticated money. It is a ratio of Barron's highest-grade corporate bond yield average to the Dow Jones composite bond yield average. When sophisticated investors are gloomy they supposedly switch to higher quality bonds, pushing the index down; when optimistic, they buy lower-grade bonds, pushing the index up.

BASE BUILDING. A term used by technicians, or chartists, to indicate a narrow range for the market over an extended time frame. Theory holds that a move by the entire market, or by an individual stock, will be modest unless preceded by a good base.

BASIS. In bonds, the yield to maturity at a given price.

BEAR. A pessimist who thinks the market will decline; the opposite of *Bull*, one who believes the market is going up. An old Wall Street adage holds that "Bears make money, bulls make money, but pigs never make any." It means one can't buy at the bottom, and sell at the top. Bear Market is a sharply depressed and gloomy market.

GLOSSARY

BEARER BOND. Can be cashed by anyone since its owners name is not registered on it. Made payable to *holder* of bond. Opposite of *registered bond.*

BEAR RAID. A now-outlawed technique whereby aggressive short sellers attempt to drive out the bulls in a particular stock, or in the market, and force liquidation in overextended margin accounts. If successful, this maneuver enabled the bears to cover their short positions profitably at much lower prices.

BEAR SQUEEZE. An upswing in price of a stock at a time when bears are going short, forcing the bears to close out their short sales at a loss. Sometimes results in a *corner,* if the bears can't buy any shares to cover their short positions. Another old Wall Street adage: "He who sells what isn't his'n, buys it back or goes to prison." The panic that ensues when bears cannot buy back stock to cover their short positions generally results in arbitration, and a cash settlement.

BEATING THE GUN. A prohibited practice in which an order is accepted for a new issue before the SEC approves the prospectus. Also, the illegal issuance of significant publicity which can affect the public interest in a new issue before the Commission approves the prospectus.

BEST EFFORTS UNDERWRITING. A new issue accepted by an underwriter on consignment. He sells as much as he can, deducts his commission and gives the proceeds to the issuing company.

BETA. Volatility of a stock price or portfolio value measured against the market and signified by a term or symbol (the Greek letter B). Beta measurements are increasingly used in the stock market by analysts.

BIG BOARD. Nickname for the New York Stock Exchange, so called because it is the largest stock exchange in the world.

BLACK FRIDAY. Refers to Friday, September 24, 1869 when financiers Jay Gould and James Fisk, Jr. failed in their attempt to corner the gold market. While gold prices were soaring due to their maneuver, the United States Treasury entered the market, bought $4 million of its own bonds with gold and destroyed the corner. Gold collapsed, and some speculators committed suicide.

BLOCK. A large holding of a particular stock, usually at least 10,000 shares, traded at one time.

BLOW OFF. A short, extremely heavy buying phase which takes place after an extended rise in the price of a stock.

BLUE CHIP. An acknowledged leader in a field. Blue Chip issues normally carry very high price/earnings ratios, and take a long time to reach their important status.

BLUE LIST. List of municipal bond offerings.

BLUE SKY LAWS. State laws instituted to protect investors against securities salesmen offering nothing of value, only "blue sky." First state to introduce such a law was Kansas, in 1911.

BOARD ROOM. Customers' room in a brokerage house.

BOILER ROOM. A room from which high-pressure salesmen try to sell securities by telephone. Also called a "bucket shop." Salesmen work from telephone directories or "sucker lists." Bucket-shop operators say the best sucker lists are composed of doctors.

BOND. A debt instrument, as opposed to stock, (which is equity) in a company. An I.O.U. of a corporation or government agency, whereby the issuer promises to pay interest to the holder until the face amount, or *principal,* is paid off at maturity. Bondholders are creditors of the company, and must be paid even if assets of the company have to be sold to make good on the debt.

BORROWED STOCK. The stock borrowed by a broker to cover a short selling contract assumed by a customer.

BREAK-UP VALUE. The per share liquidation value, generally applied to the assets of an investment fund or holding company.

BREADTH OF MARKET INDEX. Measures how widespread changes are in security prices.

BROAD MARKET. Increased stock activity, featuring trading in a large number of securities, higher volume and more participation by the general public, instead of institutions.

BROAD TAPE. The Dow Jones newswire, which prints important financial news five days a week from 8 A.M. to 6 P.M. or later. The machine is most often located in a broker's office, but banned from the trading floor of the New York Stock Exchange, since immediate news would give floor traders unfair advantage over the public.

BROKER'S LOANS. Also called "margin loans," this is money borrowed by a broker (usually from banks) to finance underwritings, and

his own loans to customers who are buying "on margin."

BULL. One who is strongly optimistic about the market. Bull market is a sharply advancing market, usually backed by improving corporate earnings, increased speculation.

BUSINESS BAROMETERS. Discussed in Chapter 4, these are widely used forecasting indexes, such as prices, employment levels, profit margins.

BUSINESS CYCLE. Economic theory holds that business regularly goes through phases of prosperity, recession, depression, and recovery. The entire series comprises a cycle.

BUTTONWOOD TREE. On May 17, 1792 a group of 24 brokers met in front of what is now 69 Wall Street, under a buttonwood (sycamore) tree and founded what became The New York Stock Exchange. A plaque now marks the spot.

CALL. An option to buy a stock which the call purchaser thinks will rise. The contract calls for a fixed price and a fixed period of time—usually 30, 60, or 90 days. If the call purchaser does not exercise his call, he loses his total investment.

CALLABLE FEATURE. A feature written into some bond and preferred stock agreements whereby the company can buy in the issue before the due date, even against the wishes of the holder of the security. Companies often refinance this way when interest rates drop sharply, and they can reduce their interest charges by calling in a high-interest security. The call may provide a premium above redemption price which varies according to the number of years left to maturity.

CALL LOAN. No fixed maturity date or interest rate. Payable on demand of either lender or borrower.

CAPITAL. (1) In narrowest sense, the dollar value of the various stock issues carried in the paid-in surplus account; (2) in accounting, the term is synonymous with net worth and refers to the excess of assets over liabilities; (3) in economics, capital refers to the machinery with which to manufacture goods.

CAPITAL ASSETS. Fixed assets.

CAPITAL EXPENDITURES. Outlays of cash or equivalent to improve capital assets. The level of such spending depends upon management optimism and is a requisite before overall economic expansion.

CAPITALIZATION. The aggregate of the company's equity securities and long-term debt. A short-term obligation, due to be paid in less than a year, is considered a current liability, but it is a question of judgment as to whether shortish-term obligations not due for payment within 12 months should be treated as part of the capitalization.

CAPITAL STRUCTURE. The composition and division of the capitalization among bonds, preferred stock and common stock. Where common stock represents nearly all the capitalization, the structure is conservative; where common stock is a small part of the structure, and debt is heavy, the structure is speculative, or "leveraged."

CAPITALIZING EXPENDITURES. Some expenditures can be written off immediately, or, if management wishes, written off over the pre-sumed life of the asset. When it is written off over a period longer than a year, it is "capitalized" and does not impact current year's earnings nearly as heavily as if it were "expensed out" that year. Research and development costs, capitalized until recent accounting rules changes forbade the practice, are now expensed, and some technology companies have not shown earnings since the change.

CAPITAL GAIN. Profit from the sale of a capital asset, such as securities or real estate, or a corporation. Preferential tax rates are applied to *long-term* capital gains, to encourage investment. Until 1976, the holding period was "more than six months," meaning at least six months and one day. This was changed to "more than *nine* months" in 1977, and to "one year" in 1978.

CAPITAL REQUIREMENTS. Member firms of the New York Stock Exchange must meet Rule 325 of the Exchange, maintaining net capital great enough to service their public business. The rule forbids member firms from having total debt exceeding 15 times their net capital, and also requires these firms doing public business to have at least $100,000 in liquid capital. Member firms are also subject to "haircuts," the market term for a reduction in the value of their stock holdings when valuing them as part of net capital.

CAPITAL MARKETS. Long-term debt markets. (Money markets refer to short-term money instruments.)

CASH FLOW. Net income after taxes, plus depreciation, depletion, amortization, extraordinary charges to reserves. An important figure, because it measures the company's real ability to pay dividends. A company which is reporting modest earnings can still pay a large dividend if income pouring into the corporate treasury is great because large amounts are being written off without tax impact (explained in Chapter 5).

CATS AND DOGS. Wall Street expression meaning very speculative stocks, generally low-priced and non-dividend bearing. Some Cats and Dogs ultimately turn out to be big winners.

CEDE & CO. Nominee name for New York Stock Exchange member firms who are part of the Central Certificate Service and who put part or all of their "street name" accounts in this program. When instituted, some public companies thought they were being raided as Cede suddenly began showing up as a large holder and buyer of stock.

CERTIFICATE OF DEPOSIT (called CD's). Time deposits of $100,000 to $1,000,000 or more on which commercial banks pay interest. CD's are money market instruments, and are frequently found in short-term portfolios.

CHARTIST. A Wall Street technician who believes charts of the market and individual stocks can point to accumulation, possible break-outs, and resistance points. A fundamentalist, in contrast, believes in the underlying earning power of the company and its balance sheet, more than in technical responses to the stock.

CHEAP MONEY. Low-interest rate, and easily borrowed.

CHURNING. An illegal practice whereby some brokers buy and sell customer securities to create more commissions for themselves. Also, when applied to market as a whole, connotes aimless buying and selling, with no progress being made.

CLIMAX. End of an extended movement—up or down—in the general market or in an individual stock, generally accompanied by heavy trading. Also called blow off, if a *buying* climax.·

CLOSED-END FUND. An investment company which does not offer new shares continuously, nor redeedm them on demand. Its capital, therefore, remains relatively fixed. Its shares sell on the open market at prices which reflect a combination of investor interest and the true net asset value, although, at times, many have sold considerably below liquidation value of their marketable securities. An Open-end Fund (or Mutual Fund) sells shares continuously, and the value is determined each day by the closing prices of the assets behind each outstanding share.

COMMERCIAL PAPER. The short-term promissory notes issued by well-known corporations who are seeking interim funds, normally from 30 to 270 days, and in denominations generally above $100,000. Companies usually sell this paper through dealers, although some large finance companies handle their own sales directly.

COMMON STOCK. Share representing ownership (equity) in a corporation. Each share represents a proportionate percentage interest in the number of *outstanding* shares of common stock. In liquidation, owners of common shares receive what is left after all debts are paid and the preferred shareholders (if any) are taken care of.

CONGLOMERATE. A corporation which has diversified through the acquisition of properties in unrelated industries.

CONVERSION PARITY. The price at which the conversion value of a bond equals the current market price of the common stock into which it is convertible.

CONVERTIBLE BOND. A bond which permits the holder, at his option, to convert into shares of the common stock of the company at a fixed price for the common. Some preferred stocks also have convertible features.

COOLING OFF PERIOD. The 30-day period required by the SEC before a new issue becomes effective.

CORNER. Occurs when a person or group has acquired control over the price of a stock through ownership of much of the issue. Short sellers are badly injured when this happens.

CORRECTION. A technical (chartist) term much used to mean an adjustment in the market, or in a stock, during which it loses some of its recent gain.

CROSS. The execution of both sides of a brokerage transaction, with one broker handling both the buy and sell for his customers.

CURRENT DELIVERY. The month specified for delivery in a futures contract.

CURRENT RATIO. Ratio of current assets to current liabilities in a balance sheet. Indicates ability to meet current debt.

CYCLICAL STOCKS. Those which move directly with the business cycle, advancing as business improves, declining as business falls. Such basic industry stocks as steel, chemical, textile, and machinery groups are in this category.

DEBENTURE. A debt instrument backed only by the issuing corporation's general credit. (As opposed to a *bond,* which is backed by collateral such as plant and equipment or real estate—although Wall Street people usually use "bond" to mean either a bond or a debenture.)

DEFENSIVE STOCKS. Quality, seasoned companies, generally slow-trading and unattractive to active traders. Can withstand selling in bad markets. Such groups as food and utilities fall in this category.

DEFLATION. An economics term denoting price reductions, contraction in business loans, curtailment in consumer spending. More goods can be purchased for the same dollar during such periods.

DELAYED OPENING. An unusual accumulation of overnight buy or sell orders for a specific security often results in a delay by the specialist in opening the stock for trading so that he can bring the buying and selling into some semblance of order.

DE-LIST. The removal of a company's securities from listing on an exchange, generally caused by consistent deficits in earnings over a period of years, or too few shareholders or shares outstanding or some other violation of the listing agreement.

DEPRECIATION. The write-off of the cost of an asset over the useful life.

DILUTION. Occurs when a company issues new shares more rapidly than the growth in total earnings.

DISCOUNT RATE. Also called the "rediscount rate." Federal Reserve Bank interest charge to member banks. Higher discount rates generally lead to lower securities prices.

DISPOSABLE PERSONAL INCOME. Personal income, after Federal, state, and local taxes.

DISTRIBUTION. In speculative markets, distribution occurs near the top of a price climb when insiders and other astute investors begin to sell. Good indications that distribution is occurring are failure of the market (or a specific stock) to react to good news, and quick up and down movements in the market (or in a specific stock) accompanied by high volume.

DIVESTITURE. Disposing of a business or part of it, sometimes required of major companies by the FTC.

DIVIDEND. A disbursement of a portion of earnings, distributed to stockholders in proportion to their holdings. Dividends are declared on a *per share* basis, so that the stockholder multiplies the disbursement rate by the number of shares he owns.

DOW JONES AVERAGES. Explained more fully on page 113, there are four Averages—the industrial (composed of 30 stocks), the transportation (20 issues), utilities (15 companies) and a composite average of those 65 stocks. Usually when it is said that the Averages were up, it is meant that the 30 industrials rose on average.

DOW THEORY. Originated by the late Charles H. Dow, cofounder of the *Wall Street Journal,* the Dow Theory presumes that there are three movements occurring simultaneously in the stock market: the *primary* movement, which runs for at least a year and is the basic undercurrent—up or down; the *secondary* movement, which displays sharp rallies in a market and sharp declines in a primary *bull* market; and the tertiary movement, which consists of day-to-day fluctuations. Followers of the theory have worked out a sophisticated set of corollary circumstances where primary and secondary moves work in concert and confirm each other, and many variations. The Dow Jones Averages are used in these analyses.

DUAL FUND. A recent innovation. A closed-end investment company which sells two classes of stock: income shares, giving the company's portfolio income to holders of this class; and capital shares, whose holders receive no income during the life of the income shares, but at the conclusion own the portfolio.

DUAL LISTING. Listing of a security on more than one stock exchange.

EARNED SURPLUS (or SURPLUS). Net profit after dividends, placed in the surplus account, from which it is disbursed into other accounts, such as inventory, assets, cash, and so on.

EARNINGS PER SHARE. Computed by dividing net income after taxes and dividends on preferred stock, if any, by number of common shares outstanding.

EQUIPMENT TRUST. A trust agreement for the purchase and lease of railroad equipment, which represents an ownership interest in the property, not just a claim.

EQUIPMENT TRUST CERTIFICATES. Issued by transportation companies to finance equipment purchase, also represent ownership in the property.

EQUITY. On a corporate basis, the combined ownership interests of preferred and common stockholders. At a brokerage house, equity refers to the excess value of securities above the debit balance in a *margin account*.

EXCHANGE OF SECURITIES. Usually the result of a merger, the securities of one corporation are turned in and exchanged for those of another corporate entity.

EX-DIVIDEND. Without dividend. The buyer of a stock is entitled to the most recently declared, but not yet distributed, dividend until such date as the stock goes "Ex-dividend." On that day, the stock price should theoretically decline to reflect the dividend.

EXPIRATION DATE. The date on which rights, options or warrants expire.

EX-RIGHTS. The rights have been retained or exercised by the seller.

EXTRACTIVE INDUSTRY. One which uses up natural resources. Oil, timber, and coal are examples.

FACE VALUE. Value of a bond stated on the security. Has nothing to do with market value.

FEDERAL RESERVE ACT. Signed into law by President Wilson on December 23, 1913, establishing the Federal Reserve System. The 12 Federal Reserve Banks (see Chapter 4) are responsible for the orderly flow of credit and money.

FIFO. The standard method of determining the value of inventory on hand, the First-In, First-Out method assumes that the first items purchased are the first sold. Accelerates earnings in periods of rapid price increases. (See LIFO: Last-In, First-Out.)

FINDER'S FEE. Fee paid to a third party who brings two companies or parties together.

FISCAL YEAR. The 12-month period chosen by a company as the basis for computing and reporting earnings. Merchandising companies often select a noncalendar-year date, such as January 31, to facilitate inventory taking after peak season.

FLUSH PRODUCTION. Large production yielded by new oil wells.

FIRM COMMITMENT OFFERING. An offering of stock where the underwriter assumes the full risk of selling the issue. Still, there are many ways out—the market can be poor, company earnings can decline.

FLOAT. (1) To sell, or "float," an issue of stock. (2) The number of outstanding shares of a company not held by directors, management, friends, and relatives and presumed to be available for trading at current market prices.

FROZEN ASSETS. Assets which cannot easily be converted into cash.

FUNDAMENTALIST. As opposed to the "technical" analyst, the fundamentalist arrives at his investment decisions by analyzing business conditions, earning power, company performance.

FUNDED DEBT. Long-term indebtedness of a corporation. This contrasts with *floating debt,* due within one year.

GTC. (Good 'til cancelled.) An order to sell a stock which is valid, or good, until cancelled.

GARAGE. Nickname for the New York Stock Exchange annex, where six of the 22 trading posts are located. The Blue Room is that part of the annex where an additional four posts are located.

GENERAL OBLIGATION BOND. The largest category of municipal bonds, these securities are backed by the "full faith, credit and taxing power" of the municipality.

GINNIE MAE. Nickname for the Government National Mortgage Association, since 1970 a corporate instrument of the United States, supervised by the Secretary of Housing and Urban Development. Ginnie Mae refinances certain aspects of other government agencies, and is gaining investment favor as a special type of bond.

GLAMOUR STOCK. A very popular issue, especially one which has risen steadily in price. Also called a go-go stock.

GOING CONCERN. The value of a company on an operating basis, taking into account its earnings prospects rather than its liquidating value.

GO LONG. Buy a stock for investment. Opposite of go short.

GOOD WILL. Intangible asset allegedly reflecting an advantage in earning power accruing to a company—such as a brand name, strategic plant location, or good management. As a result, a buyer of the business may indeed pay more than book value because of the good will.

GO PUBLIC. Selling securities to the public, usually a first issue.

GO SHORT. Opposite of go long. Selling a stock not owned by the seller, who hopes to buy it back at a lower price in the future.

GROSS NATIONAL PRODUCT. Total market value of all goods and services sold in the year by the nation.

GROWTH STOCK. Analysts consider a growth stock one whose earnings have increased annually at a compounded rate of 15% for at least five years, and has the prospect of continuing. Many growth stocks pay little or no dividends, re-investing all earnings in the assets needed to propel growth in the future. Investors often are generous in awarding a high price-earnings multiplier to these issues.

HAIRCUT. Securities used by member firms of the New York Stock Exchange in connection with their capital requirements are reduced in value before being counted—given a "haircut."

HEDGE. To offset the impact of unexpected price movements, generally in commodities, commitments are hedged through both purchase and sale agreements.

HEDGE FUND. A fund which not only goes long, but sells short.

HIGH FLYERS. Go-go stocks. Volatile and generally speculative.

HI-LO INDEX. This index maintains a moving average of New York

Stock Exchange listings which each day hit new highs and lows. Indicates when the Dow Jones Averages are being kept at high levels by blue chips, with deterioration taking place in secondary issues.

HOT ISSUE. A new issue very much in demand.

HOT MONEY. Short-term funds shifting quickly from country to country seeking higher interest rates and faster profits.

HOLDING COMPANY. A corporation which owns completely or has majority control of the stock of several or more subsidiary companies.

INACTIVE STOCK. One in which there is little trading, perhaps a few hundred shares per week.

INCOME ACCOUNT. The profit and loss statement.

INCOME BOND. A bond whose payout of interest is contingent upon earnings.

INDENTURE. A legal document or contract outlining the terms under which a specific bond is issued.

INDUSTRIAL REVENUE BONDS. Issued by a municipality or other governmental body to raise funds for the construction of facilities to be used by an industrial corporation, and secured by lease payments on the facilities.

INFLATION. A business cycle term denoting a period of abnormally high and rising prices, concomitant with a decrease in purchasing power of money and soaring costs and wages. In such a period, prices are high relative to values. Opposite of deflation.

INSIDER. One who has knowledge of important events or information that, if broadly released, will likely affect the valuation of the company's securities. Significant SEC rulings affect the way insiders conduct themselves (see Chapter 7) and regulations have been extended to include tippees, those who *receive* unreleased news from insiders.

INSIDER REPORT. The monthly report filed with the SEC by officers, directors and large stockholders (10% or more) of listed corporations. Gives a quick view of what insiders think about their company's prospects, although often individuals sell for personal reasons.

INSTALLMENT BOND. In such issues, principal is paid in installments, rather than in lump sum at maturity.

INSTITUTION. In financial terms, refers to a large pool of capital controlled by an organization, generally for purposes of investing, rather than assets in control of an individual. Banks, mutual funds and insurance companies are examples of institutions which invest in securities.

INTERIM REPORT. A report issued quarterly or semiannually to shareholders.

INTERNATIONAL BANK FOR RECONSTRUCTION AND DEVELOPMENT (World Bank). Consists of 110 member nations. The Bank guarantees and participates in loans, issues long-term bonds with the purpose of helping improve trade and living standards of member countries.

INTERPOSITIONING. An illegal act under securities law, this is a make-work arrangement whereby a brokerage intermediary is inserted between two principal firms simply to create another commission for the intermediary.

IN THE BLACK. Operating at a profit, as opposed to "In the Red," operating at a loss.

INTRADAY HIGH AND LOW. The highest and lowest price achieved by a stock or the market on any particular day under review. Chartists pay special attention to such statistics.

INTRASTATE SECURITIES. Stocks issued and distributed only within a state, and subject at first to the state attorney general's office.

INVERTED MARKET. Refers to commodity futures markets where near-term contracts sell at higher prices than contracts due many months from now.

INVESTMENT ADVISERS ACT OF 1940. An SEC act which extends to investment advisers the responsibility to conduct business with the same standards as those who conform to the earlier Acts of 1933 and 1934.

INVESTMENT BANKERS. Financial specialists who help companies raise money, either through negotiations with banks and other financial institutions, or through underwritings, which they themselves might undertake. Some investment bankers price a deal, negotiate it and offer it to other underwriters.

ISSUE PRICE. The price at which an underwriter offers a new issue of securities.

JOINT VENTURE. A new organization established by two going con-

cerns to develop a third enterprise, partially owned by each.

JUNIOR SECURITIES. An issue whose claims are subordinate to those of a senior security, such as a bond subordinate to another bond; second mortgages are subordinate to first mortgages and in liquidation common shares are junior to preferred.

KITING. An illegal act related to pushing stocks to unnatural levels. Also, borrowing money from a bank to pay off a debt to another bank.

KNOW YOUR CUSTOMER RULE. Rule 405 of the New York Stock Exchange under which members are occasionally prosecuted. Members must know the financial condition and other pertinent facts about their customers so they can advise them prudently, and partners must diligently supervise all accounts.

LATE TAPE. Occurs when trading is so heavy that the exchange ticker tape cannot print the sales rapidly enough to keep up with the action.

LEGAL LIST. Some institutions are forbidden by their own indentures to invest in certain types of securities, and therefore invest only in those on their legal list.

LEASEHOLD IMPROVEMENTS. The cost of improving a property which is being leased from an owner. The improvements normally belong to the owner at the end of the lease period, and their cost is amortized over the period of the lease.

LETTER STOCK. (Also called "legend" stock). Securities which have not been registered for sale with the SEC, and which have restrictions stamped on their face. Insider's stock—that of management and directors—is letter stock (purchased under terms of an "investment" letter) and, with the exception of Rule 144 sales, must be registered to be sold. Rule 144 permits each insider to sell each six months stock equivalent to 1% of the total capitalization of the company, but not more than the average trading in the three weeks preceeding the sale. Some institutions in the late 1960s were badly hurt by the then new practice of purchasing letter stock from insiders at sharp discounts from market price, because the market declined badly in many of these securities by the time the institutions were legally able to register and sell the shares.

LEVERAGE. Augmenting the common equity through the addition of fixed obligations; there is no leverage involved if a company only has common shares outstanding. In an expanding business, leverage can be advantageous to common stockholders since the return on borrowed funds is greater than the interest charges, and accrues to the benefit of the owners of the company; in situations where earnings are stable or deteriorating, leverage hurts the common shareowner, because it diminishes his opportunity for increased dividends, since interest charges must be paid first.

LIFO. Last-In, First-Out method of evaluating inventory, it levels out reported earnings by minimizing inventory profits and losses, and therefore reduces tax impact. The most recently acquired items are charged against sales. (See FIFO.)

LIQUID ASSETS. Money, inventory or other property which can be quickly converted into cash. Also called quick assets.

LOADING CHARGE. The premium above net asset value charged by open-end investment funds on the sale of new shares. Used to cover selling costs.

LIQUIDATION. In a market sense, panic selling accompanied by heavy volume, with prices being pounded down. In a corporate sense, the dissolution of a business and conversion of its assets to cash. In the commodities market, the term refers to the sale of a previously purchased contract, or the *repurchase* of a stopped contract to cover a short position.

LIQUIDITY. A term related to the market's ability—or that of a single stock—to absorb selling without sharp price changes.

LISTED SECURITIES. Those securities which have been accepted for trading on various stock exchanges, and have passed the listing requirements. Some exchanges are much less rigorous in their requirements than others. Being listed does not guarantee dividends, or the worth of a security—only that information will be forthcoming on a regular basis, generally quarterly.

LOAN PRICE. The cost of a government loan to growers under price support programs.

LOANED STOCK. Securities which have been loaned to a short seller, or his broker acting on his behalf, to meet the terms of his short selling contract.

LONG-TERM. Under the Tax Reform Act of 1976, the long-term capital gain tax calls for a holding period of "more than nine months" in 1977 (as opposed to "more than six" previously) and in 1978 became "more than 12 months." The six-months-plus-one-day rule remains applicable for commodities futures transactions.

LOT. The unit of trading in the stock market. A round lot is 100 shares, an odd lot less than that. Some brokers charge an additional commission for handling an odd-lot purchase or sale. See odd-lot index.

MAJORITY STOCKHOLDERS. Holders of more than 50% of the shares of a company. With stocks broadly distributed throughout the country, and held in many small accounts, control of a company can be maintained with far less than 50%. In very large companies, with millions of shares and tens of thousands of shareholders, effective control can be had by an incumbent management holding as little as 5% to 10%, although for practical purposes in medium-sized situations control requires 30 to 35%.

MAKING A MARKET. An over-the-counter dealer makes a market in a security when he is willing to put up his own money to inventory a stock against the time that he can sell it. With the decline of the over-the-counter market in the early 1970s, many smaller companies found it difficult—sometimes impossible—to find market makers, and consequently their shareholders discovered they had limited marketability. Stocks with fewer market makers generally sell at lower price/earnings ratios than those with greater visibility and marketability, and therefore corporate managements consider an important part of their job to be the consistent release of honest information to keep market makers, specialists (if listed), stockholders, bankers and journalists apprised of corporate developments.

MARGIN. The amount of money or value of securities put up by a client to finance part of the cost of listed securities, or those over-the-counter securities approved for margin by the Federal Reserve Board. The Fed sets the margin rate (at times as high as 90%, currently at 50%.)

MARGIN CALL. When a margined stock declines in price, the broker may find it necessary to require additional cash or securities to bring the value of the account up to the current margin rate.

MARKET AVERAGES. Those indexes used to give a quick picture of the current stock market. They are very sensitive to news, and mirror public sentiment rather than reality, although at times these are consistent. The more important averages are the four Dow Jones indexes, Standard & Poor's 500-Stock Price Index, the New York Stock Exchange Index and the American Stock Exchange Index.

MARKET LETTERS. The reports issued by brokerage firms or investment advisers offering their current opinions on various stocks and industries.

MERGER. The amalgamation of two or more companies into a single company.

MONEY MANAGER. One who manages investment portfolios. Generally an analyst, who does his own investigation of companies, buys research from other sources as well, and works independently or is affiliated with a brokerage house.

MORTGAGE. A lien on the fixed property of a company.

MUTUAL FUND. An investment company which sells its own shares to the public and uses the funds thus raised to invest in the securities of other public companies. Types of funds include: closed-end, dual fund, closed-end fund, growth fund, hedge fund, no-load, performance, among others.

NARROW MARKET (also called a "thin" market.) Low volume, modest changes in price.

NATIONAL ASSOCIATION OF SECURITIES DEALERS (NASD). An association of over-the-counter brokers and dealers, with its own automated quotation system (NASDAQ) which permits members to quote many issues currently.

NATIONAL SECURITY TRADERS ASSOCIATION. A trade organization for over-the-counter dealers.

NEAR-TERM. In Wall Street parlance, a two-month period or less. Same as short-term (although for tax purposes, starting in 1978 short-term is anything up to 12 months).

NEGOTIATED OFFERING. Negotiated offering creates a price for an issue determined by the investment banker and the company; as opposed to a competitive bid, where the best offer wins. Rarely done on equity deals, but bidding is common on debt issues.

NET ASSET VALUE. Investment companies compute their net asset value once or twice daily by subtracting all liabilities from the current asset value of securities in the portfolio, then dividing by the number of shares outstanding in the investment company itself. Important since many mutual fund shares are sold at net asset value plus commission.

NET EARNINGS. Profits available for dividends (but not necessarily disbursed this way) after deducting operating costs, charges and interest. Distinction must be made between earnings before taxes and earnings after taxes, the latter figure being the one on which a price/earnings multiplier is fixed.

NET WORTH. Assets minus liabilities, equal to capital and earned surplus.

NONCUMULATIVE DIVIDEND. One which does not accrue if the regular payment is missed.

NON-MEMBER FIRM. A brokerage house which is not a member of the New York Stock Exchange, but which executes buy and sell orders of listed securities in what is known as the *third market*. (The exchanges represent the first market, over-the-counter the second, and exchange-listed stocks selling OTC the third). Commissions charged in third-market trades are generally less than on the exchanges.

NON-RECURRENT EXPENSE. An unusual corporate cost not likely to be repeated. Example, expenses caused by a flood. Some companies, however, seem to have a new example of a non-recurrent expense every year to explain a lack of earnings. Wall Street jesters call these "recurring non-recurring expenses."

NON-VOTING STOCK. Any class of stock other than voting. The New York Stock Exchange since 1926 has refused to list non-voting shares, with the exception in 1970 of A.T.&T. warrants.

NO-PAR STOCK. A stock without an assigned dollar value per share. See par value.

OBSOLESCENCE. The reduction in value of a capital asset caused by new developments.

ODD LOT. Less than 100 shares of a stock.

ODD-LOT BROKER. One who specializes in executing orders for less than 100 share lots, working on behalf of other brokers and maintaining no contact of his own with the public.

ODD-LOT INDEX. An index used to measure public psychology, arrived at by dividing total odd-lot sales by odd-lot purchases on a ten-day moving average. When sales are greater than purchases, it indicates public is pessimistic. When purchases outweigh sales, the reverse is true. Professional wisdom holds that the public is always wrong, and that when the odd-lot index indicates confidence, it is time for the professional to sell. In a way this is less unflattering than it seems, since it is only an updating of an axiom attributed at various times to the Rothchilds' and at other times to Bernard Baruch: Buy stocks when nobody wants them, and sell them when they do. *This is also called the theory of contrary opinion.*

OPTION. A contract to buy or sell a security at a specific price within a stated period of time. Company executives are often given options on common stock, exercisable over ten years at current prices, as an incentive.

OPTION WRITER. An investor, usually with a larger portfolio, who allows a broker to sell options against his portfolio in exchange for a commission. Sometimes the purchaser of the option sees a good rise in the stock and exercises the option; at other times, he allows the option to lapse, leaving the writer intact.

OUT-THE-WINDOW. A new issue which has sold quickly.

OVERBOUGHT. A technician's term meaning the stock market is too high, responding to aggressive buying and creating a price/earnings multiplier inconsistent with historic ratios. The opposite of *Oversold.*

OVERCAPITALIZED. A situation which exists when a company has too much cash in the bank, or sitting in unused plant. The stockholder could get a higher return on invested capital if management would properly use some of the funds in a profitable venture. There is a thin line between business caution and overconservatism, and a good manager has to be prudent while using assets to the best advantage.

OVER-THE-COUNTER (OTC). The oldest and largest securities market, this is where all new issues are initially traded. Some major companies prefer having their stocks trade in a dealer market, rather than an auction market, and thus never seek a listing on an exchange.

PAINTING THE TAPE. Constant

trading in and out, which causes excitement as the ticker tape records the apparent increasing volume of the trades. An illegal maneuver.

PAPER PROFITS. A gain in a security not yet translated into cash. Wall Streeters caution against "living on your paper profits." Noted Special Situations Analyst Raphael Yavneh once wrote, "Don't count your investment chickens until they've shelled out."

PAR. The dollar amount assigned to a share of stock by the founders, originally computed by dividing the paid-in capital by the number of shares first issued. Nowadays, few companies do this, most assigning an arbitrary value since transfer taxes are computed on the par value. In bonds, par is the face value, usually $1000 per bond.

PARTICIPATING BOND (it is also known as a "profit-sharing bond"). A bond which carries both a minimum fixed interest rate, and the enforceable right to a share of profits (unlike "income" bonds where the maximum rate of interest is fixed but contingent upon earnings).

PENNY STOCKS. Extremely speculative stocks selling below $1.

PINK SHEETS. Pink quotation sheets distributed daily to over-the-counter houses in which dealers give indications of buy and sell interest in specific over-the-counter stocks.

POINT. Stocks and bond movements are measured in points. In stocks, one point is $1 (and stocks sell at ⅛ fractions, equivalent to 12½ cents. A stock selling at 10⅜ is selling for $10.375). In bonds, one point is usually $10 (a bond moving up a point, from 90 to 91, really is moving from $900 to $910).

POINT-AND-FIGURE CHART. A method of charting securities prices. Technicians consider the point and figure chart a basic tool in forecasting further price movement in a stock.

POOL. A group of persons who put their effort behind a stock to move it up or down. Now outlawed.

PORTFOLIO. The group of diversified securities owned by an institution or individual.

PRE-EMPTIVE RIGHT. The right of a stockholder to purchase additional shares of a company in which he is a shareholder, before the new issues offered to the general public. Few companies give this privilege to shareholders although it was once common. A shareholder can generally sell his right if he does not wish to exercise it.

PRICE-EARNINGS RATIO. Market price divided by current annual earnings per share. To be significant, it has to be measured against the multipliers of competitors, the stock market as a whole and against the historic multiplier of the particular company being assessed. One must also look at the current condition of the company since a low multiplier, by historic standards, may simply reflect the fact that company prospects are now poor.

PRIMARY OFFERING. The sale of stock for the account of the company. The sale for insiders is considered a "Secondary." A first-time primary is an "initial" offering of stock.

PRIVATE PLACEMENT. The sale of shares to an institution or a few large individual investors.

PRO FORMA. The accounting treatment obtained by putting together two financial statements to see how the combination would look—or would have looked had it been in effect in a prior period. (It is referred to as a "giving effect" statement—giving effect to the possibility of a merger of the two companies.)

PROSPECTUS. Selling pamphlet containing information filed with the Securities and Exchange Commission. The sale of securities cannot take place until the effective date listed on the prospectus. Earlier versions leading up to the one approved by the SEC are called "Red Herrings," and each prospect who has received a Red Herring must receive a final prospectus, even if he is not interested in buying the stock.

PROXY STATEMENT. An informational brochure which must be sent to shareholders when soliciting their written vote on some corporate matter, most often the election of officers at the annual meeting.

PRUDENT MAN RULE. Varies from state to state, but essentially requires trustees and other fiduciaries to invest only in securities on the *legal list* or in a security which a prudent man would find acceptable. Makes it virtually impossible for institutions to invest in small growth companies which carry great risk, but possibly offer great rewards.

PUTS AND CALLS. Options which give the holder the right to trade a certain amount of stock at a fixed price in a given period of time. The holder of a *put* has the right to "put" the stock to the person named in the contract at the price mentioned, and the holder of the *call* has the right to "call" the stock away from the owner according to the terms of the agreement.

PYRAMIDING. A dangerous but legal practice whereby some speculators put up unrealized paper profits as additional margin to buy still more securities or commodities. In corporate finance, pyramiding refers to the practice of creating a highly leveraged capital structure through holding companies, whereby a small amount of voting stock in the parent controls a large conglomeration of companies and assets.

QUICK ASSETS. Current assets excluding inventories. Generally, the cash or other liquid portion of the current asset category. The quick ratio—quick assets to current liabilities—helps lenders appraise a credit risk.

QUANTITATIVE AND QUALITATIVE FACTORS (in securities analysis). Quantitative refers to items which can be stated in figures, such as earnings and balance sheet position, various key ratios; qualitative refers to intangible considerations, such as management capabilities, company's penetration of market for its key products and labor conditions.

RAID. An attempt to gain control of another company against the wishes of the incumbent management.

REGISTRATION STATEMENT. The information form which a corporation files with the Securities and Exchange Commission.

RECAPITALIZATION. A type of reorganization calling for the exchange of the outstanding capital stock of a company for a new issue, possibly of a different type, with different covenants.

RECEIVERSHIP. The state of being delivered to a receiver, a court appointed representative who will reorganize or liquidate a sick or dying company.

RECORD DATE. The date by which a stockholder's name must be on the books of a company for him to be entitled to receive the most recent dividend, and to have rights to vote on corporate activities.

RED HERRING. A preliminary prospectus.

REGISTRAR. A bank or trust company which maintains the shareholder list and prevents the issuance and distribution of unauthorized shares. See Transfer Agent.

REGULATED INVESTMENT COMPANY. One which, under the tax law, can avoid income tax on ordinary income and capital gains by acting as a conduit and distributing these profits to shareholders as dividends.

REGULATION T AND Q. Regulation T of the Federal Reserve Board governs the amount of credit that brokers and dealers can advance to clients for purchasing securities on margin. Regulation Q sets maximum interest rates that commercial banks can pay their depositors.

RESISTANCE LEVEL. Chartist's term indicating level where stock has previously encountered selling pressure and above which it has not been able to rise in the past. *Opposite of support level.*

RESTRICTED STOCK. Same as letter stock.

REVERSE SPLIT. Reduction in the number of outstanding shares, resulting in the increase of the price per share but not a change in the percentage ownership by each shareholder. If a stock were selling at $10 and a three-for-one reverse split were declared, a holder of 100 shares would own 33⅓ shares each selling for $30 per share.

ROUND-LOT. One hundred shares or more.

SCRIP CERTIFICATE. Ownership of a fractional share of stock, which may be turned in for cash or converted into a full share when enough scrip is gathered to do so.

SDR's. These SPECIAL DRAWING RIGHTS are used, instead of dollars or gold, to settle international financial transactions and are accepted by central banks as an appropriate substitute for currency and gold.

SEAT. An individual membership on an exchange.

SECURITIES AND EXCHANGE COMMISSION. This is a Government agency created by Congress in 1933 to look after the welfare of investors. See Chapter 7.

SELLING AGAINST THE BOX. A stock market term for a practice used to protect paper profits, while postponing taxes into another year. The owner of a stock sells short, knowing he can deliver the stock at the same price without having to go back into the market to purchase it. *He* is the *box.* Can only be used on a long-term situation; cannot convert short-term to long-term, but can postpone year of taxation.

SELLING CLIMAX. Panic dumping of securities, generally characterizing the final stages of a bear market.

SELLING GROUP. A group of securities dealers brought together by the syndicate department of an underwriting firm to join in the public sale and distribution of a new issue. They are not part of the *management group* handling the sale, and each usually takes only a small part of the issue. The ad ("Tombstone") which announces the successful sale of an issue is generally headed by the management group, the lead underwriter, or underwriters, and then the selling group, alphabetically and by categories indicating their status in the financial community. There is as much jockeying over position in the ad as in the billing awarded to movie stars, and occasionally an underwriter will refuse to participate in the syndicate because he is being listed in a grouping lower in the ad than he thinks he deserves.

SELL SHORT. Sale of a stock which is not owned. Stock is borrowed from a lender, who is protected by being given cash equal to the current value. When the stock is returned (the short position is covered) the cash is given back to the short seller. If the stock has indeed gone down, the short seller is able to acquire it at a lesser price in the open market and has made a profit.

SINKING FUND. The periodic deposit of cash to pay off a debt not due to mature for a number of years.

SHELL. A company which is public but no longer has assets. A *clean* shell has no liabilities. Some privately owned companies which do not need cash occasionally go public through merger into a shell, of which they end up owning the majority position. This saves them legal, accounting, and printing costs, but is considered an unwise move since the shell into which they have merged obviously has disgruntled shareholders and a poor investment image.

SHELF REGISTRATION. A registration, generally by insiders, of some of their stock which will not be offered to the public immediately, but kept current and sold when market conditions are better. Shelf registrations generally make investors nervous, and put a damper on the price of the stock since no one knows when the additional shares will pour into the market and saturate it.

SHORT INTEREST. The total number of shares sold short in expectation of a decline in prices. The short interest figure is carefully scrutinized, because it ultimately can mean buying support for a stock by short sellers who have to cover if the shares start to go up.

SIA. The Securities Industry Association, the professional trade group made up of brokerage and underwriting firms, some banks and insurance companies and executives from various exchanges.

SECURITIES INDUSTRY PROTECTION CORPORATION (SIPC). Agent which provides insurance against brokerage house failure.

SIZE OF THE MARKET. A stock market term which indicates the total number of round-lots bid *at the highest price* now on the specialists book, and the total number offered for sale *at the lowest price,* any given time. Size might be reported back as "eight by two," meaning 800 at the highest bid, versus 200 at the lowest offering.

SPECIAL BID. A bid entered on the floor of the exchange by an institution trying to get a large block of stock. Has to be executed at price equal to or above last transaction.

SPECIALIST. Broker-dealer member of the stock exchange who uses his own cash to buy and sell stocks which he is assigned as a permanent monopoly. He must maintain fair and orderly markets in these stocks, matching bids and offers and using his own cash when required.

SPECIAL OFFERING. The sale of a large block of stock through special exchange approval, so as not to disrupt the market price. The exchange has strict rules about the type of offering and the method.

SPECIAL SITUATIONS. Description given to securities which have the capability of developing large followings and moving sharply upward because of some unusual feature in the company.

SPIN-OFF. The distribution of a portion of a company's assets to its shareholders, as a special dividend. The newly created spin-off is thus a public company on its own. Also, the sale to another company of a division, subsidiary or portion of corporate assets in exchange for shares in the acquiring company.

SPLIT. The division of a corporation's shares into a larger number, generally to improve the "float" or to give the shareholder a stock dividend.

SPONSORSHIP. The term denoting who stands behind an issue, or who is currently strongly in favor and recommending the purchase of the stock. The quality of sponsorship is important in creating support of a stock.

SPREAD. The difference between the bid-and-asked prices.

STAND-BY UNDERWRITING. Used in conjunction with a rights offering. The group or syndicate "standing by" and willing to take that part of the issue not subscribed to by shareholders exercising their rights.

STOCKHOLDER LIST. Alphabetical list of shareholders. Insurgents generally demand this list in preparation for proxy battle, and management seeks court order to prevent it. However, all stockholders are entitled to stockholder lists.

STRADDLE. A double stock-option contract, including one put and one call. It has identical striking prices (the price the stock might be *put*, or *called*), and gives the holder the option of moving in either direction.

STRAP. Combination of two calls and one put. A strategic device. See Strip.

STREET NAME. Securities bought on margin are carried in the name of the broker ("street name").

STRIP. Combination of two puts and one call. See Strap.

SUBSIDIARY. A company controlled by another corporation, usually a parent company. Subsidiaries operate more formally than do divisions, sometimes having their own board of directors and independent financing capabilities.

SUPPORT LEVEL. A chartist's term denoting the price range where buying has historically come in to support the stock.

SUSPEND TRADING. An indefinite halt in the trading of a listed security.

TAPE READING. Ability to sense price movements from the action on the ticker tape. The good tape reader makes judgments based on price, volume and breadth of market without much regard for fundamental or other technical factors.

TAX-EXEMPT BOND. A government obligation on which interest is tax-free. City and state bonds are generally also free of local taxes.

TAX SELLING. The sale of securities which show a current loss to reduce anticipated taxes. Tax selling is heaviest in November and December, especially in years when the market has been declining and investors have broad losses.

TENDER. A formal offer to shareholders of a company inviting them to sell their shares at a price higher than the current market, for a limited period of time. Sometimes companies make tender offers to their own shareholders to reduce the number of shares outstanding—especially if there are many odd-lot holders, since the cost of servicing owners of less than 100 shares is expensive on a per-share basis (mailing and printing costs of shareholder reports and proxy statements). More frequently, a tender offer is made by an unfriendly raider who wants to take over the company, and the initial tender offer is the beginning of a proxy battle and legal entanglements.

THIN MARKET. Volatile market where price fluctuations are wide, generally because there are not enough shares outstanding to make an orderly market. The "float" is thin.

TICKER SYMBOLS. Each listed security has its own symbol (any brokerage house will give you the list) so that abbreviations can be printed on the ticker, speeding up the dissemination of trading information. American Telephone & Telegraph, the most widely owned common stock, is represented by the letter "T."

TIME DEPOSITS. Money on deposit at a bank, withdrawable at the end of a short period of time, instead of on demand.

TREASURY STOCK. The unissued or repurchased stock held in the treasury of a corporation which it can issue for additional funds or for an acquisition. The amount available for this purpose is determined by checking the balance sheet surplus statement, and subtracting the number of *outstanding* shares from the number *authorized* for issuance. To issue more than the authorized, management must request permission from shareholders at a stockholders' meeting.

TOMBSTONE. Advertisement placed by an underwriting syndicate in which the syndicate members are listed, plus details of the underwriting.

TRADER'S MARKET. One which moves in a narrow range, generally considered advantageous for a skillful and active trader willing to rake up a series of small profits.

TRANSFER AGENT. Generally a bank, but sometimes a company official, entrusted with holding a corporation's stock certificates and handling the housekeeping associated with cancelling old certificates, mailing new ones to new holders, mailing dividends and various shareholder reports and notices.

TRANSFER TAXES. Taxes paid on the sale and transfer of securities, levied on each share and computed as a percentage of par value, or in some cases as a specific amount per share.

TREASURY BILLS, NOTES AND BONDS. (1) *Treasury bills* are short-term bearer obligations of the United States Government, sold on a discount basis, and redeemed at face value at maturity, without additional interest (minimum $10,000); (2) *treasury notes* are United States Government obligations, paying semiannual interest, maturing in one to seven years and issued in bearer or registered form; and (3) *treasury bonds* are United States Government obligations maturing in more than seven years, paying semi-annual interest, callable at par five years before maturity (and presently constituting the largest segment of the public debt).

TREND LINES. A chartist's term, referring to two straight lines drawn on a chart, one connecting the highest points reached by a stock or a market average, the other connecting the lowest points. They are supposed to indicate the direction in which a stock or the market is heading.

TRIPLE BOTTOM. One of the more frequently quoted technician's terms, a triple bottom supposedly indicates a resistance barrier through which the market or a stock cannot penetrate until conditions change. A triple bottom on a chart is the third time the same level has been reached.

TWO-DOLLAR BROKER. A broker who executes orders for other more busy brokers, or for firms who do not have their own partners on the exchange floor. Although his fee varies with the price of stock, he used to receive $2 per hundred shares.

UNDERWRITER. One who distributes new issues of securities.

UNISSUED STOCK. Authorized shares being retained in the company's treasury for future use.

UNLISTED SECURITIES. Securities which trade over-the-counter.

UNREGISTERED STOCK. Letter stock. Companies occasionally sell blocks in private placement, bypassing the registration process and the cost of an underwriting.

UP TICK. A price higher than the previous sale of a stock. Short sales can only be done on an up tick (called a "plus tick"). Each New York Stock Exchange trading post places a plus or minus sign alongside the last price of each stock traded at that post, throughout the day.

VENTURE CAPITAL. Risk capital, generally involved in start-up businesses and receiving a larger share of capital stock than one would receive in an established company.

VOTING TRUST. An agreement whereby stockholders grant voting rights to a trustee for a fixed period.

The trustees exchange certificates for shares owned by stockholders, and these may be traded as shares are. When the trust ends, the certificates are again exchanged for stock. Voting trusts generally come about as a result of reorganizations.

WALL STREET. A street name which connotes much more—the financial district of New York City, at times almost a generic name for American capitalism. The Dutch originally built a stockade, or wall, along the current Wall Street demarcation. The purpose was to protect against Indian raids and to keep cattle within the confines of lower Manhattan.

WARRANTS. A right to purchase shares of stock in a company, generally with a longer life than ordinary rights. Often attached to other securities to make their sale easier (common stock with warrants attached, bonds with warrants attached), the warrants are detachable and can be sold or exercised independently.

WHEN ISSUED. Securities authorized but not actually issued, occurring sometimes as a result of a stock split or merger. The stock is traded "w.i." which means it will be delivered when in proper form.

WINDOW DRESSING. The process of dressing up the balance sheet just before issuing it to shareholders. Can be done by disposing of unproductive assets and building up cash. Mutual funds are sometimes accused of selling losing investments just before the end of the latest quarterly or annual period, so that their portfolios do not have to show the losers.

WIRE HOUSE. Term refers to a large brokerage house with numerous branch offices and correspondent firms, linked by private communication wires.

WORKING CAPITAL. Current assets minus current liabilities.

YANKEES. The term used for American securities on the London Stock Exchange.

YIELD. Return on an investment, shown as a percentage. Yield is computed by dividing dividend by the market price of the stock to get current yield, or by price paid to get yield on investment.

YIELD TO MATURITY. The return, expressed as an annual rate, received by holding a bond to its maturity, including interest and any deviation from par. Usually requires a bond yield table.

CHAPTER NINE

Reference Sources

Sources of information available to the financial journalist run into the thousands. To simplify and abbreviate this gold mine, the more important reference sources are listed below and divided into three categories: information on companies, industries and individuals.

COMPANIES

1. *SEC Reports.* As indicated in Chapter 7, the eight required and two optional forms filed with the SEC by public companies comprise the single most intensive research tool for the financial journalist. Mandated are the 10-K, 10-Q, 8-K, Proxy Statement, Registration Statement, Prospectus, N-1R and N-1Q. Optional are the Annual Report to Shareholders and the Listing Application.

The SEC offices are located at:

26 Federal Plaza
New York, NY 10007
(212) 264-1614

500 N. E. Capitol Street
Washington, DC 20549
(202) 523-5506

1375 Peachtree Street, N. E.
Suite 788
Atlanta, GA 30309
(404) 881-2524

150 Causeway Street
Room 1204
Boston, MA 02114
(617) 223-2721

Everett McKinley Dirksen Building
219 South Dearborn Street
Chicago, IL 60604
(312) 353-7390

1020 Standard Building
1370 Ontario Street
Cleveland, OH 44113
(216) 522-4060

2 Park Central (Room 640)
1515 Arapahoe Street
Denver, CO 80202
(303) 837-2071

1044 Federal Building
Detroit, MI 48226
(313) 226-6070

503 U. S. Court House
Tenth & Lamar Streets
Fort Worth, TX 76102
(817) 334-3393

Federal Office & Court Building
515 Rush Avenue (Room 5615)
Houston, TX 77002
(713) 226-4986

10960 Wilshire Boulevard
Suite 1710
Los Angeles, CA 90024
(213) 473-4511

DuPont Plaza Center
300 Biscayne Blvd. Way (Suite 1114)
Miami, FL 33131
(305) 350-5765

600 Arch Street (Room 2204)
Philadelphia, PA 19106
(215) 597-2278

Federal Reserve Bank Building
120 South State Street
Salt Lake City, UT 84111
(801) 524-5796

450 Golden Gate Avenue
P. O. Box 36042
San Francisco, CA 94102
(415) 556-5264

3040 Federal Building
915 Second Avenue
Seattle, WA 98174
(206) 442-7990

210 North 12th Street (Room 1452)
St. Louis, MO 63101
(314) 425-5555

2. *Disclosure, Inc.* (a subsidiary of the publicly owned Reliance Group) is the official agent for the reproduction and distribution of all SEC reports on companies. Reports are made available to subscribers ten days after being filed with the SEC, and are issued

monthly as part of the *Disclosure Journal*, 4827 Rugby Avenue, Bethesda, MD 20014.

3. *Funk & Scott Index of Corporations and Industries* reports company news on a weekly basis. Funk & Scott, 11001 Cedar Avenue, Cleveland, OH 44106.

4. *F & S Index of Corporate Change*, a quarterly digest of corporate news that has appeared in newspapers and periodicals. *F & S*, 11001 Cedar Avenue, Cleveland, OH 44106.

5. *Standard & Poor's Corporation Records*, loose-leaf volumes containing writeups on thousands of publicly owned companies. Revised every couple of months. S & P also offers an updating service in between revisions in *Corporation Records*.

Standard & Poor's one-page stock reports on thousands of listed and over-the-counter companies are used by brokers and financial analysts as basic guides to these companies, and are useful to journalists as well. Standard & Poor's Corporation, 345 Hudson Street, New York, NY 10014.

6. *Moody's Investors Service*, which publishes the most popular manuals offering corporate financial statistics, also updates these manuals with a twice-weekly news service. Moody's, 99 Church Street, New York, NY 10006.

7. *Value Line Survey* covers 1500 companies from an investment viewpoint, offering in-depth studies of individual companies and their potential. Value Line, 5 East 44th Street, New York, NY 10017.

8. The *Wall Street Transcript*, a weekly newspaper ($15 per issue), reprints selected brokerage house reports on various public companies. The *Wall Street Transcript*, 120 Wall Street, New York, NY 10005.

9. *Fortune*, 1271 Avenue of the Americas, New York, NY 10020. Prestigious in-depth publication which in early 1978 switched from monthly to biweekly. Articles on important executives, and profiles on companies and industries. Ranges broadly over societal problems, international trade, technological breakthroughs. Economic forecasts much respected. Fortune's annual list of top 500 industrial companies (May), second largest 500 corporations (June), largest United States non-industrial corporations (July), and top foreign corporations (August) sell-out issues.

10. Professional securities analysts are generally conversant with trends in companies and industries, and are worth cultivating for that purpose. Sell-side analysts (those who prepare and analyze information which their firms present to banks, mutual funds and other large institutions) are broken down into generalists, special-situations analysts (who cut across all industries) and industry specialists. Buy-side analysts work for the financial institutions and most frequently are generalists who are in effect money managers. They may also be specialists in particular industries, since most came from the "sell-side."

The Financial Analysts Federation sells for $50 an annual directory listing all members of the 48 constituent societies throughout the United States and Canada. There are now some 15,000 professional analysts in the U.S. and Canada.

Each of the analysts societies holds meetings to which it invites corporate managements to tell their stories. The New York Society of Security Analysts, which boasts 5,200 members, holds daily meetings throughout the year; some groups only hold one meeting per month. It would pay for the financial journalist to attend the scheduled meetings of the nearest analyst society.

Member Societies of the Financial Analysts Federation

An annual directory is published by The Financial Analysts Federation, Tower Suite, 219 East 42nd Street, New York, NY 10017, (212) 557-0055.

Atlanta Society of Financial Analysts, Inc.

The Austin-San Antonio Society of Financial Analysts

Baltimore Security Analysts Society, Inc.

The Boston Security Analysts Society, Inc.

The Financial Analysts Society of Central Florida, Inc.

The Investment Analysts Society of Chicago, Inc.

The Cincinnati Society of Financial Analysts, Inc.

The Cleveland Society of Security Analysts

The Columbus Society of Financial Analysts, Inc.

The Dallas Association of Investment Analysts

The Denver Society of Security Analysts, Inc.

The Des Moines Society of Financial Analysts, Inc.

The Financial Analysts Society of Detroit, Inc.

The Hartford Society of Financial Analysts, Inc.

Houston Society of Financial Analysts, Inc.

The Indianapolis Society of Financial Analysts, Inc.

The Jacksonville Financial Analysts Society, Inc.

The Kansas City Society of Financial Analysts

The Los Angeles Society of Financial Analysts, Inc.

The Louisville Society of Financial Analysts, Inc.

The Financial Analysts Society of Miami, Inc.

Milwaukee Investment Analysts Society, Inc.

Montreal Society of Financial Analysts

The Nashville Society of Financial Analysts, Inc.

Financial Analysts of New Orleans

The New York Society of Security Analysts, Inc.

The North Carolina Society of Financial Analysts, Inc.

The Oklahoma Society of Financial Analysts

The Omaha-Lincoln Society of Financial Analysts, Inc.

Phoenix Society of Financial Analysts

The Pittsburgh Society of Financial Analysts, Inc.

Portland Society of Financial Analysts

The Providence Society of Financial Analysts

The Richmond Society of Financial Analysts

Rochester Society of Security Analysts, Inc.

The Saint Louis Society of Financial Analysts

The Financial Analysts Society of San Diego, Inc.

The Security Analysts of San Francisco

The Seattle Society of Financial Analysts

The Financial Analysts Society of Toledo

The Toronto Society of Financial Analysts

The Twin Cities Society of Security Analysts, Inc.

The Vancouver Society of Financial Analysts

The Washington Society of Investment Analysts, Inc.

Western Michigan Society of Financial Analysts

Financial Analysts of Wilmington, Inc.

The Winnipeg Society of Financial Analysts

Financial Analysts of Philadelphia, Inc.

INDUSTRIES

1. Probably the most important source of information on a given industry is the trade association which serves it, and these are to be found in the *Encyclopedia of Associations,* published by Gale Research Co., 700 Book Building, Detroit, MI 48226.

2. *The National Trade and Professional Associations of the*

United States and Labor Unions, published by Columbia Books, Inc., 734 15th Street N.W., Washington, DC 20005, provides union sources which are helpful in many business stories.

3. Standard & Poor's, which publishes individual stock reports, also produces *Industry Surveys,* a two-volume publication which analyzes 40 major industries on a current basis, and breaks down into about a thousand corporations. Standard & Poor's Corporation, 345 Hudson Street, New York, NY 10014.

4. *Value Line* also produces analytical studies on an industry and individual corporation basis. Value Line, 5 East 44th Street, New York, NY 10017.

5. *Forbes,* in its *Annual Report on American Industry,* published as its first January issue each year, gives excellent in-depth information on manufacturing in the United States, broken down by industry. Forbes, 60 Fifth Avenue, New York, NY 10011.

6. A Government publication, *The U.S. Industrial Outlook 197- with Projections to 197-,* offers detailed analyses of more than 200 industries, which are responsible for about 85% of manufacturing sales in the nation. Available from the Superintendent of Documents, U.S. Government Printing Office, Washington, DC 20402.

7. Market surveys of individual industries or product lines are often prepared by such consulting firms as Arthur D. Little, Frost & Sullivan and Predicasts, as well as others. These are generally expensive studies to purchase, and are reviewed in *Marketing Information Guide,* published by Hoke Communications, Inc., 224 Seventh Street, Garden City, NY 11530.

8. *The Monthly Catalog of U.S. Government Publications* offers the most comprehensive list of government publications, amongst which one generally finds specifics on particular industries. As an example, the government periodicals generally considered the most authoritative in their fields include: *Construction Review; Containers and Packaging; Copper; Printing & Publishing* and *Pulp, Paper, and Board.* Available from the Government Printing Office.

9. *The Business Service Checklist,* published by the Government Printing Office, is a weekly guide to U.S. Commerce Department publications, and includes key business indicators and comparative data.

10. *The Standard Industrial Classification Manual,* also available from the Government Printing Office, codes by number and lists alphabetically every aspect of United States economic activity by product, process and service.

11. Both the *U.S. Census of Business* (in three parts including retail trade, wholesale trade and selected services) and the *U.S. Census of Manufactures* (in two parts covering some 430 manufacturing industries) break down information by geographic region and state, employment size, and product specialization. Specialized publications are also available, such as *Growth Pace Setters in American Industry,* a detailed study of 55 United States industries, and *Industry Profiles,* a comprehensive statistical report comparing the 1957-1970 performance of the nation's 409 manufacturing industries. All from the Government Printing Office.

12. *Commodity Prices—A Source Book and Index,* by Gale Publishing, lists newspapers and trade periodicals which regularly publish prices for specific commodities. 700 Book Building, Detroit, MI 48226.

13. Financial and operating ratios for various industries can be found in an interesting publication, *Sources of Financial Data,* published by Robert Morris Associates, Philadelphia National Bank Building, Philadelphia, PA 19107.

14. Forecasts by industry are available from Predicasts, Inc., 11001 Cedar Avenue, Cleveland, OH 44106, presented on a statistical and abstract basis, covering more than 500 trade journals, government documents and financial services. Sources are listed.

15. The National Planning Association, 1606 New Hampshire Avenue, Washington, DC 20009 issues a monthly, *Looking Ahead,* which gives detailed forecasts on the economy and industry, plus two expensive series, *National Economic Projections* and *Regional Economic Projections.*

INDIVIDUALS

1. *The Federal Statistical Directory,* offered by the Government Printing Office, lists by agency the names and location of key persons involved in statistical programs.

2. Financial analysts (also called "securities analysts" or "security analysts") are listed in the *Financial Analysts Directory,* by name, keyed to specialty, firm, location and telephone number. From the Financial Analysts Federation, 219 East 42nd Street, New York, NY 10017 ($50).

3. Compensation of leading executives is listed annually by Forbes, in its annual directory issue, as well as *Business Week,* in a special annual issue, and by the American Management Association, 135 West 50th Street New York, NY 10020, in an expensive service.

4. *Poor's Register,* a service of Standard & Poor's, lists officers and directors of thousands of companies, with biographical sketches. Also, this annual volume contains listings of thousands of companies and their officers and directors.

5. *Who's Who in Finance and Industry,* published by Marquis Who's Who, 200 East Ohio Street, Chicago, IL 60611, is an annual volume containing listings of important executives, with biographical sketches. Specialized Who's Who volumes, such as *Who's Who in Banking,* by Business Press, Inc., 200 Park Avenue, New York, NY 10017, provide biographical data on those who might not be in the Marquis volumes. Many industries have specialized biographical publications.

MISCELLANEOUS

Needless to say, many reference sources focus on categories which do not fall within our simple division of companies, industries, and individuals. But you ought to be aware of them, because they are useful.

1. *Bibliography of Publications of University Bureaus of Business and Economic Research,* covering the excellent research being done at graduate schools of business. Published by the Association for University Business and Economic Research, University of Colorado, Boulder, CO 80309.

2. *Cumulative Index of the Conference Board,* covers business management and business economics. The Conference Board, 845 Third Avenue, New York, NY 10020.

3. The National Bureau of Economic Research publishes monographs on economic topics. 261 Madison Avenue, New York, NY 10017.

4. *Dictionary of Economic and Statistic Terms,* published by The Government Printing Office, covers the language of economics.

5. McGraw-Hill *Dictionary of Modern Economics,* one of the best dictionaries in the field of economics, is published by McGraw-Hill Book Co., 1221 Avenue of the Americas, New York, NY 10020.

6. The *Media General Financial Weekly,* The M/G Financial Weekly, P.O. Box 26991, Richmond, VA 23261, offers the most comprehensive weekly group of charts, statistics, and quotations of economic and financial figures.

7. The *Wall Street Journal Index* and the *New York Times Index* provide a valuable guide to the business news published in each of these topnotch newspapers.

8. The *Business Periodicals Index,* published by H.W. Wilson Co., 950 University Avenue, Bronx, NY 10452, indexes about 170 business publications, and indexes book reviews as well.

9. *The Fed in Print,* a quarterly update of articles on the Federal Reserve Bank, published by the Federal Reserve Bank of Philadelphia, PA 19106, and free.

10. Major banks all issue monthly newsletters loaded with economic detail on state and federal programs. Contact the leading local banks.

12. Computerized economic and financial data banks are becoming increasingly useful. Data Resources Inc., Lexington, Massachusetts (macro-economic statistics for 79 industries, FRB indices for 41 indices and 7,000 economic and industry time series); Bunker-Ramo Corp., Trumbull, Connecticut (stock quotations); Interactive Data Corporation, Waltham, Massachusetts (analyzes economic, financial data); Computer Directions Advisors, Inc., Silver Spring, Maryland (beta coefficients, stock market analyses); Wharton Econometric Forecasting Associates Inc., Philadelphia, Pennsylvania (GNP studies, macro-model prediction and simulation activities); Lionel D. Edie & Company, Incorporated, New York, New York (economic data base for economic and financial analyses); Telerate Systems Inc., New

ECONOMICS

1. *Economic Indicators,* published monthly by the Council of Economic Advisors, provides the monthly statistics which end up in news stories. Executive Office Building, 17th & Pennsylvania Avenue N.W., Washington, DC 20506.

2. *Business Conditions Digest,* a monthly, published by the U.S. Department of Commerce, Washington, DC 20230, provides illustrative charts and explanations of the leading, coincident and lagging indicators on a current basis.

3. *Survey of Current Business,* monthly, U.S. Department of Commerce.

4. *Treasury Bulletin,* monthly, U.S. Treasury Department, Washington, DC 20220.

5. *Federal Reserve Bulletin,* monthly, Board of Governors of the Federal Reserve System, Washington, DC 20551.

6. *Statistical Abstract,* annual, U.S. Department of Commerce.

7. Bank bulletins, such as those published by the First National City Bank of New York, the Cleveland Trust Company, the Morgan Guaranty Trust Company, and each of the 12 Federal Reserve Banks.

8. *Business Economics,* quarterly published by the National Association of Business Economists, 28349 Chagrin Boulevard, Cleveland, OH 44122.

FINANCIAL PERIODICALS

1. *Barron's* (published by Dow Jones & Co.), 22 Cortlandt Street, New York, NY 10007. A weekly newsmagazine. The leading investment periodical, *Barron's* publishes a lengthy article each week on prospects for a particular industry. Also "News and Views" profiles of several publicly owned companies demonstrating strong growth.

2. *Commercial & Financial Chronicle,* 120 Broadway, New York, NY 10005. Weekly newsmagazine, heavy on statistics.

3. *Financial Analysts Journal,* 219 East 42nd Street, New York, NY 10017. Scholarly bimonthly published by the Financial Analysts Federation.

4. *Financial World,* 919 Third Avenue, New York, NY 10022. Survey articles on industry, with emphasis on publicly owned components. Statistics include money indicators and basic business indicators. First issues of March, June, September and December carry "Independent Appraisals of Listed Stocks," and last issue in August is devoted to "Directory of Top Growth Companies."

5. *Institutional Investor,* 488 Madison Avenue, New York, NY 10022. Monthly magazine with big impact in brokerage and institutional markets. Each year picks top securities analysts in each speciality—"The All-America Team."

6. *Investment Dealers' Digest,* 150 Broadway, New York, NY 10038. Weekly newsmagazine of finance. Trade publication for traders. Carries three or four articles on public companies. Lists all issues in registration for new financings.

7. *Journal of Portfolio Management,* 509 Madison Avenue, New York, NY 10022. Quarterly containing sophisticated professional articles on security selection, timing, risk management.

8. The *Market Chronicle,* 160 Broadway, New York, NY 10008. Lively weekly newspaper, recently broadened from over-the-counter stocks to include listed stock reviews. Gives extensive price quotations of OTC stocks.

9. *Over-The-Counter Securities Review,* Box 110, Jenkintown, PA 19046. Monthly devoted to news and reviews of over-the-counter companies.

10. The *Wall Street Journal,* 22 Cortlandt Street, New York, NY 10007. The leading U.S. daily financial newspaper, with five editions throughout the nation. Circulation is 1,600,000.

11. The *Journal of Commerce,* 99 Wall Street, New York, NY 10005. Tops in shipping, insurance, and chemical coverage on daily basis, read by financial analysts and business executives.

12. *Business Week,* 1221 Avenue of the Americas, New York, NY 10020. Top business weekly, contains series of short articles on management, industries, marketing, international business, government, and so forth. Also statistics and business indicators. Last issue of year is "Investment Outlook," with a statistical table for 890 large corporations.

13. *Conference Board Record,* 845 Third Avenue, New York,

NY 10022. This monthly contains short articles by staff members on recent research.

14. *Dun's Review,* 666 Fifth Avenue, New York, NY 10019. Short, readable articles on management topics aimed at executive readers. Financial ratios for some 125 businesses are carried in September (retailers), October (wholesalers) and November (manufacturers).

15. The *Economist,* 25 Saint James Street, London, SWAI 1 HG. Highly respected weekly with feature articles and news on economic and political trends, mostly about the United Kingdom, but with important section on the United States.

16. *Fortune,* 1271 Avenue of the Americas, New York, NY 10020. Prestigious in-depth publication which in early 1978 switched from monthly to biweekly. Articles on important executives, profiles on companies and industries. Ranges broadly over societal problems, international trade, technological breakthroughs. Economic forecasts much respected. *Fortune's* annual list of top 500 industrial companies (May), second largest 500 corporations (June), largest U.S. industrial corporations (July) and top foreign corporations (August) are sell-out issues.

17. *Industry Week,* 1111 Chester Avenue, Cleveland, OH 44114. Increasingly popular since it converted to management book from former orientation as publication for metalworking executives. Contains four or five stories weekly on current business and management topics. March issue carries "Financial Analysis of Industry," profiles of 17 manufacturing industries with earnings of leading companies.

18. *Journal of Business,* University of Chicago Press, 5801 South Ellis Avenue, Chicago, IL 60637. Quarterly academic journal, well regarded. Original research on business and economic theory.

19. *Nation's Business,* 1615 H Street, N.W., Washington, DC 20062. Chamber of Commerce. Monthly. Articles from business viewpoint on economic and political subjects.

20. *American Banker,* 525 West 42nd Street, New York, NY 10036.

21. *Business Leader,* PO Box 369, Hialeah, FL 33011.

22. The *Exchange,* 20 Broad Street, New York, NY 10005. Magazine of the New York Stock Exchange.

23. *Burroughs,* 605 Third Avenue, New York, NY 10016.

24. *Journal of Finance,* 100 Trinity Place, New York.

25. *Harvard Business Review,* Teele Hall, Soldiers' Field, Boston, MA 02163.

26. *Kiplinger Washington Letter,* 1729 H Street N.W., Washington, DC 20006.

27. *Money & Commerce,* PSF Bldg. 12 South 12th Street, Philadelphia, PA 19107.

28. *Pensions & Investments,* 708 Third Avenue, New York, NY 10017.

29. *Western Financial Journal,* 607 South Hobart Boulevard, Los Angeles, CA 90005.

30. *California Business,* 1060 Crenshaw Boulevard, Los Angeles, CA 90019.

31. *Securities Digest,* 1100 Glendon Avenue, Suite 805, Los Angeles, CA 90024.

32. *Business Economics,* 888 17th Street, N. W., Washington, DC 20006.

33. *Forbes,* 60 Fifth Avenue, New York, NY 10011. One of the "Big 3" of business magazines *(Fortune* and *Business Week* are the others), *Forbes* is noted for a breezy style (some call it the *"Time* Magazine" of business publications) in which it mixes company features, some in-depth industry studies and short profiles of important individuals in business and finance. Also an excellent balance of columnists, a number of them partners at Wall Street houses.

TRADE PUBLICATIONS AND ORGANIZATIONS

The New York Society of Security Analysts has compiled a list of trade publications and organizations useful in gathering statistical and business information on the specialized industries covered by its membership. Since it is also extremely useful to journalists, it is mentioned here. For fuller information regarding trade publications, one can turn to *N.W. Ayer's & Sons Directory of Newspapers and Periodicals* (Ayer Press, 210 West Washington

Square, Philadelphia, PA 19106), *Standard Periodicals Directory* (Oxbridge Publishing Co., Inc. 1345 Avenue of the Americas, New York, NY 10019), *Standard Rate & Data Service* (5201 Old Orchard Road, Skokie, IL 60077). For overseas periodicals, *Ulrich's International Periodicals Directory* (R.R. Bowker Company, 1180 Avenue of the Americas, New York, NY 10036) is a useful directory.

COURTESY OF THE NEW YORK SOCIETY OF SECURITY ANALYSTS

PUBLISHED	SOURCE	ADDRESS

ADVERTISING

PERIODICALS

Weekly (Magazine)	Advertising Age	740 North Rush Street Chicago, IL 60611
Weekly (Newsletter)	Gallagher Reports, Inc.	230 Park Avenue New York, NY 10017
Weekly (Newsletter)	Jack O'Dwyer's Newsletter (Public Relations)	271 Madison Avenue New York, NY 10016
Daily (Newspaper)	The New York Times Company	207 West 43d Street New York, NY 10036
THE STANDARD DIRECTORY OF ADVERTISING AGENCIES Quarterly (Directory)	National Register Publishing Co.	20 East 46th Street New York, NY 10017

BOOKS

| WHAT ADVERTISING AGENCIES ARE—WHAT THEY DO AND HOW THEY DO IT 1970 (7th Edition) | Frederic R. Gamble American Association of Advertising Agencies | 200 Park Avenue New York, NY 10017 |
| THE ADVERTISING AGENCY BUSINESS 1964 | Kenneth Groesbeck Advertising Publications, Inc. — Advertising Age | Chicago, IL |

AIRLINES

PERIODICALS

| AIR CARRIER TRAFFIC STATISTICS Monthly (Statistics) | Civil Aeronautics Board (Publications Services Section) | Washington, DC 20428 |

PUBLISHED	SOURCE	ADDRESS
AIR CARRIER FINANCIAL STATISTICS		
Quarterly	Civil Aeronautics	Washington, DC 20428
(Statistics)	Board (Publications	
	Services Section)	
AIRLINE INDUSTRY DATA		
1. All Cargo Supplemental		
Carriers		
2. Regional Carriers		
3. U.S. Trunkline Carriers		
and Pan American		
Quarterly (each)	McDonnell Douglas	3855 Lakewood Blvd.
(Statistics)	Finance Corp.	Long Beach, CA 90801
	Airline Credit	
	Analysis	
AIRLINE INDUSTRY ECONOMIC REPORT		
Quarterly (Booklet)	Civil Aeronautics	Washington, DC 20428
	Board	
AIRLINE INDUSTRY FINANCIAL REVIEW		
AND OUTLOOK		
Irregular, Usually	Air Transport Assn.	1000 Connecticut
Annual (Booklet)	of America	Avenue, N.W.
		Washington, DC 20036
AEROSPACE DAILY	Ziff-Davis Publish-	1156 Fifteenth Street,
	ing Co.	N.W.
		Washington, DC 20005
AVIATION DAILY	Ziff-Davis Publish-	1156 Fifteenth Street,
Daily	ing Co.	N.W.
(Newsletter)		Washington, DC 20005
AVIATION WEEK & SPACE TECHNOLOGY		
Weekly	McGraw-Hill, Inc.	1221 Ave. of the
(Magazine)		Americas
		New York, NY 10020

OTHER

FORECAST OF SCHEDULED INTERNATIONAL		
AIR TRAFFIC OF U.S. FLAG CARRIERS		
1971-1980	Civil Aeronautics	Washington, DC 20428
	Board	

ALUMINUM

PERIODICALS

ALUMINUM		
Annual	Bureau of Mines	4800 Forbes Avenue
(Magazine)		Pittsburgh, PA 15213

PUBLISHED	SOURCE	ADDRESS
ALUMINUM ASSOCIATION YEARBOOK & RELEASES Quarterly and Annually (Reports)		750 Third Avenue New York, NY 10017

AMERICAN BUREAU OF METAL STATISTICS
YEARBOOK
Annually
(Statistical
  Yearbook)
	American Bureau of
	  Metal Statistics
	  Yearbook
		50 Broadway, 30th fl.
		New York, NY 10004

AMERICAN METAL MARKET Daily (Newspaper)	American Metal Market Co.	7 East 12th Street New York, NY 10003

COMMODITY YEARBOOK STATISTICAL ABSTRACT
SERVICE
Annually
(Statistical
  Yearbook)
	Commodity Research
	  Bureau
		140 Broadway
		New York, NY 10005

ENGINEERING & MINING JOURNAL Monthly (Journal)	McGraw-Hill, Inc.	1221 Ave. of the Americas New York, NY 10020
JAPAN METAL BULLETIN Three times per week (Newspaper)	Sangyo Press, Ltd.	104 East 40th Street New York, NY 10016
METAL STATISTICS Annually (Yearbook)	American Metal Market Co.	7 East 12th Street New York, NY 10003
METALS WEEK Weekly (Magazine)	McGraw-Hill, Inc.	1221 Ave. of the Americas New York, NY 10020
MINING JOURNAL Weekly (Newspaper)	Mining Journal, Ltd.	15 Wilson Street London EC2 London, U.K.
MINING JOURNAL Annually	Mining Journal, Ltd.	15 Wilson Street London EC2 England, U.K.

MINERALS YEARBOOK VOLUMES 1 & 2
METALS, MINERALS, & FUELS
Annually
(Yearbook)
	Superintendent of
	  Documents
	U.S. Government
	  Printing Office
		Washington, DC

MINERALS YEARBOOK VOLUME 3, AREA REPORTS—
DOMESTIC; VOLUME 4 AREA REPORTS—INTERNATIONAL
Annually
(Yearbook)
	Superintendent of
	  Documents
	U.S. Government
	  Printing Office
		Washington, DC

PUBLISHED	SOURCE	ADDRESS

AUTOMOTIVE INDUSTRY

PERIODICALS

AUTOMOTIVE FACTS & FIGURES
Annual
(Pamphlet)

Automobile Manufac-
turers Assn., Inc.

320 New Center Bldg.
Detroit, MI 48202

AUTOMOTIVE MARKET REPORT
Weekly
(Magazine)

Automotive Publish-
ing, Inc.

1101 Fulton Bldg.
Pittsburgh, PA 15222

AUTOMOTIVE NEWS
Weekly
(Newspaper)

Crain Communications

965 E. Jefferson Ave.
Detroit, MI 48207

SINDLINGER AUTOMOTIVE REPORT
Weekly
(Newsletters)

Sindlinger & Co.

Howard & Yale Avenues
Swarthmore, PA 19081

WARD'S ADVANCE SCHEDULE & INVENTORY REPORT
Monthly
(Statistical Release)

Ward's Communications

28 W. Adams
Suite 1805
Detroit, MI 48226

WARD'S AUTO WORLD
Monthly
(Magazine)

Ward's Communications

28 W. Adams
Suite 1805
Detroit, MI 48226

WARD'S AUTOMOTIVE REPORTS
Weekly
(Newsletter)

Ward's Communications

28 W. Adams
Suite 1805
Detroit, MI 48226

BOOKS

PLANNING, REGULATION AND COMPETITION:
AUTOMOTIVE INDUSTRY—1968
HEARINGS BEFORE SUBCOMMITTEES OF THE
SELECT COMMITTEE ON SMALL BUSINESS
(U.S. Senate)
1968

U.S. Government
Printing Office

Washington, DC

BANKS AND FINANCE COMPANIES

PERIODICALS

THE AMERICAN BANKER
Daily
(Newspaper)

American Banker, Inc.

525 West 42nd Street
New York, NY 10036

PUBLISHED	SOURCE	ADDRESS
THE BANKERS MAGAZINE Quarterly (Magazine)	Warren, Gorham & Lamont, Inc.	870 Seventh Avenue New York, NY 10019
BANKERS MONTHLY Monthly (Magazine)	Bankers Monthly, Inc.	601 Skokie Blvd. Northbrook, IL 60062
BANKING Monthly (Magazine)	Simmons-Boardman Publishing Corp.	350 Broadway New York, NY 10013
BANKING LAW JOURNAL Monthly (Journal)	Warren, Gorham & Lamont, Inc.	870 Seventh Avenue New York, NY 10019
BANK OF NEW YORK—FINANCE COMPANY STATISTICS Semiannually (Stat. Abstract)	Bank of New York	48 Wall Street New York, NY 10005
BURROUGHS CLEARING HOUSE Monthly (Magazine)	Burroughs Clearing House	P.O. Box 418 Detroit, MI 48232
COMMENTS ON CREDIT, BOND MARKET SURVEY Weekly (Newsletter)	Salomon Brothers	60 Wall Street New York, NY 10005
FEDERAL RESERVE BULLETIN Monthly (Bulletin)	Board of Governors Federal Reserve Board	Washington, DC 20551
FEDERAL RESERVE DISTRICT BANK BULLETINS Monthly (Magazine)	Individual Reserve Banks	Atlanta Boston Chicago Cleveland Dallas Kansas City Minneapolis New York Philadelphia Richmond St. Louis San Francisco
FEDERAL STATISTICAL RELEASE H 4.2 (CONDITIONS OF LARGE COMMERCIAL BANKS) Weekly (Bulletin)	Federal Reserve Board	Washington, DC

PUBLISHED	SOURCE	ADDRESS
FINANCE FACTS YEARBOOK Annually (Yearbook)	National Consumer Finance Assn.	100 Sixteenth Street, N.W. Washington, DC 20003
FINANCE MAGAZINE Monthly (Magazine)	IFB Communications	8 West 40th Street New York, NY 10018
FIRST NATIONAL BANK OF CHICAGO, FINANCE COMPANY COMPOSITE STATISTICS Semiannually (Stat. Abstract)	First National Bank of Chicago	Dearborn, Monroe & Clark Streets Chicago, IL
NATIONAL BANKING REVIEW Quarterly (Journal)	Controller of the Currency U.S. Treasury Dept.	Washington, DC
NATIONAL ECONOMIC TRENDS Weekly (Bulletin)	Federal Reserve Bank of St. Louis	St. Louis, MO
NEW YORK CLEARING HOUSE DEPOSIT STATISTICS Weekly (Stat. Abstract)	New York Clearing House Assn.	100 Broad Street New York, NY 10004
QUARTERLY BANK SURVEY Quarterly (Magazine)	M.A. Shapiro & Co.	1 Chase Manhattan Pl. New York, NY 10005
ST. LOUIS FEDERAL MONETARY TRENDS Weekly (Bulletin)	Federal Reserve Bank of St. Louis	St. Louis, MO

BOOKS

HOW TO ANALYZE A BANK STATEMENT, 6th EDITION 1966	F.L. Garcia Bankers Publishing	Boston, MA
MANAGEMENT OF BANK FUNDS, 2nd EDITION 1962	Roland I. Robinson McGraw-Hill, Inc.	New York, NY
MANAGEMENT POLICIES FOR COMMERCIAL BANKS, 2nd EDITION 1973	Howard Crosse Prentice-Hall, Inc.	New York, NY

PUBLISHED	SOURCE	ADDRESS

BEVERAGES

PERIODICALS

| BEVERAGE INDUSTRY (Biweekly) | Magazines for Industry | 777 Third Avenue New York, NY 10017 |

BREWING AND DISTILLING

PERIODICALS

BEVERAGE EXECUTIVE Monthly (Magazine)	Brewers' Digest	4049 W. Peterson Ave. Chicago, IL
BREWERS INDUSTRY SURVEY Annually (Annual Report)	Research Co. of America	654 Madison Avenue New York, NY 10021
DISTILLED SPIRITS INDUSTRY ANNUAL STATISTICAL REVIEW Annually (Statistical Yearbook)	Distilled Spirits Institute	425 Thirteenth St. Washington, DC 20004
LBI FACTS BOOK Annually (Fact Book)	Licensed Beverage Industries, Inc.	485 Lexington Avenue New York, NY 10017
LIQUOR HANDBOOK Annually (Handbook)	Gavin Jobson Associates	820 Second Avenue New York, NY 10017
WINE HANDBOOK Annually (Handbook)	Gavin Jobson Associates	820 Second Avenue New York, NY 10017

BUILDING MATERIALS

PERIODICALS

| CONSTRUCTION REVIEW Monthly (Journal) | U.S. Department of Commerce Government Printing Office | Washington, DC 20402 |
| F.W. DODGE CONSTRUCTION STATISTICS Monthly (Journal) | McGraw-Hill, Inc. | 1221 Ave. of the Americas New York, NY 10020 |

PUBLISHED	SOURCE	ADDRESS
ECONOMIC SERVICES REPORT Semiannually (Journal)	Western Wood Products Assoc.	Yeon Building Portland, OR 97204
ENGINEERING NEWS-RECORD Weekly (Magazine)	McGraw-Hill, Inc.	1221 Ave. of the Americas New York, NY 10020
FOREST INDUSTRIES Monthly (Magazine)	Miller Freeman Publications	500 Howard Street San Francisco, CA 94105
HOUSING COMPLETIONS Monthly (Journal)	U.S. Department of Commerce U.S. Government Printing Office	Washington, DC 20402
HOUSING STARTS Monthly (Journal)	U.S. Department of Commerce U.S. Government Printing Office	Washington, DC 20402
HOUSING STARTS BULLETIN Weekly (Journal)	National Assn. of Homebuilders	1625 L Street, N.W. Washington, DC 20036
MINERAL INDUSTRY SURVEYS (VAR. MATERIALS) Monthly & Yearly (Surveys)	U.S. Department of Interior Bureau of Mines	Washington, DC 20240
PROFESSIONAL BUILDER & APARTMENT BUSINESS Monthly (Magazine)	Cahners Publishing Co., Inc.	5 S. Wabash Avenue Chicago, IL 60603
ROCK PRODUCTS Monthly (Magazine)	Maclean-Hunter Publishing Corp.	300 W. Adams Street Chicago, IL 60606
SHORT RANGE FORECASTS Quarterly (Journal)	Portland Cement Association	Old Orchard Road Skokie, IL 60070

BOOKS

DIRECTORY OF THE FOREST PRODUCTS INDUSTRY 1972	Miller Freeman Publications	500 Howard Street San Francisco, CA 94105

PUBLISHED	SOURCE	ADDRESS
TIMBER TRENDS IN THE UNITED STATES 1965	Forest Service, U.S. Dept. of Agric. U.S. Government Printing Office	Washington, DC 20402

OTHERS

BUILDING CONSTRUCTION INFORMATION SOURCES 1964	Howard B. Bentley Gale Research Co.	Book Tower Detroit, MI
OUTLOOK FOR THE FOREST PRODUCTS INDUSTRY 1970	Arthur D. Little, Inc.	Acorn Park Cambridge, MA 02140
PORTLAND CEMENT PLANTS—U.S, CANADA, & MEXICO Map of Portland Cement Plants	Pit & Quarry Pub- lications	105 W. Adams Street Chicago, IL 60603

CHEMICALS

PERIODICALS

CHEMICAL AND ENGINEERING NEWS Weekly (Magazine)	American Chemical Society	1155 Sixteenth Street, N.W. Washington, DC 20036
CHEMICAL ENGINEERING Biweekly (Magazine)	McGraw-Hill, Inc.	1221 Ave. of the Americas New York, NY 10020
CHEMICAL HORIZONS Monthly (Abstracts)	Predicasts, Inc.	200 University Circle Research Center 11001 Cedar Avenue Cleveland, OH 44106
CHEMICAL MARKETING REPORTER (INCLUDING OIL, PAINT & DRUG REPORTER) Weekly (Newspaper)	Schnell Publishing Co., Inc.	100 Church Street New York, NY 10007
CHEMICAL WEEK Weekly (Magazine)	McGraw-Hill, Inc.	1221 Ave. of the Americas New York, NY 10020

PUBLISHED	SOURCE	ADDRESS
CURRENT INDUSTRIAL REPORTS—SHIPMENTS OF SELECTED PLASTIC PRODUCTS SERIES M A 30B Monthly (Stat. Release)	Bureau of the Census	Washington, DC 20233
EUROPEAN CHEMICAL NEWS Weekly (Magazine)	Int'l Publishing Corp., Ltd.	300 East 42nd Street New York, NY 10017
FARM CHEMICALS Monthly (Magazine)	Meister Publishing Company	37841 Euclid Avenue Willoughby, OH 44094
INDUSTRY REPORTS Monthly (Stat. Release)	Superintendent of Documents Government Printing Office	Washington, DC 20402
INORGANIC CHEMICALS & GASES (CURRENT INDUSTRIAL REPORTS—SERIES M-28-A) Monthly (Stat. Release)	Bureau of the Census	Washington, DC 20233
MODERN PLASTICS Monthly (Magazine)	McGraw-Hill, Inc.	1221 Ave. of the Americas New York, NY 10020
MODERN PLASTICS ENCYCLOPEDIA Annually (Encyclopedia)	McGraw-Hill, Inc.	1221 Ave. of the Americas New York, NY 10020
PLASTICS WORLD Monthly (Magazine)	Cahner's Publishing Company	221 Columbus Avenue Boston, MA 02116
TEXTILE ORGANON Monthly (Stat. Newsletter)	Textile Economics Bureau, Inc.	489 Fifth Avenue New York, NY 10017

COAL

PERIODICALS

BITUMINOUS COAL FACTS Biennial (Factbook)	National Coal Assn.	1130 Seventeenth St. Washington, DC 20036
COAL AGE Monthly (Magazine)	McGraw-Hill, Inc.	1221 Ave. of the Americas New York, NY 10020

PUBLISHED	SOURCE	ADDRESS
COAL CHRONICLE Irregular (Catalogue)	United States Bureau of Mines Publications Distri- bution Section	4800 Forbes Avenue Pittsburgh, PA 15213
COAL DIRECTORY Annual (Directory)	McGraw-Hill, Inc.	1221 Ave. of the Americas New York, NY 10020
COAL NEWS Weekly (Newspaper)	National Coal Assn.	1130 Seventeenth St. Washington, DC 20036
MINERAL INDUSTRY SURVEY—BITUMINOUS COAL Monthly (Magazine)	U.S. Bureau of Mines	4800 Forbes Avenue Pittsburgh, PA 15213
MINERALS YEAR BOOK VOL. 1-2 METALS, MINERALS, AND FUELS Annually (Book)	Superintendent of Documents U.S. Government Printing Office	Washington, DC 20402
MINERALS YEAR BOOK VOL. 3 AREA REPORTS— DOMESTIC MINERALS YEAR BOOK VOL. 4 AREA REPORTS— INTERNATIONAL Annually (Book)	Superintendent of Documents U.S. Government Printing Office	Washington, DC 20402

BOOKS

MINERAL FACTS AND PROBLEMS 1970 (4th Edition)	U.S. Bureau of Mines	Washington, DC

COMMUNICATIONS

PERIODICALS

AMERICAN GROWTH STORY Annually (Booklet)	U.S. Independent Telephone Assn.	438 Pennsylvania Bldg. Washington, DC 20004
ANNUAL STATISTICAL VOLUME ONE Annually (Booklet)	U.S. Independent Telephone Assn.	438 Pennsylvania Bldg. Washington, DC 20004

PUBLISHED	SOURCE	ADDRESS
ANNUAL STATISTICAL VOLUME TWO		
Annual	U.S. Independent	438 Pennsylvania Bldg.
(Booklet)	Telephone Assn.	Washington, DC 20004
FROM THE STATE CAPITALS		
Weekly	Bethune Jones	321 Sunset Avenue
(Newsletter)		Ashbury Park, NJ
NARUC BULLETIN		
Weekly	Nat'l Assn. of	3327 Interstate
(Newsletter)	Regulatory Utility	Commerce Bldg.,
	Commissions	P.O. Box 684
		Washington, DC 20044
PUBLIC UTILITY REPORTS—ADVANCE SHEETS		
Bimonthly	Public Utility Re-	1828 L Street, N.W.
(Pamphlet)	ports, Inc.	Suite 502
		Washington, DC 20036
PUBLIC UTILITY REPORTS EXECUTIVE INFORMATION SERVICE		
Weekly	Public Utility Re-	1828 L Street, N.W.
(Newsletter)	ports, Inc.	Washington, DC 20036
TELECOMMUNICATIONS REPORTS		
Weekly	Telecommunications	Nat'l Press Bldg.
(Newsletter)	Reports	Room 1204
		Washington, DC 20004

CONSTRUCTION MATERIALS

PERIODICALS

CONSTRUCTION ACTIVITY—SERIES C30		
Monthly	Superintendent of	Washington, DC 20402
(Report)	Documents	
	U.S. Government	
	Printing Office	
CONSTRUCTION REVIEW		
Monthly	U.S. Department of	Constitution Ave. &
(Magazine)	Commerce	E Street, N.W.
		Washington, DC 20402
CROW'S FOREST PRODUCTS DIGEST		
Monthly	C.C. Crow Pub-	Terminal Sales Bldg.
(Magazine)	lications, Inc.	1220 S.W. Morrison
		Portland, OR 97205
ELEVATOR WORLD		
Monthly	William C. Sturgeon	Box 6523, Loop
(Magazine)		Branch
		Mobile, AL 36606

PUBLISHED	SOURCE	ADDRESS
ENGINEERING NEWS-RECORD Weekly (Magazine)	McGraw-Hill, Inc.	1221 Ave. of the Americas New York, NY 10020
HOUSE AND HOME Monthly (Magazine)	McGraw-Hill, Inc.	1221 Ave. of the Americas New York, NY 10020
HOUSING STARTS—SERIES C20 Monthly (Report)	Superintendent of Documents U.S. Government Printing Office	Washington, DC 20402
INDUSTRIAL OUTLOOK Annually (Book)	U.S. Department of Commerce	Constitution Ave. & E Street, N.W. Washington, DC 20037
MINERALS YEARBOOK VOL. 1-2 METALS, MINERALS, & FUELS Annually (Book)	Superintendent of Documents U.S. Government Printing Office	Washington, DC 20402
MINERALS YEARBOOK VOL. 3—AREA REPORTS—DOMESTIC VOL. 4—AREA REPORTS—INTERNATIONAL Annually (Book)	Superintendent of Documents U.S. Government Printing Office	Washington, DC 20402
MODERN CONCRETE Monthly (Magazine)	Pit and Quarry Publications, Inc.	105 W. Adams Street Chicago, IL 60603
PIT AND QUARRY Monthly (Magazine)	Pit and Quarry Publications, Inc.	105 W. Adams Street Chicago, IL 60603
SAVINGS & LOAN FACT BOOK Annually (Fact Book)	U.S. Savings & Loan League	221 N. LaSalle Street Chicago, IL 60601
SURVEY OF CURRENT BUSINESS Monthly (Magazine)	U.S. Department of Commerce Office of Business Economics	Constitution Ave. & E Street, N.W. Washington, DC 20402

PUBLISHED	SOURCE	ADDRESS

OTHERS

F.W. DODGE ECONOMICS DEPARTMENT

1221 Ave. of the Americas
New York, NY 10020

NATIONAL ASSOCIATION OF HOMEBUILDERS

1625 L Street, N.W.
Washington, DC 20036

U.S. DEPARTMENT OF COMMERCE

Constitution Ave. & E Street, N.W.
Washington, DC 20402

DEFENSE

PERIODICALS

PUBLISHED	SOURCE	ADDRESS
AIAA BULLETIN Monthly (Bulletin)	American Institute of Aeronautics & Astronautics	1290 Sixth Avenue New York, NY 10019
AEROSPACE DAILY Daily (Newsletter)	Ziff Davis Publishing Co.	1156 Fifteenth Street, N.W. Washington, DC 20005
AEROSPACE FACTS AND FIGURES Annually (Booklet)	Aerospace Industries Assn. of Americas	1725 DeSales Street, N.W. Washington, DC 20036
AEROSPACE MAGAZINES Quarterly (Magazine)	Aerospace Industries Assn. of America	1725 DeSales Street, N.W. Washington, DC 20036
AEROSPACE MARKET INTELLIGENCE REPORTS 1. MILITARY AND CIVIL AIRCRAFT 2. ROCKETS, MISSILES, AND SPACECRAFTS 3. AEROSPACE INDUSTRY DOSSIER Monthly (Newsletter)	DMS, Inc.	71 Lewis Street Greenwich, CT 06830
AIR FORCE & SPACE DIGEST Monthly (Magazine)	Air Force Assn.	1750 Pennsylvania Ave., N.W., Suite 400 Washington, DC 20006

PUBLISHED	SOURCE	ADDRESS
ASTRONAUTICS & AERONAUTICS Monthly (Magazine)	American Institute of Aeronautics & Astronautics	1290 Ave. of the Americas New York, NY 10019
AVIATION DAILY Daily (Newsletter)	Ziff-Davis Publish- ing Co.	1156 15th Street, N.W. Washington, DC 20005
AVIATION WEEK & SPACE TECHNOLOGY Weekly (Magazine)	McGraw-Hill, Inc.	1221 Sixth Avenue New York, NY 10020
DEFENSE MANAGEMENT JOURNAL Quarterly (Bulletin)	Superintendent of Documents U.S. Government Printing Office	Washington, DC 20402

DRUGS AND COSMETICS

PERIODICALS

AMERICAN DRUGGIST Biweekly (Magazine)	Hearst Corp.	224 West 57th Street New York, NY 10019
BEAUTY FASHION Monthly (Magazine)	Beauty Fashion Inc.	48 East 43rd St. New York, NY 10019
COSMETIC WORLD Weekly (Newsletter)	Beauty Fashion Inc.	48 East 43rd Street New York, NY 10019
DRUG & COSMETIC INDUSTRY Monthly (Magazine)	Harcourt, Brace, Jovanovich	757 Third Avenue New York, NY 10017
DRUG TOPICS Semiweekly	Medical Economics	680 Kinderkamack Road Orodell, NJ 07649
FDC REPORTS Weekly (Newsletter)		1152 Nat'l Press Bldg. Washington, DC
HOSPITALS Bimonthly (Magazine)	American Hospital Assn.	840 N. Lakeshore Dr. Chicago, IL 60611

PUBLISHED	SOURCE	ADDRESS
JOURNAL OF AMERICAN MEDICAL ASSOCIATION Weekly (Magazine)		535 N. Dearborn Street Chicago, IL 60610
MEDICAL LETTER ON DRUGS & THERAPEUTICS Weekly (Newsletter)	Drug & Therapeutics Information, Inc.	305 E. 45th Street New York, NY 10017
MEDICAL TRIBUNE Weekly (Newspaper)	Medical Tribune, Inc.	641 Lexington Avenue New York, NY 10022
MODERN DRUGS ENCYCLOPEDIA Annually (Encyclopedia)	Dun. Donnelly Corp.	466 Lexington Avenue New York, NY 10017
HOSPITAL-PRACTICE Monthly (Magazine)	HPH Publishing Co.	575 Lexington Avenue New York, NY 10022
NEW PRODUCT SURVEY Monthly (Magazine)	Paul De Haen, Inc.	11 West 42nd Street New York, NY 10036
PHARMACEUTICAL NEWSLETTER Weekly (Newsletter)	Pharmaceutical Manufacturers Assn.	1155 Fifteenth St.,N.W. Washington, DC
WOMEN'S WEAR DAILY Daily (Newspaper)	Fairchild Publica- tions	7 East 12th Street New York, NY 10003
U.S. DEPARTMENT OF HEALTH, EDUCATION & WELFARE	Nat'l Center for Health Statistics	Washington, DC

ELECTRONICS INDUSTRY

<u>PERIODICALS</u>

AVIATION WEEK & SPACE TECHNOLOGY Weekly (Magazine)	McGraw-Hill, Inc.	1221 Ave. of the Americas New York, NY 10020
ELECTRONIC BUYERS' GUIDE Annually (Directory)	McGraw-Hill, Inc.	1221 Ave. of the Americas New York, NY 10020

PUBLISHED	SOURCE	ADDRESS
ELECTRONIC DISTRIBUTING & MARKETING Monthly (Magazine)	Electronic Period- icals, Inc.	33405 Aurora Road Cleveland, OH 44139
ELECTRONIC COMPONENT NEWS Monthly	Chilton Co.	Chilton Way Radnor, PA 19089
ELECTRONIC MARKET DATA BOOK Annually (Data Book)	Electronic Industries Assn.	2001 I Street, N.W. Washington, DC 20006
ELECTRONIC NEWS Weekly (Newspaper)	Fairchild Publica- tions, Inc.	7 East 12th Street New York, NY 10003
ELECTRONIC NEWS FINANCIAL FACTBOOK AND DIRECTORY Annually (Factbook)	Fairchild Book Division	7 East 12th Street New York, NY 10003
ELECTRONIC TRENDS—INTERNATIONAL Monthly (Magazine)	Electronic Industries Assn.	2001 I Street, N.W. Washington, DC 20006
ELECTRONIC TRENDS—USA Monthly (Magazine)	Electronic Industries Assn.	2001 I Street, N.W. Washington, DC 20006
ELECTRONICS Biweekly	McGraw-Hill, Inc.	1221 Ave. of the Americas New York, NY 10020
IEEE SPECTRUM Monthly (Magazine)	Institute of Elec- trical & Electronic Engineers, Inc.	345 East 47th Street New York, NY 10017
LASER FOCUS Monthly (Magazine)	Advanced Technology Publications	385 Elliot Street Newton, MA 02164
NEDA JOURNAL Monthly (Journal)	National Electronic Distributors Assn.	343 South Dearborn St. Chicago, IL 60604
TELEVISION DIGEST WITH CONSUMER ELECTRONICS Weekly (Newsletter)	Television Digest	1836 Jefferson Pl.,N.W. Washington, DC 20036
TELEVISION FACTBOOK Annually (Factbook)	Television Digest	1836 Jefferson Pl.,N.W. Washington, DC 20036

PUBLISHED	SOURCE	ADDRESS

AVIONICS/ASTRONICS/ELECTRONIC WARFARE

PERIODICALS

AIR FORCE & SPACE DIGEST
Monthly   Air Force Assn.   1750 Pennsylvania
(Magazine)   Avenue, N.W.
                                                              Washington, DC 20006

ASTRONAUTICS & AERONAUTICS
Monthly   American Institute   1290 Ave. of the
(Magazine)   of Aeronautics &   Americas
                                   Astronautics   New York, NY 10019

MARKET INTELLIGENCE REPORTS
Monthly   DMS, Inc.   100 Northfield St.
(Reports)   Greenwich, CT 06830

DEPARTMENT OF DEFENSE
MILITARY POSTURE STATEMENT (SECRETARY OF
DEFENSE)
Annually   OASD (Public Affairs) Pentagon
(Newsletter)   Washington, DC 20301

DEFENSE INDUSTRY BULLETIN
11 times annually   Business & Labor   Pentagon
(Bulletin)   Division OASD (PA)   Washington, DC 20301

SELECTED ECONOMIC INDICATORS
Monthly   OASD (Comptroller)   Pentagon
(Statistics)   Directorate for   Washington, DC 20301
                                   Stat. Services

STATUS OF FUNDS (MONTHLY REPORT BY
FUNCTIONAL TITLE)
Monthly   OASD (Comptroller)   Pentagon
(Report)   Directorate for   Washington, DC 20301
                                   Financial Analysis
                                   and Control

FARM MACHINERY

PERIODICALS

CANADIAN FARM EQUIPMENT DEALER
Monthly   Southam Business   1450 Don Mills Rd.
(Bulletin)   Publications, Ltd.   Don Mills, Ontario
                                                              Canada

PUBLISHED	SOURCE	ADDRESS
CURRENT INDUSTRIAL REPORTS SERIES M355		
Monthly (Statistical Bulletin)	Bureau of Census	Washington, DC 20233
CURRENT INDUSTRIAL REPORTS SERIES M35A		
Quarterly (Statistical Bulletin)	Bureau of Census	Washington, DC 20233
FARM EQUIPMENT		
Monthly	Johnson Hill Press	1233 Janesville Ave. Fort Atkinson, WI 53538
FARM AND POWER EQUIPMENT		
Monthly (Magazine)	National Farm & Power Equipment Dealers Assn.	10877 Watson Road St. Louis, MO 63127
IMPLEMENT & TRACTOR		
Semiweekly (Magazine)	Intertec Publishing	P.O. Box 12901 Overland Park, KS 66212
NORTHWEST FARM EQUIPMENT JOURNAL		
Monthly (Magazine)	Northwest Farm Equipment Journal	1011 Upper Midwest Building Minneapolis, MN 55401
SOUTHERN FARM EQUIPMENT		
Quarterly (Magazine)	United Publishing Company	100 Oaks Tower Nashville, TN 37204
WESTERN FARM EQUIPMENT		
8 times annually (Magazine)	M.A. Johnson	P.O. Box 1657 Lake Oswego, OR 97034

FIXED INCOME SECURITIES

PUBLISHED	SOURCE	ADDRESS
PERIODICALS		
BOND MARKET ROUNDUP Weekly (Market Letter)	Salomon Brothers	One New York Plaza New York, NY 10004
BOND & MONEY MARKET LETTER BiMonthly (Market Letter)	Goldsmith-Nagan, Inc.	National Press Bldg. Washington, DC 20004
BOND OUTLOOK Weekly (Market Letter)	Standard & Poors Corp.	345 Hudson Street New York, NY 10014
COMMENTS ON CREDIT Weekly (Market Letter)	Salomon Brothers	One New York Plaza New York, NY 10004
CONVERTIBLE FACT FINDER Weekly (Statistical Summary)	Kalb, Voorhis, & Co.	27 William Street New York, NY 10005
GUIDE TO FIXED INCOME MARKETS Monthly (Market Letter)	Merrill Lynch, Pierce, Fenner, & Smith, Inc.	One Liberty Plaza New York, NY 10006
INVESTMENT DEALERS DIGEST Weekly (Magazine)	IDD, Inc.	150 Broadway New York, NY 10038
KIPLINGER WASHINGTON LETTER Weekly (Market Letter)	Kiplinger Washington Editors	1729 H. Street, N.W. Washington, DC 20006
MOODY'S BOND RECORD Monthly (Statistical Summary)	Moody's Investors Service	99 Church Street New York, NY 10007
MOODY'S BOND SURVEY Weekly (Market Letter)	Moody's Investors Service	99 Church Street New York, NY 10007
MOODY'S CONVERTIBLE BONDS Monthly (Statistical Summary)	Moody's Investors Service	99 Church Street New York, NY 10007
REPORTING ON GOVERNMENTS Weekly (Market Letter)	Ben Weberman	80 Park Avenue New York, NY 10016

PUBLISHED	SOURCE	ADDRESS
STANDARD & POORS BOND GUIDE Monthly (Statistical Summary)	Standard & Poors Corp.	345 Hudson Street New York, NY 10014
STANDARD & POORS STANDARD BOND REPORTS Weekly (Investment Advisory Service)	Standard & Poors Corp.	345 Hudson Street New York, NY 10014
U.S. FINANCIAL DATA Weekly (Statistical Summary)	Federal Reserve Bank of St. Louis	St. Louis, MO
THE DAILY BOND BUYER (Newspaper)	The Bond Buyer	One State Street Pl. New York, NY 10004
THE WEEKLY BOND BUYER Weekly (Newspaper)	The Bond Buyer	One State Street Pl. New York, NY 10004
THE VALUE LINE CONVERTIBLE SURVEY Weekly	Arnold Bernhard & Co.	5 E. 44th Street New York, NY 10017

BOOKS

BEAT THE MARKET: A SCIENTIFIC STOCK MARKET SYSTEM 1967	E.O. Thorp and S.T. Kassouf Random House	New York, NY
HANDBOOK OF CONVERTIBLE SECURITIES 1971	Kalb, Voorhis, & Co.	New York, NY
MORE PROFIT, LESS RISK - CONVERTIBLE SECURITIES AND WARRANTS 1971	Robert E. Brown & Ronald D. Bechky Arnold Bernhard & Co.	New York, NY

FOOD PROCESSING

PERIODICALS

ACREAGE AND ESTIMATED PRODUCTION OF
PRINCIPAL COMMERCIAL CORPS.
Monthly
(Catalogue)
	Crop Reporting Board
	U.S. Dept. of Agri-
	  culture
		14th & Independence
		  Avenue, S.W.
		Washington, DC 20250

PUBLISHED	SOURCE	ADDRESS
AGRICULTURAL PRICES Monthly (Bulletin)	U.S. Dept. of Agri- culture	14th & Independence Avenue, S.W. Washington, DC 20250
AGRICULTURAL SITUATION Monthly (Mar.-Dec.) BiMonthly (Jan.-Feb.) (Bulletin)	U.S. Dept. of Agri- culture Statistical Reporting Service	Washington, DC 20250
AGRICULTURAL STATISTICS Annually (Bulletin)	Superintendent of Documents U.S. Government Print- ing Office	Washington, DC 20402
ANNUAL SUMMARY (FRESH MARKET VEGETABLES) Annually (Catalogue)	Crop Reporting Board U.S. Dept. of Agri- culture	14th & Independence Avenue, S.W. Washington, DC 20250
ANNUAL COFFEE STATISTICS Annually (Annual Report)	Pan American Coffee Bureau	1350 Ave. of the Americas New York, NY 10019
CANNED FOOD REPORT Five times per year (Bulletin)	Bureau of Census Business Division Department of Commerce	Washington, DC 20233
COMMODITY YEARBOOK STATISTICAL ABSTRACT SERVICE Yearbook	Commodity Research Bureau	140 Broadway New York, NY 10005
COTTON SITUATION Jan., Mar., May, Aug., Nov.	U.S. Dept. of Agri- culture	14th & Independence Avenue, S.W. Washington, DC 20250
DAIRY SITUATION Five times per year (Bulletin)	Economic Research Service Dept. of Agriculture	14th & Independence Avenue, S.W. Washington, DC 20250
DEMAND & PRICE SITUATION Quarterly (Bulletin)	Economic Research Service Dept. of Agriculture	14th & Independence Avenue, S.W. Washington, DC 20250

PUBLISHED	SOURCE	ADDRESS
DIRECTORY OF FROZEN FOOD PROCESSORS Annually (Directory)	Cahner Publishing Co.	205 E. 42nd Street New York, NY 10017
DIRECTORY OF WHOLESALE DISTRIBUTORS Annually (Directory)	Cahner Publishing Co.	205 E. 42nd Street New York, NY 10017
FEEDSTUFFS Weekly (Newspaper)	Miller Publishing Co.	P.O. Box 67 Minneapolis, MN 55440
FOOD ENGINEERING Monthly (Magazine)	Chilton Co.	Chilton Way Radnor, PA 19089
MARKETING & TRANSPORTATION SITUATION Quarterly (Catalogue)	Economic Research Service Dept. of Agriculture	14th & Independence Avenue, S.W. Washington, DC 20250
NATIONAL FOOD SITUATION Quarterly (Bulletin)	Economic Research Service Dept. of Agriculture	14th & Independence Avenue, S.W. Washington, DC 20250
POULTRY & EGG SITUATION Five times per year (Bulletin)	Economic Research Service Dept. of Agriculture	14th & Independence Avenue, S.W. Washington, DC 20250
PROGRESSIVE GROCERS MARKETING GUIDE BOOK Annually (Yearbook)	Progressive Grocers Marketing Guide Book	708 Third Avenue New York, NY 10017
QUICK FROZEN FOODS Monthly (Magazine)	Harcourt, Brace, Jovanovich	757 Third Avenue New York, NY 10017
QUICK FROZEN FOODS - INTERNATIONAL Monthly (Magazine)	E.W. Williams Publication, Inc.	757 Third Avenue New York, NY 10017
SUGAR REPORTS Monthly (Catalogue)	Agricultural Stabilization and Conservation Service	14th & Independence Avenue, S.W. Washington, DC 20250
VEGETABLES (PROCESSING) Fifteen times per year (Bulletin)	Crop Reporting Board Dept. of Agriculture	14th & Independence Avenue, S.W. Washington, DC 20250

PUBLISHED	SOURCE	ADDRESS
WASHINGTON FOOD REPORT Weekly (Digest)	American Institute of Food Distribution	28-06 Broadway Fairlawn, NJ 07410
WHEAT SITUATION Four times per year (Bulletin)	Economic Research Service Dept. of Agriculture	14th & Independence Avenue, S.W. Washington, DC 20250
WOOL SITUATION Quarterly (Review)	Economic Research Service Dept. of Agriculture	14th & Independence Avenue, S.W. Washington, DC 20250

GLASS AND CONTAINER INDUSTRY

PERIODICALS

BDSA QUARTERLY INDUSTRY REPORTS – CONTAINERS & PACKAGING Quarterly (Booklet)	Dept. of Commerce	Washington, DC
CURRENT INDUSTRIAL REPORTS – GLASS CONTAINERS Monthly (Stat. Summary)	Dept. of Commerce	Washington, DC
FIBRE BOX ASSOCIATION STATISTICAL BULLETIN Weekly (Stat. Summary)	Fibre Box Association	224 S. Michigan Ave. Chicago, IL 60611
GLASS CONTAINERS Annually (July) (Booklet)	Glass Container Manu- facturing Institute	330 Madison Avenue New York, NY 10017
MODERN PACKAGING Monthly (Magazine)	Morgan-Grampian Pub- lishing	205 E. 42nd Street New York, NY 10017
PAPERBOARD PACKAGING Monthly (Magazine)	Magazines for Industry	777 Third Avenue New York, NY 10017
PAPERBOARD STATISTICS Weekly (Stat. Summary)	American Paper Insti- tute, Inc.	260 Madison Avenue New York, NY 10017

HOME FURNISHING INDUSTRY

PUBLISHED	SOURCE	ADDRESS

PERIODICALS

ADVERTISING AGE Weekly (Marketing Publication)	Crain Communications, Inc.	740 Rush Street Chicago, IL 60611
APPLIANCE MANUFACTURER Monthly	Cahner's Publishing Co.	5 S. Wabash Avenue Chicago, IL 60603
HOME FURNISHINGS DAILY Daily	Fairchild Publications	7 E. 12th Street New York, NY 10003
MERCHANDISING Weekly	Billboard Publications	1515 Broadway New York, NY 10036

CURRENT INDUSTRIAL REPORTS		
Carpets and Rugs	MQ-22Q	
Electric Housewares	MA-36E	
Home Radio Receivers and Television Sets, etc.	MA-36M	
Household Furniture	MA-25D	
Major Household Appliances	MA-36F	
Selected Electronic and Associated Products	MA-36N	
(Statistical Reports)	Dept. of Commerce Social & Economics Statistics Administration Bureau of the Census Industry Division	Washington, DC 20233

ASSOCIATION OF HOME APPLIANCE MANUFACTURERS	20 N. Wacker Drive Chicago, IL 60606
CARPET AND RUG INSTITUTE	208 W. Cuyler Street Dalton, GA 30720
SEIDMAN & SEIDMAN	110 Union Bank Bldg. Grand Rapids, MI 49502
SOUTHERN FURNITURE MANUFACTURERS ASSOCIATION	P.O. Box 951 High Point, NC 27261
VACUUM CLEANER MANUFACTURERS ASSOCIATION	1615 Collamer Street Cleveland, OH 44110

HOTELS/MOTELS

PUBLISHED	SOURCE	ADDRESS
PERIODICALS		
LODGING & FOOD SERVICE NEWS Weekly (Newspaper)	Hotel Service, Inc.	131 Clarendon Street Boston, MA 02116
LODGING INDUSTRY Annually (Survey)	Laventhol & Horwath	919 Third Avenue New York, NY 10022
THE TRAVEL AGENT Semi-Weekly (Magazine)	American Traveler, Inc.	2 W. 46th Street New York, NY 10036
TRENDS IN THE HOTEL/MOTEL BUSINESS Annually (Report)	Harris, Kerr, Forster & Co.	420 Lexington Ave. New York, NY 10017
TRENDS OF BUSINESS - HOTELS Monthly (Newsletter)	Laventhol & Horwath	919 Third Avenue New York, NY 10022

INSURANCE

PERIODICALS		
BEST'S REVIEW (LIFE EDITION, FIRE & CASUALTY EDITION) Monthly (Journal)	Alfred M. Best & Co.	Park Avenue Morristown, NJ 07960
BEST'S WEEKLY NEWS DIGEST Weekly (Journal)	Alfred M. Best & Co.	Park Avenue Morristown, NJ 07960
FINAL REPORT FROM THE COMMITTEE ON LIFE INSURANCE EARNINGS ADJUSTMENTS 1970	The Association of Insurance and Financial Analysts c/o Mr. David Seifer Jas. H. Oliphant & Co., Inc.	61 Broadway New York, NY 10005
INSURANCE ADVOCATE Weekly (Magazine)	Robert's Publishing	45 John Street New York, NY 10038
INSURANCE MAGAZINE Weekly (Magazine)	Bayard Publications	300 Broad Street Stamford, CT 06901

PUBLISHED	SOURCE	ADDRESS
MONTHLY BULLETIN Monthly (Newsletter)	Insurance Department State of New York	123 William Street New York, NY 10038
NATIONAL UNDERWRITER (LIFE EDITION, FIRE & CASUALTY EDITION) Weekly (Magazine)	National Underwriter	420 E. 42nd Street Cincinnati, OH 45202
THE TALLY OF LIFE INSURANCE STATISTICS Monthly (Newsletter)	Institute of Life Insurance Div. of Statistics & Research	277 Park Avenue New York, NY 10017

BOOKS

THE ECONOMIC THEORY OF RISK AND INSURANCE 1951	Allan H. Willett Richard D. Irwin, Inc.	Homewood, IL 60430
INSURANCE: PRINCIPLES AND PRACTICES 1962	Frank J. Angell Ronald Press Co.	New York, NY
LIFE COMPANY ANNUAL STATEMENT HANDBOOK 1962	Chas. H. Beardsley H.W. Satchell & Co.	Columbus, OH
LIFE INSURANCE (TEXT EDITION) 1958	John H. Magee Richard D. Irwin, Inc.	Homewood, IL 60430
SOURCES OF INSURANCE STATISTICS 1965	Elizabeth Ferguson Special Libraries Assn.	New York, NY
TRANSITION TO MULTIPLE-LINE INSURANCE COMPANIES 1961	D.L. Bickelhaupt Richard D. Irwin, Inc.	Homewood, IL 60430

LEISURE INDUSTRY

PERIODICALS

R.V. MARKETING REPORT Monthly (Newsletter)	Recreational Vehicle Institute, Inc.	2720 Des Plaines Ave. Des Plaines, IL 60018
SELLING SPORT GOODS Monthly (Magazine)	National Sporting Goods Assn.	717 N. Michigan Ave. Chicago, IL 60611

PUBLISHED	SOURCE	ADDRESS
TOY & HOBBY WORLD Semimonthly (Newsletter-Newspaper)	Charleston Publishing	124 E. 40th Street New York, NY 10016
TOYS Semimonthly (Magazine)	Harcourt, Brace, Jovanovich	757 Third Avenue New York, NY 10017

MACHINE TOOL INDUSTRY

PERIODICALS

AMERICAN MACHINIST Monthly (Magazine)	McGraw-Hill	1221 Ave. of the Americas New York, NY 10020
ECONOMIC HANDBOOK OF THE MACHINE TOOL INDUSTRY Annually (Handbook)	National Machine Tool Builders Assn.	7901 Westpark Drive McLean, VA 22101
INDUSTRIAL MACHINERY NEWS Monthly (Magazine)	I.M.N. Corp.	29516 Southfield Rd. Southfield, MI 48037
MACHINE TOOL INDUSTRY: SHIPMENTS AND ORDERS Monthly (Statistics)	National Machine Tool Builders Assn.	7901 Westpark Drive McLean, VA 22101
METALWORKING NEWS EDITION (AMERICAN METAL MARKET) Weekly (Newspaper)	Fairchild Publishing	7 E. 12th Street New York, NY 10003

BOOKS

MACHINE SHOP THEORY FOR TOOL, DIE, AND MACHINIST APPRENTICES 1965	National Tool, Die and Precision Machinery Assn.	Washington, DC
SHOP GUIDE FOR APPRENTICE TRAINING 1972	National Tool, Die, and Precision Machinery Assn.	Washington, DC

PUBLISHED	SOURCE	ADDRESS

MOBILE HOMES

PERIODICALS

CONSTRUCTION REPORTS - HOUSING
STARTS (C20)
Monthly   U.S. Government   Washington, DC 20402
(Gov't. Stat. Bulletin)   Printing Office
     Superintendent of
     Documents

DIRECTORY - MOBILE & MODULAR HOMES
Annually   Hanley Publishing Co.   1718 Sherman Avenue
(Consumer Product Directory)   Evanston, IL 60201

HOUSING & REALTY INVESTOR
Twice Monthly   Audit Investment   230 Park Avenue
(Investment Analysis   Research   New York, NY 10017
  Service)

MOBILE HOME PARK MANAGER & DEVELOPER
Bimonthly   Trailer Dealer Pub-   6229 N. Northwest Hwy.
(Trade Magazine)   lishing Co.   Chicago, IL 60631

MOBILE HOME SALES TRENDS
Monthly   Mobile Home Manu-   6650 N. Northwest Hwy.
(Trade Assn. Bulletin)   facturers Assn.   Chicago, IL 60631

MOBILE-MODULAR HOUSING DEALER
Twice Monthly   Trailer Dealer Pub-   6229 N. Northwest Hwy.
(Trade Magazine)   lishing Co.   Chicago, IL 60631

SUPPLIER NEWS BULLETIN
Monthly   Mobile-Modular Housing   6229 N. Northwest Hwy.
(Trade Assn. Statistics)   Dealer Magazine   Chicago, IL 60631

MOTOR CARRIER INDUSTRY

PERIODICALS

AMERICAN TRUCKING TRENDS
Annually   American Trucking   1616 P Street, N.W.
(Annual Report)   Association, Inc.   Washington, DC 20036

ANNUAL REPORT (INTERSTATE COMMERCE
COMMISSION)
Annually   U.S. Government   Washington, DC
(Annual Report)   Printing Office

CARRIER REPORTS
Quarterly   Carrier Reports   369 Main Street
(Financial Statistics)   Old Saybrook, CT 06475

PUBLISHED	SOURCE	ADDRESS
DAILY TRAFFIC WORLD Daily (Newspaper)	The Traffic Service Corp.	815 Washington Bldg. Washington, DC
TRANSPORT TOPICS Weekly (Newspaper)	American Trucking Association, Inc.	1616 P Street, N.W. Washington, DC 20036
TRINC'S BLUE BOOK Annual (Company Data)	Trinc Associates, Ltd.	485 L'Enfant Pl., S.W. Washington, DC 20024
TRINC'S RED BOOK Quarterly (Statistics)	Trinc Associates, Ltd.	485 L'Enfant Pl., S.W. Washington, DC 20024

BOOKS

BANKER'S ANALYSIS OF THE MOTOR CARRIER
INDUSTRY

	Peter Douglas Chase Manhattan Bank	New York, NY

FINANCING THE MOTOR CARRIER INDUSTRY

	American Trucking Association	Washington, DC

OTHER

AMERICAN TRUCKING ASSOCIATION

		1616 P Street, N.W. Washington, DC 20036

TRANSPORTATION ASSOCIATION OF AMERICA

		60 E. 42nd Street New York, NY 10017

TRANSPORTATION CENTER

	Northwestern Univer- sity	619 Clark Street Evanston, IL 60611

NONFERROUS METALS (SEE ALSO ALUMINUM)

PERIODICALS

ALUMINUM MONTHLY Monthly (Statistics)	Bureau of Mines	Washington, DC
AMERICAN METAL MARKET Daily (Newspaper)	American Metal Market Company	7 E. 12th Street New York, NY 10003

PUBLISHED	SOURCE	ADDRESS
COPPER INDUSTRY MONTHLY Monthly (Statistics)	Bureau of Mines	Washington, DC
CURRENT INDUSTRIAL REPORT M 33-2 ALUMINUM INGOT AND MILL PRODUCT SHIPMENTS Monthly (Statistics)	Dept. of Commerce	Washington, DC
ENGINEERING & MINING JOURNAL Monthly (Magazine)	McGraw-Hill, Inc.	1221 Ave. of the Americas New York, NY 10020
HANDY & HARMAN ANNUAL REVIEW OF SILVER Annually (Yearbook)	Handy & Harman	850 Third Avenue New York, NY 10022
METAL STATISTICS Annually (Stat. Yearbook)	American Metal Market Fairchild Publications	7 E. 12th Street New York, NY 10003
METAL STATISTICS Annually (Stat. Yearbook)	Metallgesellschaft AG	6000 Frankfort A.M. Main Reuterweg 14, Germany
METALS WEEK Weekly (Newspaper)	McGraw-Hill, Inc.	1221 Ave. of the Americas New York, NY 10020
MINERALS YEARBOOK VOL. 1-2 METALS, MINERALS & FUELS Annually (Yearbook)	U.S. Government Printing Office	Washington, DC 20402
MINERALS YEARBOOK VOL. 3 AREA REPORTS - DOMESTIC VOL. 4 AREA REPORTS - INTERNATIONAL Annually (Yearbook)	U.S. Government Printing Office	Washington, DC 20402
MINING JOURNAL Weekly (Newspaper)	Mining Journal, Ltd.	15 Wilson Street London E.C.2 England, U.K.
NICKEL MONTHLY Monthly (Statistics)	Bureau of Mines	Washington, DC

PUBLISHED	SOURCE	ADDRESS
QUARTERLY INDUSTRY REPORT - COPPER		
Quarterly (Magazine)	Superintendent of Documents U.S. Government Printing Office	Washington, DC 20402
YEARBOOK OF THE AMERICAN BUREAU OF METAL STATISTICS		
Annually (Stat. Compendium)	American Bureau of Metal Statistics	50 Broadway New York, NY 10004

BOOKS

MINERALS FACTS AND PROBLEMS		
1970	Superintendent of Documents U.S. Government Printing Office	Washington, DC 20402

OTHERS

ALUMINUM ASSOCIATION		750 Third Avenue New York, NY 10017
AMERICAN BUREAU OF METAL STATISTICS		50 Broadway New York, NY 10004
AMERICAN ZINC INSTITUTE, INC.		292 Madison Avenue New York, NY 10017
BUREAU OF CENSUS		Washington, DC 20233
COPPER DEVELOPMENT OF COMMERCE		405 Lexington Avenue New York, NY 10017
U.S. DEPARTMENT OF COMMERCE	BDSA	Washington, DC 20230
U.S. DEPARTMENT OF THE INTERIOR	Bureau of Mines	Washington, DC 20240

OFFICE EQUIPMENT

PERIODICALS

COMPUTERS AND AUTOMATION		
Monthly (Magazine)	Computers and Automation	815 Washmaton Street Newtonville, MA 02160

PUBLISHED	SOURCE	ADDRESS
COMPUTERWORLD Weekly (Newspaper)	Computerworld	797 Washmaton Street Newtonville, MA 02160
DATAMATION Monthly (Magazine)	Technical Publishing Company	1801 S. LaCienega Boulevard Los Angeles, CA 90035
DATAPRO 1972 Monthly (Reference Supplements)	Datapro Research Corp.	2204 Walnut Street Philadelphia, PA 19103
DMS ELECTRONICS & GENERAL SUPPORT Monthly (Reference Supplements)	Defense Market Service	71 Lewis Street Greenwich, CT 06830
EDP INDUSTRY REPORT Semiweekly (Newsletter)	International Data Publications Co.	214 Third Avenue Waltham, MA 02154
ELECTRONIC NEWS Weekly (Newspaper)	Fairchild Publications	7 E. 12th Street New York, NY 10003
ELECTRONICS Biweekly (Magazine)	McGraw-Hill, Inc.	1221 Ave. of the Americas New York, NY 10020
INFOSYSTEMS MAGAZINE Monthly (Magazine)	Hitchcock Publishing	Hitchcock Bldg. Wheaton, IL 60187

OTHER

BUSINESS EQUIPMENT MANUFACTURERS ASSOCIATION

Washington, DC

OIL AND NATURAL GAS

PERIODICALS

ENERGY MEMO Quarterly (Newsletter)	First National City Bank	399 Park Avenue New York, NY 10022
NATIONAL PETROLEUM NEWS BULLETIN Monthly	McGraw-Hill, Inc.	1221 Ave. of the Americas New York, NY 10020

PUBLISHED	SOURCE	ADDRESS
OFFSHORE Monthly (Magazine)	Petroleum Publi- cations Co.	1200 S. Post Oak Rd. Houston, TX 77056
THE OIL DAILY Daily (Newspaper)	Whitney Communications	373 National Press Building Washington, DC 20045
OIL AND GAS JOURNAL Weekly (Journal)	The Petroleum Pub- lishing Co.	P.O. Box 1260 Tulsa, OK 74101
OIL STATISTICS BULLETIN Biweekly (Bulletin)	Oil Statistics Co., Inc.	Babson Park, MA
OIL WEEK Weekly (Magazine)	Maclean-Hunter, Ltd.	200-918 6th Avenue Calgary, Alberta, Canada T2P0V5
PETROLEUM ENGINEER Monthly (Magazine)	Petroleum Engineer Publishing Co.	P.O. Box 1589 Dallas, TX 75221
PETROLEUM SITUATION Monthly (Fact Sheet)	Chase Manhattan Bank	1 Chase Manhattan Pl. New York, NY 10015
PETROLEUM TIMES Biweekly (Newsletter)	IPC America, Inc.	205 E. 42nd Street New York, NY 10017
PLATT'S OILGRAM NEWS SERVICE Daily (Newsletter)	McGraw-Hill, Inc.	1221 Ave. of the Americas New York, NY 10020
WORLD OIL Monthly (Magazine)	Gulf Publishing Co.	P.O. Box 2608 Houston, TX 77001

OTHER

AMERICAN PETROLEUM INSTITUTE		1271 Sixth Avenue New York, NY 10019
INDEPENDENT PETROLEUM ASSOCIATION OF AMERICA		1101 16th St., N.W. Washington, DC 20036
NATIONAL PETROLEUM COUNCIL		1625 K Street, N.W. Washington, DC 20006

PUBLISHED	SOURCE	ADDRESS
	PAPER	

PERIODICALS

CAPACITY SURVEY
Annually
(Survey)
American Paper Institute, Inc. — 260 Madison Avenue, New York, NY 10016

THE DEMAND AND PRICE SITUATION FOR
FOREST PRODUCTS
Annually (Nov.)
(Survey)
U.S. Forest Service Department of Agriculture — Washington, DC 20250

LOCKWOOD'S DIRECTORY OF THE PAPER &
ALLIED TRADES
Annually
(Directory)
Lockwood Trade-Journal Co., Inc. — 551 Fifth Avenue, New York, NY 10017

MONTHLY STATISTICAL SUMMARY
Monthly
(Fact Sheet)
American Paper Institute, Inc. — 260 Madison Avenue, New York, NY 10016

PAPERBOARD STATISTICS NEWS RELEASE
Weekly
(Statistics)
American Paper Institute, Inc. — 260 Madison Avenue, New York, NY 10016

PAPER TRADE JOURNAL
Weekly
(Magazine)
Vance Publishing Co. — 133 E. 58th Street, New York, NY 10022

PHOTOGRAPHY INDUSTRY

AUDIO VISUAL COMMUNICATIONS
Monthly
(Magazine)
United Business Publications — 750 Third Avenue, New York, NY 10017

GRAPHIC ARTS PROGRESS
Monthly
(Magazine)
Graphic Arts Research Center Rochester Institute of Technology — One Lomb Memorial Dr., Rochester, NY 14623

GRAPHIC COMMUNICATIONS WORLD
Biweekly
Technical Information, Inc. — P.O. Box 775, S. Lake Tahoe, CA 95705

INDUSTRIAL PHOTOGRAPHY
Monthly
(Magazine)
United Business Publications, Inc. — 750 Third Avenue, New York, NY 10017

INFOSYSTEMS MAGAZINE
Monthly
(Magazine)
Hitchcock Publishing — Hitchcock Building, Wheaton, IL 60187

PUBLISHED	SOURCE	ADDRESS
THE JOURNAL OF MICROGRAPHICS Bimonthly (Journal)	The National Micro- film Assn.	8728 Colesville Rd. Silver Spring, MD 20910
THE JOURNAL OF THE SMPTE Monthly (Journal)	Society of Motion Picture and Tele- vision Engineers, Inc.	9 E. 41st Street New York, NY 10017
MICROFILM TECHNIQUES Bimonthly (Magazine)	PTN Publishing	250 Fulton Avenue Hempstead, NY 11550
MODERN PHOTOGRAPHY Monthly (Magazine)	Leisure Magazines, Inc.	130 E. 59th Street New York, NY 10022
PETERSON'S PHOTOGRAPHIC MAGAZINE Monthly (Magazine)	Peterson Publishing Company	8490 Sunset Blvd. Los Angeles, CA 90069
PHOTO MARKETING Monthly (Magazine)	Master Photo Dealers' & Finishers' Assn.	603 Lansing Avenue Jackson, MI 49202
PHOTO WEEKLY Weekly (Newspaper)	Billboard Publications	1515 Broadway New York, NY 10036
PHOTOGRAPHIC TRADE NEWS Biweekly (Magazine)	PTN Publishing	250 Fulton Avenue Hempstead, NY 11550

PUBLISHED	SOURCE	ADDRESS
PHOTOGRAPHIC SCIENCE & ENGINEERING Bimonthly (Magazine)	Society of Photographic Scientists & Engineers	1411 K Street, N.W. Washington, DC 20005
POPULAR PHOTOGRAPHY Monthly (Magazine)	Ziff-Davis Publishing Company	One Park Avenue New York, NY 10016
TECHNICAL PHOTOGRAPHY Monthly (Journal)	PTN Publishing	250 Fulton Avenue Hempstead, NY 11550
WOLFMAN REPORT ON THE PHOTOGRAPHIC INDUSTRY IN THE UNITED STATES Annually (Magazine)	Modern Photography	165 W. 46th Street New York, NY 10036

BOOKS

FUNDAMENTALS OF HOTOGRAPHIC THEORY 1968	T.H. James, Ph.D. George C. Higgins Morgan & Morgan, Inc.	Hastings-on-Hudson, NY
INTRODUCTION TO PHOTOGRAPHIC PRINCIPLES 1965	Lewis Larmore, Ph.D. Dover Publications	New York, NY
PHOTOGRAPHIC CHEMISTRY 1965	George T. Eaton Morgan & Morgan, Inc.	Hastings-on-Hudson, NY
THE U.S. PHOTOGRAPHIC INDUSTRY 1970-75 1971	Ian D. Robinson Elliott D. Novak Arthur D. Little, Inc.	
WORLD REPORT OF PHOTOGRAPHY 1968	L.A. M.A. Mannheim Staples Printers, Ltd.	Rochester Kent, England
YOUR GUIDE TO PHOTOGRAPHY 1969	Helen Finn Bruce Barnes & Noble, Inc.	New York, NY

OTHERS

THE ENCYCLOPEDIA OF PHOTOGRAPHY	Willard D. Morgan, Ed. The Greystone Press	New York, NY
LIFE LIBRARY OF PHOTOGRAPHY 1971	The Editors of Time- Life Books	New York, NY

THE POLLUTION CONTROL INDUSTRY

PUBLISHED	SOURCE	ADDRESS

PERIODICALS

CHEMICAL ENGINEERING BiWeekly (Trade Journal)	McGraw-Hill, Inc.	1221 Avenue of the Americas New York, NY 10020
ENVIRONMENTAL SCIENCE & TECHNOLOGY Monthly (News Magazine)	American Chemical Society	1155 16th Street,N.W. Washington, DC 20036
CHEMICAL WEEK Weekly (Trade Journal)	McGraw-Hill, Inc.	1221 Avenue of the Americas New York, NY 10020
WATER & WASTES DIGEST Monthly (Trade Journal)	Scranton Publishing Company	434 S. Wabash Avenue Chicago, IL 60605

BOOKS

THE BUDGET OF THE UNITED STATES GOVERNMENT 1972	U. S. Government Printing Office	Washington, DC 20402
ECONOMIC REPORT OF THE PRESIDENT 1972	U. S. Government Printing Office	Washington, DC 20402
A PERSPECTIVE OF REGIONAL AND STATE MARINE ENVIRONMENTAL ACTIVITIES, NO. PB 177765 1968	National Technical Information Service	Springfield, VA
ENVIRONMENTAL QUALITY (The Second Annual Report of the Council on Environ- mental Quality) August 1971	U. S. Government Printing Office	Washington, DC 20402

OTHERS

SUBCOMMITTEE ON AIR AND WATER POLLUTION	Senator Edmund S. Muskie, Chairman Copies of Hearings & Bills	Senate Office Bldg. Washington, DC 20402

PUBLISHED	SOURCE	ADDRESS
GENERAL REGISTER (The National Archives of the United States) Daily	Superintendent of Documents U. S. Government Printing Office	Washington, DC 20402

PUBLIC UTILITY COMPANIES

PERIODICALS

PUBLISHED	SOURCE	ADDRESS
ELECTRICAL WORLD Fortnightly (Magazine)	McGraw-Hill, Inc.	1221 Avenue of the Americas New York, NY 10020
FPC NEWS Weekly (Newsletter)	Federal Power Commission Office of Public Information	Washington, DC 20426
GENERAL POWER COMMISSION ELECTRIC POWER STATISTICS Monthly (Bulletin)	Superintendent of Documents U. S. Government Printing Office	Washington, DC 20402
NATIONAL ELECTRIC RATE BOOK Annually (Booklets) 50 in all; one per state	Superintendent of Documents U. S. Government Printing Office	Washington, DC 20402
PUBLIC UTILITIES FORTNIGHTLY Fortnightly (Magazine)	Public Utilities Report, Inc.	1828 L Street, N.W. Suite 502 Washington, DC 20036
PUBLIC UTILITIES REPORTS Fortnightly (Bulletin)	Public Utilities Reports	332 Pennsylvania Bldg. 425 13th Street, N.W. Washington, DC 20004
STATISTICAL RELEASES Weekly-Monthly (Statistical Yearbook)	Edison Electric Institute	90 Park Avenue New York, NY 10016
UTILITY SPOTLIGHT Weekly (Newsletter)	Corporate Intelligence	74 Trinity Place New York, NY 10004

PUBLISHED	SOURCE	ADDRESS

WEEKLY NEWSLETTER
Weekly   McGraw-Hill, Inc.   1221 Avenue of the
(Newsletter)   Americas
                                           New York, NY 10020

OTHER

AMERICAN GAS ASSOCIATION

                                           1515 Wilson Blvd.
                                           Arlington, VA 22209

EDISON ELECTRIC INSTITUTE

                                           90 Park Avenue
                                           New York, NY 10016

FEDERAL COMMUNICATION COMMISSION

                                           1919 M Street, N.W.
                                           Washington, DC 20554

FEDERAL POWER COMMISSION

                                           441 G Street, N.W.
                                           Washington, DC 20426

PUBLISHING INDUSTRY

PERIODICALS

ADVERTISING AGE
Weekly   Crain Communications   740 North Rush Street
(Magazine)   Chicago, IL 60611

BOOK PRODUCTION INDUSTRY
Monthly   BPI Publishing   21 Charles Street
(Magazine)   Westport, CT 06880

EDUCATION U.S.A. AND SUPPLEMENT WASHINGTON
MONITOR
Weekly   National School Public 1201 16th Street, N.W.
(Newsletter)   Relations Assn.   Washington, DC 20036

THE GALLAGHER REPORT
Weekly   The Gallagher Report,   230 Park Avenue
(Newsletter)   Inc.   New York, NY 10017

INLAND PRINTER/AMERICAN LITHOGRAPHER
Monthly   Maclean-Hunter   300 West Adams Street
(Magazine)   Publishing Corp.   Chicago, IL 60606

KNOWLEDGE INDUSTRY REPORT
Weekly   Knowledge Industry   56 Doyer Avenue
(Newsletter)   Publications, Inc.   White Plains, NY 10605

PUBLISHED	SOURCE	ADDRESS
MEDIA INDUSTRY NEWSLETTER Weekly (Newsletter)	MIN Publishing Inc.	156 East 52nd St. New York, NY 10022

PRINTING AND PUBLISHING
Monthly
(Newsletter)
	U.S. Department of
	  Commerce
	Superintendent of
	  Documents
	U.S. Government
	  Printing Office
		Washington, DC 20402

PUBLISHERS WEEKLY Weekly (Magazine)	R. R. Bowker Co.	1180 Avenue of the Americas New York, NY 10036

BOOKS

THE ART AND SCIENCE OF BOOK PUBLISHING 1970	Herbert Bailey Harper & Row	New York, NY
BOOK PUBLISHING IN AMERICA 1966	Charles A. Madison McGraw-Hill Book Co.	New York, NY
THE BOWKER ANNUAL OF LIBRARY AND BOOK TRADE INFORMATION 1978 (latest edition)	Phyllis Steckler R. R. Bowker Co.	New York, NY
DIGEST OF EDUCATIONAL STATISTICS 1977–78 (latest edition)	Kenneth A. Simon & W. Vance Grant U.S. Government Printing Office	Washington, DC
A GUIDE TO BOOK PUBLISHING 1966	Datus C. Smith R. R. Bowker Co.	New York, NY
THE PRINTING INDUSTRY 1967	Victor Strauss Printing Industries of America, Inc.	Washington, DC
PROJECTIONS OF EDUCATIONAL STATISTICS TO 1980–81 1972	Kenneth A. Simon U.S. Government Printing Office	Washington, DC

PUBLISHED	SOURCE	ADDRESS

RAILROAD AND RAILROAD EQUIPMENT INDUSTRY

PERIODICALS

ANNUAL REPORT (INTERSTATE COMMERCE COMMISSION)
Annually   U.S. Government   Washington, DC
(Annual Report)   Printing Office

TRAFFIC WORLD
Weekly   The Traffic Service   815 Washington Bldg.
(Newspaper)   Corp.   Washington, DC

RAILWAY AGE
SemiWeekly   Simmons-Boardman   350 Broadway
(Magazine)   Publishing Corp.   New York, NY 10013

TRAINS
Monthly   Kalmbuck Publishing   1027 North 7th Street
(Magazine)   Co.   Milwaukee, WI 53233

TRANSPORT ECONOMICS
Monthly   Interstate Commerce   Washington, DC
(Statistics)   Commission

YEARBOOK OF RAILROAD FACTS
Annually   Assn. of Am. Railroads   1920 L Street, N.W.
(Yearbook)   Washington, DC 20036

ASSOCIATIONS, ETC.

AMERICAN RAILWAY CAR INSTITUTE
     11 East 44th Street
     New York, NY 10017

ASSOCIATION OF AMERICAN RAILROADS
     1920 L Street, N.W.
     Washington, DC 20036

RAILWAY PROGRESS INSTITUTE
     801 North Fairfax
     Alexandria, VA 22314

OTHER

"ON THE ESTIMATION OF RAILROAD EARNINGS"
Nov. - Dec. 1966   Karl Ziebarth
     Financial Analyst Jour-
     nal (pp.54-55)

PUBLISHED	SOURCE	ADDRESS

REAL ESTATE AND REITS

PERIODICALS

CONSTRUCTION REVIEW
Monthly   U.S. Government   Washington, DC
(Stat. Review)   Printing Office

HOUSE AND HOME
Monthly   McGraw-Hill, Inc.   1221 Avenue of the
(Magazine)   Americas
                                                     New York, NY 10020

HOUSING AND REALTY INVESTOR
Twice Monthly   Audit Investment   230 Park Avenue
(Investment Letter)   Research, Inc.   New York, NY 10017

HUD NEWS
Irregular   U.S. Department of   Washington, DC 20410
(News Releases)   Housing and Urban
                               Development

MOBILE-MODULAR HOUSING DEALER
Monthly   Trailer-Dealer   6229 North Highway
(Magazine)   Publishing Company   Chicago, IL 60631

PROFESSIONAL BUILDER & APARTMENT BUSINESS
Monthly   Cahners Publishing   5 South Wabash Ave.
(Magazine)   Company   Chicago, IL 60603

REAL ESTATE REVIEW
Quarterly   Warren, Gorham &   P.O. Box 1019
(Magazine)   Lamont, Inc.   Manhasset, NY 11030

REALTY TRUST REVIEW
Twice Monthly   Audit Investment   230 Park Avenue
(Investment Letter)   Research, Inc.   New York, NY 10017

BOOKS

REAL ESTATE TRUSTS: AMERICA'S NEWEST
BILLIONAIRES
                            Kenneth Campbell   New York, NY
                            Audit Investment
                               Research, Inc.

OTHER

The US. Department of Housing and Urban
Development and the U.S. Government Printing
Office offer a large variety of Statistical
information on request.

PUBLISHED	SOURCE	ADDRESS

RETAIL TRADE

PERIODICALS

AUTOMOTIVE NEWS
Weekly   Crain Communications   965 E. Jefferson Ave.
(Magazine)   Inc.   Detroit, MI 48207

CLOTHES
SemiWeekly   Prads, Inc.   380 Madison Avenue
(Magazine)   New York, NY 10017

DAILY NEWS RECORD
Daily   Fairchild Publications 7 East 12th Street
(Newspaper)   New York, NY 10003

DISCOUNT STORE NEWS
BiWeekly   Lebhar-Friedman Inc.   425 Park Avenue
(Newspaper)   New York, NY 10022

FINANCIAL AND OPERATING RESULTS OF
DEPARTMENT AND SPECIALTY STORES
Annually   National Retail   100 West 31st Street
(Book)   Merchants Assn.   New York, NY 10017

FOOTWEAR NEWS
Weekly   Fairchild Publications 7 East 12th Street
(Newspaper)   New York, NY 10003

HFD - RETAILING HOME FURNISHINGS
Weekly   Fairchild Publications 7 East 12th Street
(Newspaper)   New York, NY 10003

MERCHANDISING AND OPERATING RESULTS
Annually   National Retail   100 West 31st Street
(Books)   Merchants Assn.   New York, NY 10017

MERCHANDISING
Weekly   BillBoard Publications 1515 Broadway
(Magazine)   New York, NY 10036

OPERATING RESULTS OF FOOD CHAINS
Annually   Dr. Earl Brown   Warren Hall
(Book)   Department of Agricul- Cornell University
                               tural Economics   Ithaca, NY 14850

OPERATING RESULTS OF SELF SERVICE DISCOUNT
DEPARTMENT STORES
Annually   Mr. Kurt Barmard   570 Seventh Avenue
(Book)   Mass Retailing Inst.   New York, NY 10018

PUBLISHED	SOURCE	ADDRESS
PROGRESSIVE GROCER Monthly (Magazine)	Butterick Division of American Can Co.	708 Third Avenue New York, NY 10017
RETAIL SALES STATISTICS Weekly, Monthly, & Annually	U.S. Department of Commerce Superintendent of Documents	Washington, DC
SUPERMARKETING Monthly (Magazine)	Gralla Publications	1515 Broadway New York, NY 10036
SUPERMARKET NEWS Weekly (Newspaper)	Fairchild Publications	7 East 12th Street New York, NY 10003
WOMEN'S WEAR DAILY Daily (Newspaper)	Fairchild Publications	7 East 12th Street New York, NY 10003

RUBBER/TIRES

PERIODICALS

AUTOMOBILE FACTS AND FIGURES Annually (Statistics)	Motor Vehicle Manufac- turer's Assn. of the U.S.	320 New Center Bldg. Detroit, MI 48202
AUTOMOTIVE INDUSTRIES Monthly (Magazine)	Chilton Co.	Chilton Way Radnor, PA 19089
CURRENT INDUSTRIAL REPORT-RUBBER: SUPPLY & DISTRIBUTION FOR THE U.S. Monthly (Report)	U.S. Department of Commerce Bureau of the Census Industry Division	Washington, DC 20233
INTERNATIONAL RUBBER DIGEST Monthly (Magazine)	International Rubber Study Group	5-6 Lancaster Place Strand London W.C.2, England
MODERN TIRE DEALER Monthly (Magazine)	Bill Communications Inc.	77 N. Miller Road Akron, OH 44313

PUBLISHED	SOURCE	ADDRESS
MOTOR TRUCK FACTS Annually (Statistics)	Motor Vehicle Manufac- turer's Assn. of the U.S.	320 New Center Bldg. Detroit, MI 48202
N T D R A DEALER NEWS 36 Times Yearly (Magazine)	National Tire Dealers & Retreaders Assn.	1343 L Street, N.W. Washington, DC 20005
NATIONAL PETROLEUM NEWS Monthly (Magazine)	McGraw-Hill, Inc.	1221 Avenue of the Americas New York, NY 10020
NATURAL RUBBER NEWS Monthly (Magazine)	Natural Rubber Bureau	Hudson, OH 44236
QUARTERLY INDUSTRIAL FINANCIAL REPORTS Quarterly (Statistics)	Federal Trade Commis- sion	Washington, DC 20590
RUBBER AGE Monthly (Magazine)	B. J. Kotsher	461 Eighth Avenue New York, NY 10001
RUBBER & PLASTIC NEWS SemiWeekly (Magazine)	Crain Communications Inc.	One Cascade Plaza Akron, OH 44308
RUBBER INDUSTRY FACTS Annually (Statistics)	Rubber Manufacturers Association	444 Madison Avenue New York, NY 10022
RUBBER RED BOOK Annually (Statistics)	Rubber Age	101 West 31st Street New York, NY 10001
RUBBER STATISTICAL BULLETIN Monthly (Statistics)	International Rubber Study Group	5-6 Lancaster Place Strand London, E.C.2, England
RUBBER WORLD Monthly (Magazine)	Babcox Automotive Publications	77 North Miller Road Akron, OH 44313
STATISTICAL HIGHLIGHTS Monthly (Statistics)	Rubber Manufacturers Association	444 Madison Avenue New York, NY 10022
TIRE REVIEW Monthly (Magazine)	Babcox Automotive Publications	11 South Forge Street Akron, OH 44304

PUBLISHED	SOURCE	ADDRESS

WHOLESALE PRICES AND PRICE INDEXES
Monthly
(Statistics)

U.S. Department of Labor
Bureau of Labor Statistics

Washington, DC 20212

OTHERS

RUBBER MANUFACTURERS ASSOCIATION

444 Madison Avenue
New York, NY 10022

SAVINGS AND LOAN

PERIODICALS

CALIFORNIA SAVINGS AND LOAN DATA BOOK
Annually
(Book)
(Stat. Abstract)

California Savings & Loan League

1444 Wentworth Ave.
P.O. Box R
Pasadena, CA 91109

CALIFORNIA SAVINGS AND LOAN JOURNAL
Monthly
(Magazine)

California Savings & Loan League

9800 S. Sepulveda Blvd
Los Angeles, CA 90045

CALIFORNIA SAVINGS AND LOAN OPERATING TRENDS
Annually
(Journal)

California Savings & Loan League

Pasadena, CA 91109

CALIFORNIA STATISTICAL ABSTRACT
Annually
(Stat. Abstract)

State of California Documents Section

P.O. Box 1612
Sacramento, CA 95807

FEDERAL HOME LOAN BANK DIGEST
Monthly
(Magazine)

Federal Home Loan Bank Board

Washington, DC 20225

MONTHLY SUMMARY OF BUSINESS CONDITIONS IN SOUTHERN CALIFORNIA, NORHTERN COASTAL COUNTIES
Monthly
(Journal)

Security Pacific National Bank
(Economics Research Department)

P.O. Box 2097
Terminal Annex
Los Angeles, CA 90054

THE MORTGAGE BANKER
Monthly

Mortgage Bankers Assn. of America

1125 15th Street , N.W.
Washington, DC 20005

RESIDENTIAL RESEARCH REPORTS
Quarterly
(Abstract)

Residential Research Committee of So. California

433 S. Spring Street
Los Angeles, CA 90013

PUBLISHED	SOURCE	ADDRESS

SAVINGS AND LOAN FACT BOOK
Annually
(Book)
(Stat. Abstract)

U.S. Savings and
Loan League

221 N. LaSalle Street
Chicago, IL 60601

STATISTICS ON STATE CHARTERED SAVINGS AND LOANS,
STATISTICAL RELEASE 67-3
Quarterly
(Stat. Abstract)

Savings and Loan
Commissioner
(Dept. of Investments)

3440 Wilshire Blvd.
Los Angeles, CA

BOOKS

CALIFORNIA REAL ESTATE FINANCE
1978

J. W. Pugh and W. H.
Hippaka
Prentice-Hall, Inc.

New York, NY
Rt. 9W
Englewood Cliffs, NJ
07632

SAVINGS AND MORTGAGE MARKETS IN CALIFORNIA
1963

Leo Grebler
California Savings &
Loan League

Pasadena, CA 91109

STEEL

PERIODICALS

AMERICAN METAL MARKET
Daily
(Newspaper)

Fairchild Publications

7 East 12th Street
New York, NY 10003

ANNUAL STATISTICAL REPORT
Annually
(Report)

American Iron & Steel
Institute

150 East 42nd Street
New York, NY 10017

INVENTORIES OF STEEL MILL SHAPES
Monthly
(Magazine)

Commerce Department
Census Bureau
(Industrial Reports)

Washington, DC 20233

IRON AGE
Weekly
(Magazine)

Chilton Co.

Chilton Way
Radnor, PA 19089

IRON ORE
Monthly
(Stat. Summary &
News Sheet)

Bureau of Mines
Division of Ferrous
Metals

Washington, DC 20240

IRON AND STEEL SCRAP
Monthly
(Magazine)

Bureau of Mines
Division of Ferrous
Metals

Washington, DC 20240

PUBLISHED	SOURCE	ADDRESS
METAL BULLETIN Monthly (Newspaper)	Metal Bulletin, Ltd.	46 Wigmore Street London W1, England

TEXTILE

PERIODICALS

CLOTHES SemiWeekly (Magazine)	Prads, Inc.	380 Madison Avenue New York, NY 10017
DAILY NEWS RECORD Daily (Newspaper)	Fairchild Publications	7 East 12th Street New York, NY 10003
HOSIERY STATISTICS Annually (Stat. Yearbook)	National Assn. of Hosiery Manufac- turers	P.O. Box 4314 Charlotte, NC 28204
MILL MARGINS Monthly (Statistics)	U.S. Department of Ag- riculture Consumer & Marketing Service Marketing News Section — Cotton Division	P.O. Box 7723 Memphis, TN 38117
TEXTILE ORGANON Monthly (Statistical Magazine)	Textile Economics Bureau, Inc.	489 Fifth Avenue New York, NY 10017
TEXTILE WORLD Monthly (Magazine)	McGraw-Hill, Inc.	1175 Peachtree St.,NE Atlanta, GA 30361
WOMEN'S WEAR DAILY Daily (Newspaper)	Fairchild Publications	7 East 12th Street New York, NY 10003

OTHER

STATISTICAL BULLETIN #455; AND RELATED DATA 1930-1969 (Stat. Booklet)	WOOL STATISTICS U.S. Department of Ag- riculture Economic Research Bureau	Washington, DC 20250

PUBLISHED	SOURCE	ADDRESS

TOBACCO AND CIGARETTES

PERIODICALS

ADVERTISING AGE
Weekly
(Magazine)

Crain Communications
Inc.

740 North Rush Street
Chicago, IL 60611

ALCOHOL AND TOBACCO SUMMARY STATISTICS
Annually
(Stat. Summary)

U.S. Treasury Dept.
Internal Revenue Service

Washington, DC 20224

ANNUAL REPORT ON TOBACCO STATISTICS
Annually
(Stat. Summary)

U.S. Department of
Agriculture

Washington, DC 20250

MONTHLY STATISTICAL BULLETIN
Monthly
(Bulletin)

Cigar Manufacturers
Association of
America, Inc.

575 Madison Avenue
New York, NY 10022

MONTHLY STATISTICAL RELEASE — CIGARS
AND CIGARETTES
Monthly
(Stat. Summary)

U.S. Treasury Dept.
Internal Revenue Service

Washington, DC 20224

TOBACCO REPORTER
Monthly
(Magazine)

Harcourt, Brace,
Jovanovich

757 Third Avenue
New York, NY 10017

TOBACCO SITUATION
Quarterly
(Stat. Summary)

Economic Research
Service
U.S. Department of
Agriculture

Washington, DC 20250

UNITED STATES TOBACCO JOURNAL
Weekly
(Journal)

BMT Publishing Co.

254 West 31st Street
New York, NY 10001

OTHER

THE CIGARETTE CONTROVERSY

The Tobacco Institute

1776 K Street, N.W.
Washington, DC 20006

FEDERAL LEGISLATION REPORT

FOREIGN TRADE REPORTS

INTERNATIONAL TOBACCO REPORT

PUBLISHED	SOURCE	ADDRESS
LEAF BULLETIN		
SPECIAL REPORTS		
STATE LEGISLATION REPORT		
TAX LETTER		
TOBACCO BAROMETER		
TOBACCO UPDATE	The Tobacco Merchants Association of the United States	Statler Hilton Hotel Seventh Ave. & 33rd Street New York, NY 10001

Securities and Exchange Commission

INTRODUCTION

The Securities and Exchange Commission (SEC) was created by an act of Congress entitled the Securities Exchange Act of 1934. It is an independent, bipartisan, quasi-judicial agency of the United States Government.

The laws administered by the Commission relate in general to the field of securities and finance, and seek to provide protection for investors and the public in their securities transactions. They include (in addition to the Securities Exchange Act of 1934) the Securities Act of 1933 (administered by the Federal Trade Commission until September 1934), the Public Utility Holding Company Act of 1935, the Trust Indenture Act of 1939, the Investment Company Act of 1940, and the Investment Advisers Act of 1940. The Commission also serves as advisor to Federal courts in corporate reorganization proceedings under Chapter X of the National Bankruptcy Act.

Organized July 2, 1934, the Commission is composed of five members not more than three of whom may be members of the same political party. They are appointed by the President, with the advice and consent of the Senate, for 5-year terms, the terms being staggered so that one expires on June 5th of each year. The Chairman is designated by the President.

The Commission's staff is composed of lawyers, accountants, engineers, security analysts and examiners, together with administrative and clerical employees. The staff is divided into Divisions and Offices (including nine Regional Offices), each under charge of officials appointed by the Commission.

The Commission reports annually to the Congress. These reports contain a review of the Commission's administration of the several laws.

SECURITIES ACT OF 1933

This "truth in securities" law has two basic objectives: (*a*) to provide investors with material financial and other information concerning securities offered for public sale; and (*b*) to prohibit misrepresentation, deceit and other fraudulent acts and practices in the sale of securities generally (whether or not required to be registered).

Registration of Securities

The first objective applies to securities offered for public sale by an issuing company or any person in a control relationship to such company. Before the public offering of such securities, a registration statement must be filed with the Commission by the issuer, setting forth the required information. When the statement has become effective, the securities may be sold. The purpose of registration is to provide disclosure of financial and other information on the basis of which investors may appraise the merits of the securities. To that end, investors must be furnished with a prospectus (selling circular) containing the salient data set forth in the registration statement to enable them to evaluate the securities and make informed and discriminating investment decisions.

Exemptions From Registration

The registration requirement applies to securities of both domestic and foreign private issuers, as well as to securities of foreign governments or their instrumentalities. There are, however, certain exemptions from the registration requirement. Among these are: (1) private offerings to a limited number of persons or institutions who have access to the kind of information registration would disclose and who do not propose to redistribute the securities, (2) offerings restricted to the residents of the State in which the issuing company is organized and doing business, (3) securities of municipal, State, Federal and other governmental instrumentalities, of charitable institutions, of banks, and of carriers subject to the Interstate Commerce Act, (4) offerings not in excess of certain specified amounts made in compliance with regulations of the Commission discussed below, and (5) offerings of "small business investment companies" made in accordance with rules and regulations of the Commission. The anti-fraud provisions referred to above, however, apply to all sales of securities involving interstate commerce or the mails, whether or not the securities are exempt from registration.

Purpose of Registration

Registration of securities does not insure investors against loss in their purchase, nor does the Commission have the power to disapprove securities for lack of merit—and it is unlawful to represent otherwise in the sale of securities. The *only* standard which must be met in the registration of securities is an adequate and accurate disclosure of the material facts concerning the company and the securities it proposes to sell. The fairness of the terms of securities (whether price, promoters' or underwriters' profits, or otherwise), the issuing company's prospects for successful operation, and other factors affecting the merits of securities, have no bearing on the question whether securities may be registered.

The purpose of registration is to provide disclosure of these and other important facts so investors may make a realistic appraisal of the merits of the securities and thus exercise an informed judgment in determining whether to purchase them. Assuming proper disclosure, the Commission cannot deny registration or otherwise bar the securities from public sale whether or not the price or other terms of the securities are fair or the issuing company offers reasonable prospects of success. These are factors which the investor must assess for himself in the light of the disclosures provided; and if the facts have been fully and correctly stated, the investor assumes whatever risks may be involved in the purchase of the securities.

Nor does registration guarantee the accuracy of the facts represented in the registration statement and prospectus. The law does, however, prohibit false and misleading statements under penalty of fine or imprisonment, or both. In addition, if an investor suffers loss in the purchase of a registered security, the law provides him with important recovery rights if he can prove that there was incomplete or inaccurate disclosure of material facts in the registration statement or prospectus. These rights must be asserted in an appropriate Federal or State court (not before the Commission, which has no power to award damages); and if such misstatements are proved, the issuing company, its responsible directors and officers, the underwriters, controlling interests, the sellers of the securities, and others (or one or more of such persons) would be liable to the purchaser of the securities for losses sustained in their purchase.

The Registration Process

To facilitate the registration of securities by different types of issuing companies, the Commission has prepared special registration forms which vary in their disclosure requirements to provide disclosure of the essential facts pertinent in a given type of offering while at the same time minimizing the burden and expense of compliance with the law. In general, the registration forms call for disclosure of information such as (1) a description of the registrant's properties and business, (2) a description of the significant provisions of the security to be offered for sale and its relationship to the registrant's other capital securities, (3) information about the management of the registrant, and (4) financial statements certified by independent public accountants.

The registration statement and prospectus become public immediately on filing with the Commission; but it is unlawful to sell the securities until the effective date. After the filing of the registration statement, the securities may be offered orally or by certain summaries of the information in the registration statement as permitted by rules of the Commission. The Act provides that registration statements shall become effective on the 20th day after filing (or on the 20th day after the filing of the last amendment thereto); but the Commission, in its discretion, may advance the effective date if, considering the adequacy of information theretofore publicly available, the ease with which the facts about the new offering can be disseminated and understood, and the interests of investors and the public, such action is deemed appropriate.

Registration statements are examined by the Division of Corporation Finance for compliance with the disclosure requirements. If a statement appears to be materially incomplete or inaccurate, the registrant usually is informed by letter and given an opportunity to file correcting or clarifying amendments. The Commission however, has authority to refuse or suspend the effectiveness of any registration statement if it finds, after hearing, that material representations are misleading, inaccurate or incomplete. Accordingly, if material deficiencies in a registration statement appear to stem from a deliberate attempt to conceal and mislead, or if the deficiencies otherwise are of such nature as not to lend themselves readily to correction through the informal letter process, the Commission may conclude that it is in the public interest to resort to a hearing to develop the facts by evidence and to determine on the evidence whether a stop order should issue refusing or suspending effectiveness of the statement.

A stop order is not a permanent bar to the effectiveness of the registration statement or sale of the securities, for the order must be lifted and the statement declared effective if amendments are filed correcting the statement in accordance with the stop order decision. The Commission may issue stop orders after the sale of securities has been commenced or completed. Although losses which may have been suffered in the purchase of securities are not restored to investors by the stop order, the Commission's decision and the evidence on which it is based may serve to put investors on notice of their rights and aid in their own recovery suits.

This examination process naturally contributes to the general reliability of the registration disclosures—but it does not give positive assurance of the accuracy of the facts reported. Even if such a verification of the facts were possible, the task, if not actually prohibitive, would involve such a tremendous undertaking (both in time and money) as to seriously impede the financing of business ventures through the public sale of securities.

Small Issue Exemption

Among the special exemptions from the registration requirement is one adopted by Congress as an aid primarily to small business. The law provides that offerings of securities not exceeding $500,000 in amount may be exempted from registration, subject to such conditions as the Commission prescribes for the protection of investors. The Commission's Regulation A permits certain domestic and Canadian companies to make exempt offerings not exceeding $500,000 in amount. Offerings on behalf of controlling persons are limited in amount to $100,000 for each such person, not to exceed $500,000 in all. Offerings on behalf of persons other than an Issuer or its affiliates are limited to $100,000 for each such person, not to exceed a total of $300,000, which is not included in the $500,000 ceiling limitation. Under certain circumstances an estate may offer up to $500,000 of securities. The exemption is available provided certain specified conditions are met, including the prior filing of a "Notification" with the appropriate Regional Office of the Commission and the use of an offering circular containing certain basic information in the sale of the securities. A similar regulation is available for offerings not exceeding $500,000 by small business investment companies licensed by the Small Business Administration. Other exemptions of a more limited nature are available for other types of offerings.

Interpretations and Rulemaking

As a part of its activities under this Act, the Division of Corporation Finance also renders administrative interpretations of the law and regulations thereunder to members of the public, prospective registrants and others, to help them decide legal questions about the application of the law and the regulations to particular situations and to aid them in complying with the law. This advice, for example, might include an informal expression of opinion about whether the offering of a particular security is subject to the registration requirements of the law and, if so, advice as to compliance with the disclosure requirements of the applicable registration form. Other Divisions render similar advice and assistance.

The Commission's objective of effective disclosure with a minimum of burden and expense calls for constant review of the practical operation of the rules and registration forms adopted by it. If experience shows that a particular requirement fails to achieve its objective, or if a rule appears unduly burdensome in relation to the benefits resulting from the disclosure provided, the Division of Corporation Finance presents the problem to the Commission for consideration of possible modification of the rule or other requirement. Many suggestions for rule modification follow extensive consultation with industry representatives and others affected. In addition, the Commission normally gives advance public notice of proposals for the adoption of new or amended rules or registration forms and affords opportunity for interested members of the public to comment thereon. The same procedure is followed under the other Acts administered by the Commission.

The scope and importance of the Commission's work in the accounting field under the several statutes are discussed below under "Office of the Chief Accountant."

Fraud Prohibitions

Generally speaking, the fraud prohibitions of the Securities Act are similar to those contained in the Securities Exchange Act of 1934, under which topic the Commission's investigation and enforcement activities are discussed.

SECURITIES EXCHANGE ACT OF 1934

By this Act, Congress extended the "disclosure" doctrine of investor protection to securities listed and registered for public trading on our national securities exchanges; and the enactment in August 1964 of the Securities Acts Amendments of 1964 applied the disclosure and reporting provisions to equity securities of hundreds of companies traded over-the-counter (if their assets exceed $1 million and their shareholders number 500 or more).

Corporate Reporting

Companies which seek to have their securities listed and registered for public trading on such an exchange must file a registration application with the exchange and the Commission. A similar registration form must be filed by companies whose equity securities are traded over-the-counter if they meet the size test referred to. The Commission's rules prescribe the nature and content of these registration statements, including certified financial statements. These data are generally comparable to, but less extensive than, the disclosures required in Securities Act registration statements. Following the registration of their securities, such companies must file annual and other periodic reports to keep current the information contained in the original filing.

Since trading by and between public investors, whether involving listed or over-the-counter securities, involves transactions between holders of outstanding securities (not an offer of securities for sale by the issuing company), there is no provision for dissemination of the reported data to investors through use of a prospectus or similar medium. However, the reported information is available for public inspection, both at the offices of the Commission and the exchanges. It is also used extensively by publishers of securities manuals, securities advisory services, investment advisers, trust departments, brokers and dealers in securities, and similar agencies, and thus obtains widespread dissemination. In addition, as indicated below, copies of any of the reported data may be obtained from the Commission at nominal cost.

The law prescribes penalties for filing false statements and reports with the Commission, as well as provision for recovery by investors who suffer losses in the purchase or sale of registered securities in reliance thereon.

Proxy Solicitations

Another provision of this law governs the solicitation of proxies (votes) from holders of registered securites (both listed and over-the-counter), whether for the election of directors or for approval of other corporate action. In any such solicitation, whether by the management or minority groups, disclosure must be made of all material facts concerning the matters on which such holders are asked to vote; and they must be afforded an opportunity to vote "Yes" or "No" on each matter. Where a contest for control of the management of a corporation is involved, the rules require disclosure of the names and interests of all "participants" in the proxy contest. Holders of such securities thus are enabled to vote intelligently on corporate actions requiring their approval. The Commission's rules require that proposed proxy material be filed in advance for examination by the Commission for compliance with the disclosure requirements.

Tender Offer Solicitations

In 1968, Congress amended the Exchange Act to extend its reporting and disclosure provisions to situations where control of a company is sought through a tender offer or other planned stock acquisition of over 10 percent of a company's equity securities. The amount was reduced to 5 percent by an amendment in 1970. These amendments and Commission rules thereunder require disclosure of pertinent information, by the person seeking to acquire over 5 percent of the company's securities by direct purchase or by tender offer, as well as by any persons soliciting shareholders to accept or reject a tender offer. Thus, as with the proxy rules, public investors who hold stock in the subject corporation may now make informed decisions on take-over bids.

Insider Trading

The protection provided the investing public through disclosure of financial and related information concerning the securities of registered companies, is supplemented by provisions of the law designed to curb misuse of corporate information not available to the general public. To that end, each officer and director of such a company, and each beneficial owner of more than 10 percent of its registered equity securities, must file an initial report with the Commission (and with the exchange on which the stock may be listed) showing his holdings of each of the company's equity securities. Thereafter, they must file reports for any month during which there was any change in such holdings. In addition, the law provides that profits obtained by them from purchases and sales (or sales and purchases) of such equity securities within any 6 months' period may be recovered by the company or by any security holder on its behalf. This recovery right must be asserted in the appropriate United States District Court. Such "insiders" are also prohibited from making short sales of their companies' equity securities.

Margin Trading

The statute also contains provisions governing margin trading in securities. It authorizes the Board of Governors of the Federal Reserve System to set limitations on the amount of credit which may be extended for the purpose of purchasing or carrying securities. The objective is to restrict the excessive use of the nation's credit in the securities markets. While the credit restrictions are set by the Board, investigation and enforcement is the responsibility of the Commission.

Market Surveillance

The Securities Exchange Act also provides a system for regulating securities trading practices in both the exchange and the over-the-counter markets. In general, transactions in securities which are effected otherwise than on national securities exchanges are said to take place "over the counter." Designed to protect the interests of investors and the public, these provisions seek to curb misrepresentations and deceit, market manipulation and other fraudulent acts and practices and to establish and maintain just and equitable principles of trade conducive to the maintenance of open, fair and orderly markets.

While these provisions of the law establish the general regulatory pattern, the Commission is responsible for promulgating rules and regulations for their implementation. Thus, the Commission has adopted regulations which, among other things, (1) define acts or practices which constitute a "manipulative or deceptive device or contrivance" prohibited by the statute, (2) regulate short selling, stabilizing transactions and similar matters, (3) regulate the hypothecation of customers' securities and (4) provide safeguards with respect to the financial responsibility of brokers and dealers.

Registration of Exchanges and Securities Associations

In addition, the law requires registration with the Commission of (1) "national securities exchanges" (those having a substantial securities trading volume); and (2) brokers and dealers who conduct an over-the-counter securities business in interstate commerce.

To obtain registration, exchanges must show that they are so organized as to be able to comply with the provisions of the statute and the rules and regulations of the Commission and that their rules contain provisions which are just and adequate to insure fair dealing and to protect investors. Among other things, exchange rules must provide for the expulsion, suspension or other disciplining of members for conduct inconsistent with just and equitable principles of trade.

While the law contemplates that exchanges shall have full opportunity to establish self-regulatory measures insuring fair dealing and the protection of investors, it empowers the Commission by order, rule or regulation to "alter or supplement" the rules of exchanges with respect to various phases of their activities and trading practices if necessary to effectuate the statutory objective. For the most part, exchange rules and revisions thereof, suggested by exchanges or by the Commission, reach their final form after discussions between representatives of the exchange and the Commission without resort to formal proceedings.

By an amendment to the law enacted in 1938, Congress also provided for creation of a self-policing body among over-the-counter brokers and dealers. This measure authorizes the registration with the Commission of an association of such brokers and dealers provided it is so organized as:

> "to prevent fraudulent and manipulative acts and practices, to promote just and equitable principles of trade, to provide safeguards against unreasonable rates of commissions or other charges, and, in general, to protect investors and the public interest, and to remove impediments to and perfect the mechanism of a free and open market . . ."

To enforce these objectives, the rules of such an association also must provide for the disciplining of members (including suspension or expulsion) for misconduct. The establishment, maintenance and enforcement of a voluntary code of business ethics is one of the principal features of this provision of the law. (Only one such association, the National Association of Securities Dealers, Inc., is registered with the Commission under this provision of the law.)

Not all broker-dealer firms are members of the NASD; thus, some are not subject to supervision and control by that agency. To equalize the regulatory pattern, Congress provided in the 1964 Amendments that the Commission should undertake to establish investor safeguards applicable to non-NASD firms comparable to those applicable to NASD members. Among the controls adopted by the Commission is a requirement that persons associated with non-NASD firms meet certain qualification standards similar to those applied by the NASD to its members.

Broker-Dealer Registration

Applications for registration as broker-dealers and amendments thereto are examined by the Office of Registrations and Reports with the assistance of the Division of Market Regulation. The registration of brokers and dealers engaged in an interstate over-the-counter securities business also is an important phase of the regulatory plan of the Act. They must conform their business practices to the standards prescribed in the law and the Commission's regulations for the protection of investors (as well as to the fair trade practice rules of their association); in addition, as will be seen later, they may violate these regulations only at the risk of possible loss of registration with the Commission and the right to continue to conduct an interstate securities business, or of suspension or expulsion from the association and of the benefits of such membership. (The broker-dealer registration requirement does not apply to firms engaged solely in a municipal securities business.)

Investigation and Enforcement

It is the duty of the Commission under the laws it administers to investigate complaints or other indications of possible law violations in securities transactions, most of which arise under the Securities Act of 1933 and the Securities Exchange Act of 1934. Investigation and enforcement work is the primary responsibility of the Commission's Regional Offices, subject to review and direction by the Division of Enforcement.

Most of the Commission's investigations are conducted privately, the facts being developed to the fullest extent possible through informal inquiry, interviewing of witnesses, examination of brokerage records and other documents, reviewing and trading data and similar means. The Commission however, is empowered to issue subpoenas requiring sworn testimony and the production of books, records and other documents pertinent to the subject matter under investigation; in the event of refusal to respond to a subpoena, the Commission may apply to a Federal court for an order compelling obedience thereto.

Inquiries and complaints of investors and the general public provide one of the primary sources of leads for detection of law violations in securities transactions. Another is the surprise inspections by Regional Offices of the books and records of brokers and dealers to determine whether their business practices conform to the prescribed rules. Still another is the conduct of inquiries into market fluctuations in particular stocks which appear not to be the result of known developments affecting the issuing company or of general market trends.

The more general types of investigations concern the sale without registration of securities subject to the registration requirement of the Securities Act, and misrepresentation or omission of material facts concerning securities offered for sale (whether or not registration is required). The anti-fraud provisions of the law also apply equally to the *purchase* of securities, whether involving outright misrepresentations or the withholding or omission of pertinent facts to which the seller was entitled. For example, it is unlawful in certain situations to purchase securities from another person while withholding material information which would indicate that the securities have a value substantially greater than that at which they are being acquired. Such provisions of the law apply not only to transactions between brokers and dealers and their customers but also to the reacquisition of securities by an issuing company or its "insiders."

Other types of inquiries relate to the manipulation of the market prices of securities; the misappropriation or unlawful hypothecation of customers' funds or securities; the conduct of a securities business while insolvent; the purchase or sale of securities by a broker-dealer, from or to his customers, at prices not reasonably related to the current market prices therefor; and violation by the broker-dealer of his responsibilty to treat his customers fairly.

The most common of the latter type of violation involves the broker-dealer who, on gaining the trust and confidence of a customer and thereby establishing an agency relationship demanding the highest degree of fiduciary duty and care, takes secret profits in his securities transactions with or for the customer over and above the agreed brokerage (agency) commission. For example the broker-

315

dealer may have purchased securities from customers at prices far below, or sold securities to customers at prices far above, their current market prices. In most such cases, the broker-dealer subjects himself to no risk of loss, since his purchases from customers are made only if he can make simultaneous sales of the securities at prices substantially in excess of those paid to the customers, and his sales to customers are made only if he can make simultaneous purchases of the securities at prices substantially lower than those charged the customer. Or the firm may engage in large-scale in-and-out transactions for the customer's account ("churning") to generate increased commissions, usually without regard to any resulting benefit to the customer.

There is a fundamental distinction between a broker and a dealer; and it is important that investors should understand the difference. The *broker* serves as the customer's *agent* in buying or selling securities *for* his customer. As such, he owes the customer the highest fiduciary responsibility and care and may charge only such agency commission as has been agreed to by the customer. On the other hand, a *dealer* acts as a *principal* and buys securities *from* or sell securities *to* his customers. In such transactions, the dealer's profit is measured by the difference between the prices at which he buys and sells securities. Since the dealer is operating for his own account, he normally may not charge the customer a fee or commission for services'rendered. Even in the case of such dealer transactions, however, the Commission and the courts have held that the conduct of a securities business carries with it the implied representation that customers will be dealt with fairly and that dealers may not enter into transactions with customers at prices not reasonably related to the prevailing market. The law requires that there be delivered to the customer a written "confirmation" of each transaction disclosing whether the securities firm is acting as a principal for its own account or as an agent for the customer (and, if the latter, the broker's compensation from all sources).

Statutory Sanctions

It should be understood that Commission investigations (which for the most part are conducted in private) are essentially fact finding inquiries. The facts so developed by the staff are considered by the Commission only in determining whether there is *prima facie* evidence of a law violation and whether an action should be commenced to determine whether, in fact, a violation actually occurred and, if so, whether some sanction should be imposed.

Assuming that the facts show possible fraud or other law violation, the laws provide several courses of action or remedies which the Commission may pursue:

a. *Civil injunction.* The Commission may apply to an appropriate United States District Court for an order enjoining those acts or practices alleged to violate the law or Commission rules.

b. *Criminal prosecution.* If fraud or other willful law violation is indicated, the Commission may refer the facts to the Department of Justice with a recommendation for criminal prosecution of the offending persons. That Department, through its local United States Attorneys (who frequently are assisted by Commission attorneys), may present the evidence to a Federal grand jury and seek an indictment.

c. *Administrative remedy.* The Commission may, after hearing, issue orders suspending or expelling members from exchanges or the over-the-counter dealers association; denying, suspending or revoking the registrations of broker-dealers; or censuring individuals for misconduct or barring them (temporarily or permanently) from employment with a registered firm.

Broker-Dealer Revocations

All of these sanctions may be applied to any person who engages in securities transactions violative of the law, whether or not he is engaged in the securities business. However, the administrative remedy is generally only invoked in the case of exchange or association members, registered brokers or dealers, or individuals who may associate with any such firm. In any such administrative proceeding, the Commission issues an order specifying the acts or practices alleged to have been committed in violation of law and directing that a hearing be held for the purpose of taking evidence thereon. At the hearing, counsel for the Division of Enforcement (normally a Regional Office attorney) undertakes to establish for the record those facts which support the charge of law violation, and the respondents have full opportunity to cross-examine witnesses and to present evidence in defense. The procedure followed in the conduct of such proceedings is discussed below under "Administrative Proceedings." If the Commission in its ultimate decision of the case finds that the respondents violated the law, it may take remedial action as indicated above. Such action may effectively bar a firm from the conduct of a securities business in interstate commerce or on exchanges, or an individual from association with a registered firm—subject to the respondents' right to seek judicial review of the decision by the appropriate United States Court of Appeals.

In its investigation and enforcement actions, the Commission cooperates closely with other Federal, State and local law enforcement officials, as well as with such private agenices as the Better Business Bureaus.

The many instances in which these sanctions of the law have been invoked present a formidable record. However, of perhaps greater significance to the investing public is the deterrent or prophylactic effect of the very existence of the fraud prohibitions of the law and the Commission's powers of investigation and enforcement. These provisions of the law, coupled with the disclosure requirements applicable to new security offerings and to other registered securities, tend to inhibit fraudulent stock promotions and operations. They also have a tendency to increase public confidence in securities as an investment medium, thus facilitating financing through the public sale of securities, which contributes to the industrial growth of the nation.

Commission Not a Collection Agency

Communications from the investing public are very helpful to the Commission in connection with its statutory duties and the Commission appreciates receiving them. However, because the Commission receives many inquiries and complaints from investors urging it to intercede in their behalf in an attempt to recover losses in the purchase of securities, it is appropriate to point out that the

Commission in no sense is to be considered a collection agency. While the laws provide investors with important recovery rights if they have been defrauded, and although the Commission's administration of the laws operates in many instances to uncover facts indicating the possible existence of such rights, recovery may be sought only through the assertion of claims by investors before a court of competent jurisdiction. Further, the Commission cannot give advice as to the merits of securities, whether or not they are registered. Through enactment of the securities laws Congress sought to provide disclosure of much of the basic information on which the merits of particular securities, and the risks inherent in their purchase, might be realistically appraised. But the responsibility for examining the information and determining the investment merit of securities and the risks involved in their purchase rests with the investor.

Administrative Interpretations and Rulemaking

As previously indicated, the Commission not only consults and advises with industry representatives and others concerning legal interpretative problems arising under the securities laws and with respect to the adoption of new or amended rules and regulations, but also gives public notice of suggested rules and invites comments and criticisms which are considered in determining the nature and scope of rules to be adopted. The Commission constantly reviews its rules in light of the experience gained in their administration, to the end that they will provide maximum investor protection with a minimum of interference with the proper functioning of the securities markets.

The examination of the periodic report and proxy statements of companies whose shares are listed or traded over-the-counter (except those of investment companies), as well as the reports of insiders, is conducted by the Division of Corporation Finance, while the investigative, enforcement and regulatory work under this law is carried on by the Division of Trading and Markets, assisted by Regional Offices—both under supervision and direction of the Commission.

PUBLIC UTILITY HOLDING COMPANY ACT OF 1935

Purpose of Act

This statute was enacted by Congress to correct the many abuses which Congressional inquiries had disclosed in the financing and operation of electric and gas public-utility holding-company systems.

When the Act became law in 1935, some 15 holding-company systems controlled 80 percent of all electric energy generation, 98.5 percent of all transmission of electric energy across State lines, and 80 percent of all natural-gas pipeline mileage in the United States. Many of the huge utility empires then in existence controlled subsidiaries operating in many widely-separated States and which had no economic or functional relationship to each other. Holding companies were pyramided layer upon layer, many of them serving no useful or economic purpose; and many systems had very complicated corporate and capital structures, with control often lodged in junior securities having little or no equity. These conditions ranked high among the abuses which the Act was designed to correct.

Registration

Interstate holding-companies which are engaged through their subsidiaries in the electric-utility business or in the retail distribution of natural or manufactured gas are subject to regulation under the statute. The Act requires that they register with the Commission and file initial and periodic reports containing detailed data about the organization, financial structure and operations of each such holding company and of its subsidiaries. Once the holding companies are registered, they and their subsidiaries become subject to regulation by the Commission in accordance with statutory standards designed for the protection of investors, consumers, and the public interest. If, however, a holding company or a subsidiary thereof meets certain specifications, it may be exempted from part or all the duties and obligations otherwise imposed on it by statute.

Integration and Simplification

From the standpoint of their impact on the electric and gas utility industries, the most important provisions of the Act are its requirements for the physical integration and corporate simplification of holding-company systems. The integration standards of the statute restrict a holding company's operations to an "integrated utility system," which is defined in the Act as one capable of economical operation as a single coordinated system confined to a single area or region in one or more states and not so large as to impair (considering the state of the art) the advantages of localized management, efficient operation and effectiveness of local regulation. Additional systems or incidental businesses are retainable only under certain limited conditions. The corporate simplification provisions of the Act require action to insure that the capital structure and the continued existence of any company in a holding-company system do not unduly or unnecessarily complicate the corporate structure of the system or unfairly or inequitably distribute voting power among security holders of the system.

The integration and simplification provisions of the Act direct the Commission to determine what action, if any, must be taken by registered holding companies and their subsidiaries to comply with these requirements; and the Commission may apply to Federal courts for orders compelling compliance with Commission directives made on the basis of such determinations. However, many divestments of nonretainable subsidiaries and properties, recapitalizations, dissolutions of companies and other adjustments required to comply with the Act have been accomplished by the holding-company systems through voluntary reorganization plans for which the Act also provides. If a voluntary plan is found by the Commission to be fair and equitable to all affected persons and to be necessary to further the objectives of the Act. the Commission may approve the plan. Thereafter, if the company requests, the Commission applies to a Federal district court for an order approving the plan and directing its enforcement. All interested persons, including State commissions and other governmental agencies, are accorded full opportunity to be heard in proceedings before the Commission and before the Federal courts.

The overall effect of the Commission's administration of the integration and simplification provisions of the law has been far-reaching and unparalleled.

During the 34 year period from 1938 to 1972, about 2,500 companies have been subject to the Act as registered holding companies or subsidiaries thereof at one time or another. Included in this total were over 227 holding companies, 1,046 electric and gas utility companies and 1,210 other companies engaged in a wide variety of pursuits. Among the latter were brick works, laundries, experimental orchards, motion picture theaters and even a baseball club. Today the picture is strikingly different. Only 17 active holding company systems are now registered. They are comprised of 13 registered holding companies which function solely as holding companies, 7 holding companies which also are engaged in utility operations, 91 electric and/or gas subsidiary companies, 57 nonutility subsidiaries and 16 inactive companies, making a total of 184 companies with aggregate assets og $19 billion. Further, these 17 systems now account for only about one-fifth of the aggregate assets of the privately-owned electric and gas utility and gas pipeline industries of the nation. Most electric and gas utility companies, which formerly were associated with registered holding companies, now operate as independent concerns.

The Commission's Continuing Jurisdiction

In enacting the statute, the Congress recognized that certain electric-utility holding company systems and certain groups of gas utility and transmission companies, which constitute physically integrated systems and are not too large or scattered to meet the integration and simplication requirements of the Act, may offer operating economies and other advantages which justify the continuation of holding-company control. Thus, the 17 systems referred to above are expected to be subject to the regulatory provisions of the Act for the indefinite future.

Financing Transactions

The issue and sale of securities by holding companies and their subsidiaries are subject to regulation by the Commission under prescribed standards of the law. The tests which a proposed security issue must meet are: (1) the security must be reasonably adapted to the security structure of the issuer and of other companies in the same holding company system; (2) the security must be reasonably adapted to the earning power of the company; (3) the proposed issue must be necessary and appropriate to the economical and efficient operation of the company's business; (4) the fees, commissions and other remuneration paid in connection with the issue must not be unreasonable; and (5) the terms and conditions of the issue or sale of the security must not be detrimental to the public interest or the interest of investors or consumers. In certain cases where there has been an approval by a State regulatory commission, the law directs the Commission to exempt security issues of subsidiary companies, subject to imposition of such terms and conditions as the Commission may deem necessary for the protection of investors or consumers.

To implement these objectives and to eliminate investment banker control and assure maintenance of competitive conditions as required, the Commission has promulgated a rule requiring (with certain exceptions) that in the sale of new securities by registered holding companies and their subsidiaries, as well as in the sale by such holding companies of securities held in their investment port-folio, the issuer or seller shall invite sealed competitive bids for the securities.

Purchases and Sales of Utility Securities and Properties

The acquisition of securities and utility assets by holding companies and their subsidiaries may not be authorized by the Commission unless the following standards are met:

1. The acquisition must not tend toward interlocking relations or concentration of control to an extent detrimental to the public interest or the interest of investors or consumers;
2. Any consideration paid for the acquisition, including fees, commissions and other remuneration, must not be unreasonable;
3. The acquisition must not complicate the capital structure of the holding company system;
4. The acquisition must not be otherwise detrimental to the public interest or the interest of investors or consumers, or to the proper functioning of the holding company system; and
5. The acquisition must tend toward the economic and efficient development of an integrated public utility system.

Sales of utility assets or securities may not be made in contravention of Commission rules and orders regarding the consideration to be received, maintenance of competitive conditions, fees and commissions, disclosure of interest and similar matters.

Other Regulatory Provisions

Other phases of the Act provide for the regulation of dividend payments (in circumstances where such payments might result in corporate abuses), inter-company loans, solicitation of proxies, consents and other authorizations, and insiders' trading. "Upstream" loans from subsidiaries to their parents and "upstream" or "cross-stream" loans from public-utility companies to any holding company in the same holding-company system are expressly forbidden. The Act also requires that all services performed for any company in a holding-company system by a service company in that system be rendered at cost fairly and equitably allocated. Thus, the Act deals effectively with the problem of excessive service charges levied on operating electric and gas companies by their parent holding companies, a problem with which State commissions had experienced considerable difficulty.

Administrative Interpretations and Advice

The Commission is assisted in the administration of the Holding Company Act by its Division of Corporate Regulation, which analyzes legal, financial, accounting, engineering and other problems arising under the Act. The Division participates in hearings to develop the factual records; where necessary, files briefs and participates in oral arguments before the Commission; and makes recommendations with respect to the Commission's findings and decisions in cases which arise in the administration of the law. All hearings are conducted in accordance with the Commission's Rules of Practice discussed below under

"Administrative Proceedings." The Division also confers with and renders advisory assistance to holding-company representatives to aid in the solution of their problems under the Act.

TRUST INDENTURE ACT OF 1939

This Act applies in general to bonds, debentures, notes, and similar debt securities offered for public sale which are issued pursuant to trust indentures under which more than $1 million of securities may be outstanding at any one time. Even though such securities may be registered under the Securities Act, they may not be offered for sale to the public unless the trust indenture conforms to specified statutory standards of this Act designed to safeguard the rights and interests of the purchasers.

The Act was passed after studies by the Commission had revealed the frequency with which trust indentures failed to provide minimum protections for security holders and absolved so-called trustees from minimum obligations in the discharge of their trusts. It requires that the indenture trustee be free of conflicting interests which might interfere with the faithful exercise of its duties in behalf of the purchasers of the securities. It requires also that the trustee be a corporation with minimum combined capital and surplus; imposes high standards of conduct and responsibility on the trustee; precludes preferential collection of certain claims owing to the trustee by the issuer in the event of default; provides for the issuer's supplying evidence to the trustee of compliance with indenture terms and conditions such as those relating to the release or substitution of mortgaged property, issuance of new securities or satisfaction of the indenture; and provides for reports and notices by the trustee to security holders. Other provisions of the Act prohibit impairment of the security holders' right to sue individually for principal and interest except under certain circumstances, and require the maintenance of a list of security holders which may be used by them to communicate with each other regarding their rights as security holders.

Applications for qualification of trust indentures are examined by the Division of Corporation Finance for compliance with the applicable requirements of the law and the Commission's rules thereunder.

INVESTMENT COMPANY ACT OF 1940

This legislation, together with the Investment Advisers Act of 1940, discussed below, resulted from a study of the activities of investment companies and investment advisers conducted by the Commission pursuant to direction of Congress contained in the Holding Company Act. The results of this study were reported to Congress in a series of reports filed in 1938, 1939 and 1940, the legislation being supported both by the Commission and the investment company industry.

Under this Act, the activities of companies engaged primarily in the business of investing, reinvesting and trading in securities and whose own securities are offered and sold to and held by the investing public, are subject to certain statutory prohibitions and to Commission regulation in accordance with prescribed

322

standards deemed necessary to protect the interests of investors and the public.

It is important for investors to understand, however, that the Commission does not supervise the investment activities of these companies and that regulation by the Commission does not imply safety of investment in such companies.

In addition to a requirement that such companies register with the Commission,* the law requires disclosure of their financial condition and investment policies to afford investors full and complete information about their activities; prohibits such companies from changing the nature of their business or their investment policies without the approval of the stockholders; bars persons guilty of security frauds from serving as officers and directors; prevents underwriters, investment bankers or brokers from constituting more than a minority of the directors of such companies; requires management contracts (and material changes therein) to be submitted to security holders for their approval; prohibits transactions between such companies and their directors, officers, or affiliated companies or persons, except on approval by the Commission as being fair and involving no overreaching; forbids the issuance of senior securities by such companies except under specified conditions and upon specified terms; and prohibits pyramiding of such companies and cross-ownership of their securities.

Other provisions relate to sales and repurchases of securities issued by investment companies, exchange offers, and other activities of investment companies, including special provisions for periodic payment plans and face-amount certificate companies.

With respect to plans of reorganization of investment companies, the Commission is authorized to prepare advisory reports as to the fairness of their terms and provisions if requested by the company or 25 percent of its stockholders; and it may institute court proceedings to enjoin a plan of reorganization if it appears grossly unfair to security holders. The Commission may also institute court action to remove management officials who may be guilty of gross misconduct or gross abuse of trust.

The securities of investment companies are also required to be registered under the Securities Act; and the companies must file periodic reports and are subject to the Commission's proxy and "insider" trading rules.

The Division of Corporate Regulation assists the Commission in the administration of this law, as well as the processing of investment company registration statements under the Securities Act as well as their proxy statements and periodic reports.

INVESTMENT ADVISERS ACT OF 1940

This law establishes a pattern of regulation of investment advisers which is similar in many respects to Securities Exchange Act provisions governing the conduct of brokers and dealers. It requires, with certain exceptions, that persons or firms who engage for compensation in the business of advising others about

---

*A list of registered investment companies, showing their classification, assets size and location, may be purchased from the Commission in photocopy form (cost furnished upon request).

their securities transactions shall register with the Commission and conform their activities to statutory standards designed to protect the interests of investors.

The registration of investment advisers may be denied, suspended or revoked by the Commission if, after notice and hearing, it finds that a statutory disqualification exists and that such action is in the public interest. Disqualifications include a conviction for certain financial crimes or securities violations, the existence of injunctions based on such activities, a conviction for violation of the Mail Fraud Statute, the wilfull filing of false reports with the Commission, and wilfull violations of this Act, the Securities Act or the Securities Exchange Act. In addition to the administrative sanction of denial, suspension or revocation, the Commission may obtain injunctions restraining violations of this law and may recommend prosecution by the Department of Justice for fraudulent misconduct or wilfull violation of the law or rules of the Commission thereunder.

The law contains anti-fraud provisions, and it empowers the Commission to adopt rules defining fraudulent, deceptive or manipulative acts and practices and designed to prevent such activities. It also requires that investment advisers disclose the nature of their interest in transactions executed for their clients; and, in effect, it prevents the assignment of investment advisory contracts without the client's consent. The law also imposes on investment advisers subject to the registration requirement the duty to maintain books and records in accordance with such rules as may be prescribed by the Commission, and it authorizes the Commission to conduct inspections of such books and records.

The Commission is aided in the administration of this law by the Office of Registrations and Reports and the Division of Investment Management Regulation.

BANKRUPTCY ACT, CHAPTER X

Under Chapter X, the Commission serves as adviser to United States district courts in connection with proceedings for the reorganization of debtor corporations in which there is a substantial public interest. It participates as a party to these proceedings, either at the request or with the approval of the courts. It renders independent, expert advice and assistance to the courts, which do not maintain their own staffs of expert consultants.

Representatives of the Commission follow closely the progress of reorganization proceedings in which it is a participant, and confer with the court-appointed trustees and their counsel and with other interested parties in the solution of the various problems which arise in the administration of the affairs of the debtor corporation and in the formulation of plans of reorganization. In addition to the advice and assistance which the Commission renders, both to the court and to the parties, in connection with the preparation of plans of reorganization, the Commission also presents its views and recommendations on such matters as the qualifications and independence of trustees and their counsel, fee allowances to the various parties, including the trustees and their counsel, sales of properties and other assets, interim distributions to security holders, and other financial or legal matters. The Commission has no independent right of appeal from court rulings.

Of primary importance is the Commission's assistance in the formulation of plans of reorganization of the debtor corporation which will provide fair and equitable treatment to the various creditors and other security holders and which will help to assure that the corporation will emerge from bankruptcy in a sound financial condition and able to carry on without the continued threat of bankruptcy. Underlying the Commission's recommendations concerning the fairness and feasibility of reorganization plans, is a thorough study and analysis of the debtor's past operations, its financial condition, its past earnings record and prospective future earning power, its competitive position in the particular industry, and related matters. In cases in which the scheduled liabilities of the debtor exceed $3 million, the plan of reorganization must be, and in other cases may be, referred by the court to the Commission for preparation of an advisory report on the fairness and feasibility of the plan. This advisory report is filed with the court for its assistance and is distributed among the creditors and security holders to enable them to exercise an informed judgment in considering whether to vote for or against acceptance of the plan. In cases where no formal advisory report is prepared, the Commission's views are stated orally at the hearing on the plan before the court.

Because of the predominantly local character of reorganization cases, court appearances, consultations with the parties, investigations and examinations are handled primarily by the Commission's Regional Offices, subject to supervision by the Division of Corporate Regulation and approval by the Commission.

ADMINISTRATIVE PROCEEDINGS

All formal administrative proceedings of the Commission are conducted in accordance with its Rules of Practice, which conform to the Administrative Procedure Act and are designed to establish procedural, "due process" safeguards which will protect the rights and interests of parties to each such proceeding. Among these are requirements for timely notice of the proceeding and for a sufficient specification of the issues or charges involved to enable each of the parties adequately to prepare his case. All parties, including counsel for the interested Division or Office of the Commission, may appear at the hearing and present evidence and cross-examine witnesses in much the same manner as in the ordinary trial of court actions. In addition, other interested persons may be permitted to intervene or be given limited rights of participation. In some cases, the relevant facts may be stipulated in lieu of the conduct of an evidentiary hearing.

Hearings are conducted before a Hearing Officer who is normally an Administrative Law Judge appointed by the Commission; he serves independently of the interested Division or Office and rules on the admissibility of evidence and on other issues arising during the course of the hearing. At the conclusion of the hearing, the parties and participants may urge, in writing, specific findings of fact and conclusions of law for adoption by the Hearing Officer. Thereupon, the Hearing Officer prepares and files an initial decision (unless waived), setting forth his conclusions as to the facts established by the evidence and including an order disposing of the issues involved in the proceeding. Copies of the initial decision are served on the parties and participants, who may seek Commission review thereof. If review is not sought and the Commission does not order review on its own motion, the initial decision becomes final and the Hearing Officer's order becomes effective.

In the event of Commission review of the initial decision, the parties and participants may file briefs and be heard in oral argument before the Commission. On the basis of an independent review of the record, the Commission prepares and issues its own decision; the Office of Opinions and Review aids the Commission in this decisional process. The laws provide that any person or firm aggrieved by a decision or order of the Commission may seek review thereof by the appropriate United States court of appeals. The initial decisions of Hearing Officers as well as the Commission's decisions are made public. Copies of Commission decisions and announcements that the initial decisions of Hearing Officers have become final also are distributed to the Commission's mailing lists. Ultimately, the Commission's decisions (as well as initial decisions which have become final and are of precedential significance) are printed by the Government Printing Office and published in the Commission's "Decisions and Reports" (see p. 24).

OFFICE OF THE GENERAL COUNSEL

The General Counsel is the chief legal officer of the Commission. The duties of his office include representing the Commission in judicial proceedings; handling legal matters which cut across the lines of work of the several operating Divisions; and providing advice and assistance to the Commission, its operating Divisions, and Regional Offices with respect to statutory interpretation, rule-making, legislative matters and other legal problems, public or private investigations, and Congressional hearings and investigations. The Office also reviews cases where criminal prosecution is recommended. The General Counsel directs and supervises all contested civil litigation (except United States district court proceedings under Chapter X of the Bankruptcy Act) and represents the Commission in all cases in the appellate courts, filing briefs and presenting oral arguments in behalf of the Commission. In addition, in cases between private parties involving the statutes the Commission administers, the Office represents the Commission where it participates as a friend of the court in cases involving legal issues of general importance.

The Commission from time to time recommends revisions in the statutes which it administers. In addition, it prepares comments on any proposed legislation which might affect its work or where it is asked for its views by Congressional Committees. The Office of the General Counsel, together with the Division assisting the Commission in the function which may be affected by such legislation, prepares this legislative material.

OFFICE OF THE CHIEF ACCOUNTANT

The Chief Accountant is the Commission's chief consulting officer on accounting matters, advising the Commission with respect to accounting problems which arise in the administration of the Acts, particularly in matters involving new accounting policy determination. The Chief Accountant has general supervision over the execution of Commission policy with respect to the accounting principles and procedures applicable to the financial statements filed with the Commission and to the auditing standards and practices observed by the independent public accountants who examine and render an opinion on these statements.

A major objective of the Commission has been to improve accounting and auditing standards and to maintain high standards of professional conduct by the independent accountants through cooperation with the accounting profession and by the rule-making process. In furtherance of this policy the Chief Accountant consults with representatives of the accounting profession regarding the promulgation of new or revised accounting and auditing standards and drafts rules and regulations which prescribe requirements for financial statements. Many of the rules are embodied in a basic accounting regulation entitled Regulation S–X adopted by the Commission which, together with a number of opinions issued as "Accounting Series Releases," governs the form and content of most of the financial statements filed with it.

The Chief Accountant also has supervisory responsibility for the drafting of uniform systems of accounts for public utility holding companies, mutual service companies and subsidiary service companies under the Holding Company Act; for accounting requirements for investment and broker-dealer companies; and for the general administration of those systems and accounting requirements.

The Chief Accountant administers the Commission's rules which require that accountants who examine financial statements filed with it be independent of their clients, and makes recommendations on cases arising under the Commission's Rules of Practice which specify that an accountant may be denied the privilege of practicing before the Commission because of lack of character or integrity or qualifications to represent others, or because of unethical or unprofessional conduct. He also supervises the procedures followed in accounting investigations conducted by the Commission's staff.

OFFICE OF ECONOMIC RESEARCH

The principal functions of this Office are three-fold: (1) to assist the Commission by analyzing legal, economic and industrial developments affecting the securities markets and by recommending to the Commission the institution or modification of programs commensurate with such developments; (2) to prepare statistical data and analyses related to the capital markets for Commission use as well as for general economic analysis and (3) to compile and publish data furnished to the general public as part of the overall Government statistical program.

Some of the more important projects of this office include: (1) development of analytical framework for anticipating developments in the securities industry and a continuing analysis of the economic and financial condition of the securities industry; (2) analysis of the impact of competitive rates on the economic and legal structure of the securities industry and on the investment process; (3) review of trends in corporate capital structure; (4) analysis of trends in capital markets worldwide, the impact of internationalization of these markets; and (5) continued study as to the role of self-regulation in the securities industry, and the possible need for change in regulatory rules or the industry itself to make the capital markets more efficient.

The Office of Management and Budget has designated the Commission as the agency best suited to make and publish certain financial studies including: (a) The Net Working Capital of Nonfinancial Corporations; (b) The financial activities of Private Noninsured Pension Funds and (c) New Security Offerings and related studies.

PUBLIC INFORMATION

Financial and other data included in registration statements, reports, applications and similar documents filed with the Commission are available for inspection in the Public Reference Room of the Commission's Headquarters Office in Washington, D.C. Copies of portions or all of any such public document may be obtained at nominal cost (the amount of the fee is established by an annual contract between the Commission and the copier who reproduces the documents; the rate for the year ended December 31, 1969, is 9¢ per page for 8½ x 14 copy). Estimates as to the cost of copies of specific reports or other information may be obtained on request to the Section of Public Reference, Office of Records and Service, Securities and Exchange Commission, Washington, D.C. 20549.

Current annual and other periodic reports (including financial statements) filed by companies whose securities are listed on exchanges also are available for inspection in the Commission's New York, Chicago and San Francisco Regional Offices, as are the registration statements (and subsequent reports) filed by those companies whose securities are traded over-the-counter which register under the 1964 Amendments to the Exchange Act. Moreover, if the issuer's principal office is located in the area served by the Atlanta, Boston, Denver, Fort Worth or Seattle Regional Office, its filings also may be examined at the particular Regional Office in question. In addition, prospectuses covering recent public offerings of securities registered under the Securities Act may be examined in all Regional Offices; and copies of broker-dealer and investment adviser registrations, as well as Regulation A notifications and offering circulars, may be examined in the particular Regional Office in which they were filed.

PUBLICATIONS

The publications described below are compiled by the Commission but printed and sold by the Superintendent of Documents. Requests for single copies or subscriptions, accompanied by the correct remittance, should be addressed to the Superintendent of Documents, United States Government Printing Office, Washington, D.C. 20402. THE COMMISSION DOES NOT MAINTAIN A MAILING LIST FOR THESE PUBLICATIONS.

NEWS DIGEST. A daily report of Commission announcements, decisions, orders, rules and rule proposals, current reports and applications filed, and litigation developments. $35.45 per year)

SEC DOCKET. A weekly compilation of the full texts of SEC releases under the following Acts: Securities Act, Securities Exchange Act, Public Utility Holding Company Act, Trust Indenture Act, Investment Advisers Act, and Investment Company Act. Also included will be the full texts of Accounting series releases, corporate reorganization releases, and litigation releases. ($21.35 per year)

OFFICIAL SUMMARY. $17.40 per year. $1.45 per copy; $4.35 additional for foreign mailing.

A monthly summary of security transactions and holdings reported under the provisions of the Securities Exchange Act of 1934, the Public Utility Holding Company Act of 1935, and the Investment Company Act of 1940 by officers, directors, and certain other persons.

STATISTICAL BULLETIN. $28.70 per year. $.60 per copy; $7.20 additional for foreign mailing.

A weekly publication containing data on odd lot and round lot transactions, block distributions, working capital of U.S. corporations, assets of noninsured pension funds, 144 filings, and 8k reports.

ACTS AND RULES AND REGULATIONS:

Compilation of Releases Dealing with matters arising under the Investment Company Act of 1940.................................

SEC ANNUAL REPORT TO CONGRESS:

First through Thirty-fourth (out of print) (Available only for reference purposes in SEC Washington, D.C., and Regional Offices.)

SEC JUDICIAL DECISIONS (Buckram bound)—Vols. 1–5, covering period
1934–48, available only for reference purposes in SEC Washington,
D.C., and Regional Offices.

SEC DECISIONS AND REPORTS (Buckram bound)—Vols. 1–41, covering
period 1934–64, available only for reference purposes in SEC Washington, D.C., and Regional Offices.

Volume 42 (June 1, 1964 to May 31, 1966) ....

Volume 43 (June 1, 1966 to June 30, 1969) ....

Directory of Companies filing Annual Reports with the Commission under
the Securities Exchange Act of 1934. Lists companies alphabetically
and classified by industry groups according to the Standard Industrial
Classification Manual of the Bureau of the Budget. Published annually.
Per copy...

A Study of Mutual Funds (Prepared for the SEC by the Wharton School
of Finance and Commerce) (1962)—595 pages H. Doc. No. 2274
(87th Cong.) (Available only for reference purposes in SEC Washington, D.C., and Regional Offices.)

Report of SEC Special Study of Securities Markets (1963).............

Commission Report on Public Policy Implications of Investment Company
Growth H. Rept. No. 2337 (89th Cong.).

Institutional Investor Study Report of the Securities and Exchange Commission (1971)—Eight Parts, H. Doc. No. 64 (92d Cong.)...........

Part 8 of the said Institutional Investor, containing the Text of the Summary and Conclusions drawn from each of the fifteen chapters of the
report ....

Study on Unsafe and Unsound Practices of Broker-Dealers, H. Doc. 231,
(92nd Cong.)...

Report of the Real Estate Advisory Committee to the SEC..............

The Financial Collapse of The Penn Central Company, Staff Report of the
SEC to the Special Subcommittee on Investigations, August, 1972.....

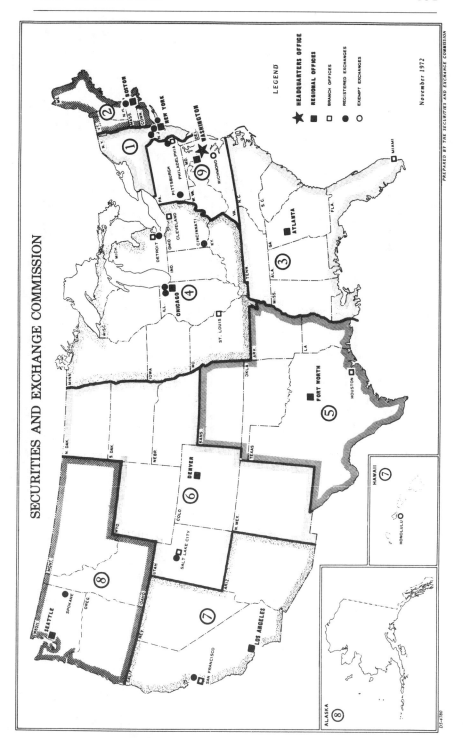

SECURITIES AND EXCHANGE COMMISSION

LEGEND

HEADQUARTERS OFFICE	★
REGIONAL OFFICES	■
BRANCH OFFICES	□
REGISTERED EXCHANGES	●
EXEMPT EXCHANGES	○

November 1972

PREPARED BY THE SECURITIES AND EXCHANGE COMMISSION

SECURITIES AND EXCHANGE COMMISSION

THE COMMISSION

- THE OFFICE OF ADMINISTRATIVE LAW JUDGES
- THE OFFICE OF OPINIONS AND REVIEW
- THE SECRETARY
- THE EXECUTIVE DIRECTOR

- THE DIVISION OF CORPORATE REGULATION
- THE DIVISION OF CORPORATION FINANCE
- THE DIVISION OF ENFORCEMENT
- THE DIVISION OF INVESTMENT MANAGEMENT REGULATION
- THE DIVISION OF MARKET REGULATION

- THE OFFICE OF THE CHIEF ACCOUNTANT
- THE OFFICE OF ECONOMIC RESEARCH
- THE OFFICE OF THE GENERAL COUNSEL
- THE OFFICE OF POLICY PLANNING

- THE OFFICE OF ADMINISTRATIVE SERVICES
- THE OFFICE OF COMPTROLLER
- THE OFFICE OF DATA PROCESSING
- THE OFFICE OF PERSONNEL
- THE OFFICE OF PUBLIC INFORMATION
- THE OFFICE OF RECORDS
- THE OFFICE OF REGISTRATIONS AND REPORTS

THE REGIONAL OFFICES

NEW YORK REGIONAL OFFICE	BOSTON REGIONAL OFFICE	ATLANTA REGIONAL OFFICE	CHICAGO REGIONAL OFFICE	FORT WORTH REGIONAL OFFICE	DENVER REGIONAL OFFICE	LOS ANGELES REGIONAL OFFICE	SEATTLE REGIONAL OFFICE	WASHINGTON, D.C. REGIONAL OFFICE
		Miami, Fla. Branch	Cleveland, Ohio Branch Detroit, Mich. Branch St. Louis, Mo. Branch	Houston, Texas Branch	Salt Lake City, Utah Branch	San Francisco, Calif. Branch		Philadelphia, Pa. Branch

Index